Chicano Detective Fiction

# Chicano Detective Fiction

*A Critical Study of Five Novelists*

Susan Baker Sotelo

McFarland & Company, Inc., Publishers

*Jefferson, North Carolina, and London*

LIBRARY OF CONGRESS CATALOGUING-IN-PUBLICATION DATA

Sotelo, Susan Baker, 1946–
    Chicano detective fiction : a critical study of five novelists /
Susan Baker Sotelo.
        p.      cm.
    Includes bibliographical references and index.

    ISBN 0-7864-2185-1 (softcover : 50# alkaline paper)

    1. Detective and mystery stories, American — History and crit-
icism.    2. American fiction — Mexican American authors— History
and criticism.    3. American fiction — 20th century — History and
criticism.    4. Mexican Americans— Intellectual life.    5. Mexican
Americans in literature.    I. Title.
    PS374.D4S69   2005
    813'.087209'0896872 — dc22                              2005007357

British Library cataloguing data are available

Manufactured in the United States of America

*McFarland & Company, Inc., Publishers*
*Box 611, Jefferson, North Carolina 28640*
*www.mcfarlandpub.com*

Para mi familia

*Sin el amor y el apoyo de mis hijos Rebecca y Emiliano,*
*su padre Abelardo y nuestra familia mexicana*
*este libro no hubiera sido posible.*

Without the example of my mother and grandmothers,
three generations of higher education,
I would have given up long ago.

*Dedico este libro a la memoria de mis madres y abuelas,*
*y a mi querido tío Humberto Roura que*
*me apoyó en mis estudios de español.*

# Acknowledgments

My thesis director, Lydia Fossa, pushed me to explore and explain my topic more than I could have imagined possible. My childhood friend Kathryn Kasch and *amiga oaxaqueña* Eda Saynes-Vazquez did initial proofreading and gave encouragement while I was struggling to complete my task. My doctorial committee, Dr. Lydia Fossa, Dr. Malcolm Compitello and Dr. Eliana Rivero, suggested that I seek the unimaginable: a publisher. Without the company and support of my "partners in crime"— fellow graduate students Nadia Avendaño, Nuria Moragado and Lourdes Gabikagojeaskoa — this road would have been lonely.

Many friends have aided me with this book by listening to my ideas and problems, and by reading my numerous drafts. Stuart Gellman's journalistic skills and Sarah Hitch's love of fiction were indispensable to the editing process.

My return to Romantic perspectives was motivated by the work of Doris Sommer and Adam Zamoyski, but my introduction to this literature and its history began in the classes of Professor John Gilabert.

My uncle Humberto Roura gave me his handwritten dictionary of Nahuatl, from *ahuacatl* to *zopítlotl*, and in the classes of Professor Lanin Gyurko I discovered pre–Columbian literature. The historical perspective of Chicano literature that I have revisited began in Professor Ana Perches' classes.

Rudolfo Anaya, Lucha Corpi, Rolando Hinojosa and Manuel Ramos were very generous with their time and insights, and I thank them for their responses to my questions about their writing process. The works of these writers and of Michael Nava have been an inspiration.

# Table of Contents

# Preface

In the United States the fastest-growing segment of our population traces its ancestry to Mexico. Chicano detective fiction introduces the reader to various contemporary portraits of members of this diverse culture. This is not insignificant, but is only part of our interest in Chicano detective fiction. These narratives also serve as critical studies of the genre itself and of one manner in which we construct national and/or ethnic identities.

The novels studied portray Chicanos, from those recently immigrated to those whose ancestors were among the first immigrants to California, Colorado, New Mexico and Texas. The books introduce the reader of whatever background to cultural diversity and deny stereotypical or homogeneous perspectives that plague all U.S. population groups. Furthermore, they accomplish this in an entertaining manner.

Teachers and mystery genre aficionados will find this critical study useful because of the historical information it contains that is relative to the contemporary situations of the characters in these novels. These novels do not need this information; they are well written and entertaining reading without it. However, too many readers have not had the opportunity to be exposed to the history and literature of Mexican Americans and therefore lack background information that can enrich their reading experience.

Reading as a leisure-time activity in the United States is declining, but popular genres continue to have a large audience. North Americans are familiar with the whodunit's formula through film and television and are less likely to feel alienated by its form than those of nongenre prose fiction. Because of detective fiction's easily recognizable formula, the changes in this genre are more discernable than in other literary works. Together with its timely subject matter and its transformations to the genre, Chicano detective fiction is a particularly suitable subject matter for the secondary and undergraduate student of literature and cultural diversity.

For the student and the whodunit aficionado, familiarity with the formula may not suffice as preparation for the Chicano transformations of the genre. This book explores these changes by investigating their relationship to Chicano social and literary history and linking these to social and literary environments that surrounded previous transformations of the genre by British and Anglo American authors. The detective genre has a 200-year-old history, and its various interpretations have reflected social and literary trends. This is not to say that the same is not true of other literary genres, but this relationship is more readily observed in the whodunit.

The detective story originated along with Romantic mid–nineteenth-century Eurocentric literatures of the old and new worlds and was closely linked with national fictional narratives prevalent at the time. National histories that develop a plot to explain the contemporary nation have gone out of style, but their underlying narratives continue to act as themes that rally and unify populations. Contemporary British and Anglo American detective fiction retains only a subtle relationship to thematic national identities. However, minority detective fictions reinvent the genre's link to the author's, or detective protagonist's community. In the United States, these novels, written by insiders and outsiders alike, have introduced readers to cultural identities of African Americans and Navajos, Cuban Americans, Central Americans and Puerto Ricans. This book includes suggestions for further reading by authors of Spanish-speaking ancestry writing in the United States. The largest group of these authors is Chicano. While clearly members of an identifiable demographic minority, these authors' perspectives toward thematic cultural identity are as varied as their individual and regional backgrounds, and therefore their works offer a broad but detailed view of Chicanos and their relationship to their native land.

In the chapters that follow, I hope to communicate my enthusiasm for the Chicano detective novel. This book is meant to inspire interest in these works, supplement the reader's experience of them and act as a resource for those who teach these texts at the secondary and undergraduate level and thus cultivate an even broader readership.

# Introduction

Writing a detective novel is like taking a couple of eggs, a pat of butter, salt and pepper, and using these basic ingredients to make a satisfying meal. The options seem limited — you can scramble, fry, or bake — but talented cooks seem to produce something tasty every time.

To successfully engage his reader, the writer of formulaic literature must work within the limitations set by the genre without boring the reader with repetition, while at the same time meeting the reader's expectations of the genre. Is this always true? Are "basic" ingredients always the same? Popular detective fiction uses whole fresh eggs, in contrast to the "metaphysical" variety that might use only the whites, or only the yolks or even a powdered variety of eggs that needs to be reconstituted. The basic Anglo American or British egg dish might be seasoned with a little catsup, but not with chile. The Chicano variety, however, tends toward the *huevos rancheros* that are part of Rudolfo Anaya's detective Sonny Baca's favorite breakfast — a complete meal: "eggs, beans, potatoes, and green chile [with] just-baked corn tortillas" (Anaya *Zia Summer* 189).

During the last 18 years, Chicano authors Rudolfo Anaya, Lucha Corpi, Rolando Hinojosa, Michael Nava and Manuel Ramos have produced a corpus of work that now includes 21 detective novels. Working within the limitations of the genre, they are able to satisfy the demands of a reader of mainstream detective fiction. Even though these are not ambiguous novels, the reader needs to be aware that these are "resistant texts" (Sommer "Textual" 147). The mainstream reader, like the blue-eyed woman who orders Sonny's "the usual," which she calls "[a] ranchero with huevos" ("a rancher with balls") will be surprised and could find "her eyes go full of tears" and even hear muffled laughter from the kitchen if she orders Chicano-style eggs and expects the Anglo American and British type (*Zia Summer* 189–190). Baca's dish is hot, *picante*, with chile. Sonny Baca's father always said, "Comida sin chile no es comida" ("Food without

3

chile isn't food.") (*Zia Summer* 191). Authors of the Chicano whodunit subscribe to the senior Señor Baca's dictum and season their whole-egg narratives with chile-flavored hot Mexican *salsa* ("sauce"), which, unlike catsup, comes in many varieties.

People of Mexican ancestry in the United States use various names to describe themselves. In this book I have not indiscriminately alternated Chicano, Mexican American, American and Mexican, but have tried to respect each author's preference. In general, "Chicano," or the female "Chicana," is used to describe a person of Mexican ancestry who identifies with the projects and goals initiated during the activism of the 1960s and 1970s. The Chicano movement concerned itself with workers' rights, equal access to social services and education. Many of these activists also opposed the war in Vietnam. Chicanas participated in this movement and later, in the 1970s, worked for women's rights in their communities and in cooperation with other women of color. It is generally accepted that post–1960 literature by authors of Mexican ancestry living in the United States is identified as "Chicano" or "Chicana" unless the author has defined his literature otherwise. People of Mexican ancestry also refer to themselves with regional terms including *Tejano Mexicano, Nuevo Mexicano* and *Californio* that I use when appropriate.

Mexican Americans have been writing in what is now the continental United States since before the forced annexation of the western states — Texas, California, New Mexico, Arizona, Nevada, Utah and parts of Colorado and Wyoming — that began in 1836 with the Lone Star State. *Recovering the U.S. Hispanic Literary Heritage*, edited by Ramón Gutiérrez and Genaro Padilla, provides an introduction to the sixteenth-century origins of this literature and the works produced during the Spanish Colonial period, the short Mexican Republic era and early U.S. era dating to the middle of the twentieth century. However, the volume of Chicano/a literature published since the 1960s overwhelms that produced in the previous four centuries.

Detective fiction written by and about Chicanos represents a small percentage of Chicano literature in general, and is a recent addition to this body of work. There was no Chicano detective protagonist until 1985, the year when Rolando Hinojosa's Rafe Buenrostro was first introduced as a homicide investigator in *Partners in Crime*. Rudy Apodaca wrote *The Waxen Image*, the first whodunit by a Chicano, in 1977. His protagonist, however, is not Chicano, and his story focuses on a mysterious "image" from Africa. (Apodaca has a new novel out that I review in Chapter 7.)

In the last two decades, educational institutions have been making efforts to introduce their students to ethnic literatures of the United States.

Many students are familiar with the works of Rudolfo Anaya, Sandra Cisneros, Rolando Hinojosa and Tomás Rivera, and these writers are becoming frequent subjects of academic writing. Conversely, academic readers of Chicano literature have written little about its detective genre. Two notable exceptions are *Chicano Renaissance: Contemporary Cultural Trends*, edited by David R. Maciel, Isidro D. Ortiz and María Herrera-Sobek (2000), and Charles M. Tatum's *Chicano Popular Culture: Que Hable el Pueblo* (2001). I hope my contribution will encourage more academic interest in Chicano detective fiction and offer the student, soon to be a general reader, ethnic literature in the form of a popular genre that is primarily marketed for its entertainment value.

Even though the Chicano whodunit to date is written almost exclusively in English, it has not captured the interest of a large U.S. audience. In his analysis of this genre, Charles Tatum focuses on the plot and the characterization of the protagonist detective, which are the principal elements emphasized by this formulaic literature. Tatum's perspective underscores an aspect of "popular" which has always been associated with detective fiction — its potential for commercial success. Readers will seek out other novels by the same author when they have enjoyed the plot or empathized with the detective protagonist, but they may be lazy in searching for new authors.

Marketing has been a factor in the lack of interest in the Chicano genre. A lurid or colorful cover along with easy availability at the local grocery checkout is the easiest way to sell a mystery novel. Commercial houses have published Anaya, Nava and Ramos. The University of Houston's Arte Público Press publishes the novels of Hinojosa and Corpi. Northwestern University Press and the University of New Mexico Press are publishing the novels of Manuel Ramos.

Academic publishers do not have the commercial clout to garner an easy access position at the supermarket and are generally more timid with their covers. Moreover, with regional exceptions, Chicano authors, even one as commercially successful as Rudolfo Anaya, are not among those whose works are placed within close proximity to the *National Enquirer*. By doing an online search for detective fiction, readers can make a dent in the dominance of the magazine rack cum bookstore at the grocery.

Four personal interests drew me to Chicano detective fiction. I have been in love with mysteries since I read about the exploits of the teenage sleuth Nancy Drew. A good mystery story grabs my attention because of its predictability, but it holds my attention because of its inventiveness. A whodunit is like a familiar old friend, but it can also be like a night on the town, full of surprises. I don't eschew the metaphysical narratives of Jorge

Luis Borges, or Umberto Eco's postmodern detective fiction, but for pure enjoyment I would rather follow the footsteps of a detective in the tradition of Miss Marple or Philip Marlowe. Although I enjoy taking a mystery tour of an exotic locale, I prefer a narrative that returns me to places I have often visited and, even more, those that transport me to my "hometown," the western United States. Chicano mysteries satisfy my needs as a reader of detective fiction and as a *romantiphile*.

First, I am a Romantic at heart. My favorite novel, *La Regenta*, by the Spaniard Leopoldo Alas, bridges the gap between Romanticism and realism. Detective fiction does the same. My all-time favorite poems are story poems, "El Moro Espósito" (1834), by Ángel Saavedra, el duque de Rivas, and a late Romantic poem from the early twentieth century, "The Highwayman," by Alfred Noyes. My dad read "The Highwayman" to me as a child, and I read Edgar Allan Poe. Detective fiction satisfies my need for a good story, wrapping a mystery around the protagonist's identity and focusing on death as a part of the plot.

Secondly, Chicano authors have successfully adopted a traditional Anglo American and British genre. More to the point, these authors have not simply plugged in "Chicano" for "Anglo," Ms. Damasco for Miss Marple or Henry Rios for Philip Marlowe; they engage in a dialogue with traditional Anglo American and British genres. Chicano detective fiction is not an exception to the genre's formula for enduring popularity. This fiction depends on an implicit agreement between the reader and the text. The reader accepts and embraces the familiarity of the formula and the text rewards him by accepting and confirming "popular" conceptions of the reader's culture.

My original culture is mainstream Anglo American, but I have Chicano children, and have spoken Spanish for more than 30 years. In my hometown of Tucson, Arizona, it is practically impossible to be unaware of the cultivation of a hybrid community where even traditional neighborhoods are no longer exclusively Mexican or Anglo. The discussion I hear when reading Anglo American and Chicano detective fiction is representative of the dialectic I observe and participate in every day. The Anglo genres, American and British, have been shown to reinforce cultural values of the Anglo-European hegemony in the United States. Chicano detective fiction contests this worldview and affirms the Chicano presence in the West without imposing an exclusive cultural perspective.

For me, Chicano detective fiction asks, "What came first, the salsa or the egg?" There were no chickens in the Americas until the Spanish arrived, and there were no chile peppers or tomatoes in Spain until the "discovery" of America.

My third interest stems from the first two: Romantic mystery and the American dialectic. In my opinion it does not necessarily follow that the individual dialectic of all of these authors' novels with the Anglo genre is the same; it can also be said that Chicano works are in dialogue with each other. I am interested in what these novels are "saying" to each other, in exploring where their dialogues differ, where they converge and what critical outline might be useful in defining these works without limiting their diversity. I hear a Romantic "national tale" (historian Adam Zamoyski's term) or a "foundational fiction" (literary critic Doris Sommer's term) in these novels, but it is not the same story in each.

The eighteenth- and nineteenth-century Romantic hero had precedents as old as the heroes of oral European folklore, pagan and biblical myth, and more recently as the protagonists of medieval tales of chivalry. The romance heroes of earlier eras, Odysseus or David and Goliath, for example, have grown in stature to where they are oftentimes seen as more universal and archetypical than their modern Romantic reincarnations. The American and European Romantics of the late eighteenth through the early twentieth centuries were interested in regional and ethnic identity. Their heroes, unlike the exemplar heroes of the Age of Enlightenment, or Neoclassicism, who preceded them, were rebellious individuals. They asserted their difference and eschewed concepts of universal laws of human behavior by favoring the primacy of individual emotional response.

A fourth reason that I chose detective fiction, and in particular Chicano detective fiction, as my topic is my belief that we are evolving into a nation of nonreaders. Furthermore, as a nation, our romance genre preferences have been dominated by the traditions of England, Scotland and Ireland with a little zest from France and Germany. The Chicano mystery has the potential to introduce a written representation of a familiar genre to the occasional reader — perhaps inspiring him to become a frequent reader — and to introduce Chicanos and the general population to the largest group of what our census has termed "Hispanic."[1]

Throughout this study I use "romance" to describe literature that transcends chronological historical divisions and "Romantic" to refer to the history and literature of the Romantic Era (from the late eighteenth century through the initiation of the twentieth century). Romantic literature is romance literature, but not all romance is Romantic. Romance literature is a universal phenomenon whether viewed from Fredric Jameson's Marxist perspective or from Northrop Frye's archetypal perspective. The chapter "The Shaman Sleuth: Rudolfo Anaya's *Shaman Winter*" discusses Jameson's and Frye's perspectives in more detail. Detective fiction and national, regional or ethnic historical fictions as we know them were given their basic formulas during the Romantic Era. Television viewers are familiar with the contemporary descendents of two Romantic Era genres: national tales (Westerns) and detective fiction (crime dramas). Two examples familiar to readers of Romantic American fiction from the United States are the tales of James Fenimore Cooper and Edgar Allan Poe.

The chapter "Chicano Romance" introduces Chicano history and its Romantic Era literature. "Chicano" is a relatively new name for a population that has lived in the confines of the current national borders of the United States of America for a period much longer than that of the Mayflower descendants. In 1850, Chicanos, then "Mexican Americans," were not unaware that their culture, like that of Native Americans, was threatened with extinction by the policies and actions of the U.S. government. Unlike the Europeans who readily assimilated, the Mexican Americans, and also Native Americans, believed that the U.S. government would honor its treaties with them by respecting their language and property. "Chicano Romance" briefly tells this story through two distinct literatures: an early Mexican American historical novel, *The Squatter and the Don* (1885), by María Amparo Ruiz de Burton, and "Elena," an example of the *corrido*, a popular oral genre.

Detective fiction is only a recent example of adaptations and transformations of literary genres by Chicano authors. *The Squatter and the Don* is a Romantic novel that, not unlike *Amalia* (1855), by Argentina's José Mármol, presents a political view in the guise of a love story. *The Squatter and the Don* tells the story of *Californios*, Mexican Americans who lost their property to Anglo European Americans following California's statehood in 1850. The *corrido* is a literary genre that surfaced either in Mexico or in the southern United States during the mid–nineteenth century. Because the *corrido* is an oral genre, a ballad, it undergoes subtle changes as it passes from place to place and from generation to generation. These changes can be indicative of the ballad's singers' perspective of themselves at a particular time and place. It is possible to interpret Chicano detective fiction as a time and circumstance adaptation of a genre whose transformations reflect current perspectives of Chicano communities.

The second and third chapters, "The Shaman Sleuth: Rudolfo Anaya's *Shaman Winter*" and "The Lieutenant and the Chevalier, Buenrostro and Dupin: Rolando Hinojosa's *Partners in Crime*," explore two unique approaches to the familiar whodunit. Anaya and Hinojosa's transformations of the whodunit typify two poles of Chicano fiction, and two poles of its detective fiction. Some Chicano fiction has been described as "realistic." Examples of this realistic literature include Tomás Rivera's novel ... *y no se lo tragó la tierra*, Sandra Cisneros's *The House on Mango Street*, *The Rain God* by Arturo Islas and all the work of Rolando Hinojosa. Other authors emphasize the supernatural or a heightened personal reality. Miguel Méndez's novel *Peregrinos de Aztlán*, *The Road to Tamazunchale* by Ron Arias, Ana Castillo's *So Far from God* and Anaya's *Bless Me, Última* are examples of what has sometimes been called "magic realism." The "reality" of these novels is a true reality from the perspective of the narrator, but may appear "magical" to the reader. Anaya is heavily indebted to Chicano folklore and an indigenous heritage. Hinojosa, influenced by folklorist and ethnographer Américo Paredes, is a narrator who listens to what the *pueblo*, the people, are saying.

Among Chicano authors, Rudolfo Anaya is perhaps the most well known. His growing-up story, a *bildungsroman*, *Bless Me, Última*, has become part of a canon of works by authors of minority American literature. Like *Bless Me, Última*, his detective novels transport the reader to a past that is infused with utopian hope contrasting with the actuality and disillusionment of the present. Anaya's mysteries combine the universalism of myth and romance with the Romantic concept of homeland, *patria*. "Shaman Sleuth" also reviews the circumstances that gave rise to "nation" as "homeland," a political union of members of a cultural community that inspired or was inspired by Romantic Era literature including national tales.

Anaya's detective novels restore foundations of New Mexico's history. Through his mysteries he explores the genealogy of the *Nuevo Mexicano* in particular and the contemporary Chicano in general. Sonny Baca, formerly a teacher and now a private detective, takes a mystical journey back through time to the origins of the *Nuevo Mexicano* in the Valley of Mexico during the pre–Columbian civilization of the Toltecs. In the first novel of Anaya's cycle, *Zia Summer*, the handsome, young and recently divorced Sonny Baca is a man about town who undergoes a spiritual transformation that coincides with his investigation of the crimes of an arch-villain named Raven. The mystery cycle takes place in and around the cities of Albuquerque and Santa Fe in Anaya's native state of New Mexico. His descriptions of the cities are detailed and his observations of nature are authentic and poetic. He establishes a balance between the two cultures, Spanish and Native American, that comprise the inherited culture of his *Nuevo Mexicano* protagonist, and that of many Mexicans and Mexican Americans.

Both Rolando Hinojosa and Rudolfo Anaya write epics. Anaya has written several series of novels, including his detective cycle, whereas Hinojosa's novels are part of the same continuing epic: *The Klail City Death Trip*.

This "macrotext," a term used by critic Rosaura Sánchez, is about a place in south Texas with the fictional name of Belken County (Sánchez 76). Hinojosa's detective stories continue a tale that he began in 1973 with the publishing of *Estampas del valle y otras obras*, the story of two cousins, Rafa Buenrostro and Jehú Malacara. Hinojosa has written the saga of Rafa and Jehú in unconventional novels, poetry, and finally as detective fiction.

Chicanos are new to the detective genre, but are experienced survivors of historical circumstances not dissimilar to those that gave rise to this genre during the Romantic Era. The third chapter, "The Lieutenant and the Chevalier, Buenrostro and Dupin: Hinojosa's *Partners in Crime*," discusses the Romantic origins of detective fiction. In part, mysteries were a fictional response to an increasingly complex world. The Industrial Revolution, major technological improvements in transportation, rural poverty, and burgeoning city populations fueled an increase in urban crime. In Hinojosa's *Rafe Buenrostro* mysteries, Belken County moves out of an isolated rural past and into an era of global communication and international drug trafficking.

In *Partners in Crime* Rafa Buenrostro is now called Rafe, the English pronunciation of his Spanish nickname. He is a homicide detective, a veteran of the Korean War and a young widower. He is a serious young man who loves to read literature but also knows his baseball. Rafe has deep roots in Belken County, where his family, original settlers in the area, has lived for centuries but was pushed aside generations before Rafe by Anglo Texans and their Mexican allies. In 1972, Rafe and his cousin Jehú, a bank officer, are in positions of power that were formerly unavailable to members of their family. In contrast to Hinojosa's earlier novels, his detective fiction was originally written in English, which has become the dominant language of Rafe and Jehú's generation.

Hinojosa, like Anaya, delves into a familiar past, to investigate the history and genealogy of another Chicano homeland. Although, Hinojosa's mysteries are not particularly symmetrical or balanced, they, in contrast to Anaya's, retain a grainy realism. Hinojosa constructs his novels with pieces of spoken language; unlike Anaya, he avoids narrative descriptions. The mystery novels of Anaya and Hinojosa are rooted in the experience of generations of Mexicans made American citizens in the mid–nineteenth century. Anaya emphasizes the traditional roots of this population in New Mexico whereas Hinojosa explores the social, political and cultural abuse suffered by generations of *Tejano Mexicanos*.

Lucha Corpi tells her story in a series of three *Gloria Damasco* detective novels and to date one *Brown Angel* mystery. In contrast to Anaya and Hinojosa, she begins with the Chicano movement of the 1960s and continues forward in time to embrace recent immigration from Mexico. The title of the fourth chapter is "Poetry in Action: Lucha Corpi's *Cactus Blood.*" Anaya and Hinojosa investigate the genealogies of a centuries-old culture. Whereas from Mexico, Corpi[2] brings—fresh and direct—the ingredients that constantly enrich the U.S. based Mexican culture. Corpi's protagonist and the characters in her mysteries return to or maintain ties with contemporary Mexico. The year 1910—the year of the initiation of the Mexican Revolution—signals a demographic shift in the U.S. Mexican population. Since that date, Mexican immigrants to the United States and their descendents began to outnumber the people whose families were settled before 1850 within the confines of the current borders of the United States. Now, in the twenty-first century, the majority of Mexican Americans are descendents of post–1910 immigrants.

Corpi, a well-known Chicana poet and novelist (*Delia's Song*) who has written in Spanish as well as English, brings metaphoric language and images to detective fiction. Her novels are as complex as *mole*, a *salsa* that combines chile and chocolate from the *mestizo*[3] heartland of Mexico. The hot *picante* taste, the crime, is the first sensation on the tongue or in the mind, but rich chocolate and poetic images of human emotions are just below the *picante* bite. Corpi's detective fiction may be an acquired taste for readers of mainstream mysteries, but it is well worth the effort. As consumers have learned, hot sauce is more interesting than catsup because it has a more complex flavor.[4]

Chicanas, women who were active in the male–directed movement of the late 1960s and women who felt confined by patriarchal family traditions, were given a voice of their own beginning in the 1970s by a group of Mexican American female authors, the majority of whom were poets. Corpi's was one of the voices of this first generation of Chicana authors.

In 1981 two Chicanas, Gloria Anzaldúa[5] and Cherríe Moraga, co-edited *This Bridge Called My Back*, a collection of essays, fiction and poetry by women of color. Their efforts defined the common ground between women of color and the outstanding differences between these women and those of the mainstream feminist movement. Anzaldúa, in her work *Borderlands/La Frontera*, combined autobiographical narrative and poetry. As a person marginalized by four distinct characteristics—woman, lesbian, Mexican American, and born into poverty—Anzaldúa provided a poetic image that has influenced the thinking of postcolonial theorists. *Borderlands/La Frontera* has been a "fundamental contribution" and is "deservedly well known" in Latin America, the United States and Great Britain (Mignolo 54; Singh and Schmidt 13). For Anzaldúa the political limen, the threshold, between Mexico and the United States was also seen as a cultural line of demarcation between peoples. The "border" sheds its "blood" that mixes with the blood of south and north, and then heals itself only to bleed and mix again. It is seen as a living open wound that has the power to heal itself through a process that combines hostile confrontation with shared experience and contemplation. In *Cactus Blood*, Lucha Corpi uses an extended metaphor analogous to Anzaldúa's bleeding border. The novel follows the life of a Mexican immigrant woman, her border crossings, national and cultural, the abuse she suffers, and her periods of sickness and healing.

Gloria Damasco is the protagonist of Corpi's first series of mysteries. She was an activist during the Chicano movement, a working mother and wife. In *Cactus Blood* as a widow and a professional woman she is making a career change by training herself, with a little professional help, to be a gun-carrying private eye. The *Gloria Damasco* detective novels tell the "now" history of Chicanas which is juxtaposed with the "then" history of their mothers and grandmothers. Gloria's former career as a speech therapist was in health care, which with the exception of the medical doctor, provides more careers for females than males. Many Romantic heroines don men's clothing to follow the idealistic goals of their lovers. Gloria embraces a dominantly male profession and her youthful activism to investigate the abuse that Chicanas and Chicanos have suffered and are suffering.

The mystery novels of Lucha Corpi, those of Anaya, Hinojosa, Nava and Ramos, do not clearly adhere to conventional models of the genre. Many analyses of detective fiction highlight a connection between hermeneutic analysis and this genre. The basic assumption of these analyses is that the majority of detective fiction is so constructed that its readings perforce lead to a search for a singular irrefutable "truth" that is revealed through plot construction and confirmed by the conclusion. In many ways, and particularly in Corpi's novels, the Chicano detective genre does not conform to this description. The chapter "Poetry in Action" briefly describes hermeneutic analysis and its application vis-à-vis the conventions of the detective genre.

With their experience as legal professionals, Michael Nava and Manuel Ramos enhance Corpi's poetic view of a post–1910 Mexican American genealogy. The detectives brought to life by these lawyers are familiar with recent immigration, the adjustments required of immigrants and their families, the assimilationist attitudes of some segments of the long-established Mexican American population and the lack of support from and abuse meted out by state and federal institutions. Nava and Ramos do not shy away from following the male-centered hard-boiled formula. My fifth and sixth chapters focus on contrasting concepts of masculinity in Mexican

U.S.A. As detectives, the lawyer-protagonists are required through the practice of law to investigative their communities' and their own concepts of masculinity.

Luis Montez, the creation of Manuel Ramos, and Michael Nava's detective Henry Rios are a pair of misfits in a traditional Chicano community that reveres strong father figures. Montez is twice divorced, his mother is dead, and he rarely sees his two sons. He does have a close relationship with his father. In Nava's mysteries, Henry Rios has lost his parents and he does not regret their deaths because he witnessed their abusive relationship as a child and young adult. He has one sibling, a sister; Luis Montez has a mountain of siblings. The relationships the two lawyer-detectives maintain with their siblings are tenuous. Both, soon to be facing middle age, are heavy-drinking, bar-hopping guys when their investigative careers begin. Luis is chasing his youth, following the hemlines of young Chicanas' skirts, while Henry is trying to find a male Cinderella lover to rescue and be adored by for the rest of his life.

Superficial characteristics of the whodunit, particularly those of the lone male private eye, devoid of family ties and close friends outside his professional life, have suggested a facile distinction between the Chicano and the Anglo American or British sleuth. The sixth chapter, "Marginalization in Aztlán," discusses constructs of white male masculinity in the hard-boiled genre, its Depression-era origin and the similarities and distinctions between these and the tortilla variety of masculinity. "Breaking the *Macho* Mold" chronicles the fabrication of traditional Chicano masculinity and contemporary changes in its construction as reflected in its current refusal to conform to a particular mold.

The Anglo male sleuth is typically a loner who may have a male associate, does not maintain close familial or intimate relationships, but who is very cognizant of his community's values, habits and geography. Francisco Lomelí and his co-authors point out that as "protagonists [Chicano detectives] behave in ways that demonstrate a strong sense of identity with and close connections to their communities" (Lomelí et al 299). It would be difficult to establish this as a defining characteristic that separates the Chicano sleuth from the male protagonists of mainstream of Anglo-American and British detective fiction. Superficially Henry Rios and Luis Montez comport themselves more in line with their hard-boiled predecessors than with a Chicano who is closely connected with family and community. In order to make a comparison between Anglo hard-boiled fiction and the Chicano genre, the respective detectives' communities must first be defined. The protagonists of Nava and Ramos have close connections to their communities, but these may or may not be the communities held up as representational of the Mexican American population, and so superficially it may appear that their communal ties are weak. The same can be said of the Anglo hard-boiled sleuth.

The detective fiction of Manuel Ramos and Michael Nava questions assumptions that have long been held about the Chicano family and community. "Marginalization in Aztlán" discusses the work of Mexican American essayist Richard Rodriguez and his relationship to the Chicano literary community. In the experience of the fictional protagonists of Nava and Ramos, and in the life experience of Richard Rodriguez, there are other recipes than *mamá's* for salsa. Family and community relationships are changing all across the United States, and Chicanos are not immune to the causes of these changes or free from their effects. It is possible to combine pineapple, avocado, jalapeños, cilantro, mango and a dash of chipotle peppers and make a great new salsa.

"More *Salsa*," my seventh chapter, lists and offers summaries of this genre fiction by Cuban Americans, Puerto Ricans, Central Americans and Chicanos whose works are not explored in the body of this study. Detective fiction written by Latinos living in the United States runs the gamut from the investigation of a Nazi torturer by a German Chicano, to a Salvadorian homicide detective in Nashville, Tennessee, to a dinosaur working out of Los Angeles. In this chapter I include biographical information of a dozen authors, summaries of their novels and brief biographies of Anaya, Corpi, Hinojosa, Nava and Ramos.

Writers of the genre have at times been free with their insights as well as their defense of mystery and detective fiction. A classic volume, *The Art of the Mystery Story*, edited by Howard Haycraft and first published in 1946, contains, among others, essays by G.K. Chesterton, Dorothy Sayers and Raymond Chandler. Following this tradition in my seventh chapter, I present some insights on the Chicano genre from some of its writers, Anaya, Corpi, Hinojosa, Nava and Ramos, gleaned from published interviews and recent communications that I have had with a number of them. This chapter also attempts to give some biographical insight into the works of the authors studied in the body of my text. These five professionals, educators and lawyers have lived and worked in northern and southern California, Texas, Colorado and New Mexico and have during the last three decades shown an active interest in some of the most pressing problems of our time.

"Identity?" is the eighth and final chapter of my study and reviews questions that have been put forth by Chicano literary criticism and those discussed in the contested space of identity politics. Akin to all identity constructs, that of a minority population is reflected in cultural, ethnic, national or geographic mirrors. However, in contrast to a member of the majority population or of an isolated minority group, the negotiation of individual identity for the hyphenated individual is more complex. He or she will perforce see "self" in a greater number of mirrors, some of which are conflicting. Critics Tey Diana Rebolledo, Eliana Rivero, José David Saldívar, Ramón Saldívar and Rafael Pérez-Torres, and autobiographers Gloria Anzaldúa, Cherríe Moraga and Richard Rodriguez have all defined processes that have led to the formation of an integrated *hyphenless* identity.

The chapter "Identity?" discusses the detective fiction of Anaya, Hinojosa, Corpi, Nava and Ramos as "foundational fictions." Doris Sommer coined this term to describe historical fiction written in Latin America during the second half of the nineteenth century and the first decades of the twentieth century. She uses "foundational fiction" to describe a literature that could not properly be called "national" when it was written because it could only suggest a national identity that was as yet unformed (*Foundational Fictions* 15).

Romantic literature and literatures that follow Romantic models have been criticized as past and present promoters of divisive worldviews. I will refer to the current debate revolving around the questionable validity of teleological, sociopolitical and literary histories that establish cultural identities. A brief discussion of current literary criticism's views of identity politics is discussed in chapter eight.

In practice, the detective genre continues to require a specific setting. Its plot may be farfetched, but its milieu must relate to a historical reality. In general the genre prefers the context of a circumscribed community. In order to write a detective story, the Chicano genre authors have had to define their particular detectives' environments in relationship to the hegemonic Anglo American community. Furthermore, they have been obligated by the genre itself to distinguish "Chicano" community in relationship to the protagonist's space. Each author goes about this differently and constructs unique definitions. These make up the matrices of an incipient, unrealized foundational tale. A single foundation has not been established. Origin is still in question. Each author proposes an origin, with a refreshing caveat for those of us who may feel burdened by a hegemonic origin tale: Chicano origin need not be fixed, sanctioned or limited.

Detective fiction is the first Chicano genre to come on the scene since the *corrido* that has the potential to reach a broad group of Mexican Americans. The *corrido* has told many stories of the Mexican American experience. Its history began in the nineteenth century during social conflict between honest hard-working people and their oppressors north and south of the border. Though it now follows the confrontation between drug traffickers and the state governments, the basic ballad has not changed: the hero still belongs to the people. He bravely faces powerful tyrants; most of the time he is generous, but sometimes he is cruel, and he is almost always dead when his song is sung. For right or wrong, his life serves as an example. What has changed in the *corrido* is the hero's environment.

The environment of the Mexican American population is no longer rural but predominately urban. In this space it is practically impossible to ignore oneself as reflected by a multiplicity of mirrors, many of which are Mexican American. My "Identities" chapter looks at images behind images for common denominators among Chicano detectives, their loves, their antagonists, their lives and their homes. These factors suggest that the prevalent self-reflection is that of a person standing between two or more mirrors. From a fixed center the image both multiplies and grows smaller. The possibilities are infinite and diminishing. Chicano detective fiction agrees that the future of this group is positive, that its identity is fluid and cannot be erased. Among them, Rudolfo Anaya, Lucha Corpi, Rolando Hinojosa, Michael Nava and Manuel Ramos have created an outline for a recipe that is deliciously open to the imagination.

# 1

## Chicano Romance
### *Histories and Mythologization*

Tales of mystery, romance and crime are not alien to Chicano literature. They just have not been written as detective fiction until recently. One rainy afternoon and on into an equally rainy evening I listened to the soggy campers of my bilingual Brownie Scout troop while away the hours telling stories. Each claimed to know the "right" version of one story and its telling was a joint effort with considerable discussion of the details. The story, familiar to many Mexican Americans, tells of a girl who went to a dance. According to the Brownies, and they all agreed on this point, the girl snuck out to the dance because she didn't have her mother's permission. Some of the girls said she'd been mean to her baby brother, others said that she hadn't done her homework and this was why she didn't have permission, but they all confirmed that she was at the dance and she danced with a mysterious stranger. They had many different descriptions of the stranger — he was cute, he was ugly, he wore really neat clothes, he had a tail. He was, however, really bad, as in evil. And then the girl disappeared. For the Brownies there was no need for an investigation. The moral was clear: Don't disobey your mother.

Seen from a different perspective, this folktale was investigated by an ethnographer. José Limón, in his book *Dancing with the Devil*. He concluded that for his subjects in south Texas the stranger was the devil. He was an Anglo sought after by the women who told the story because of the power and prosperity his race could guarantee. But he was feared because of his unknown qualities and the criticism the storytellers would receive for having danced with him. The girl who danced with the devil is only one example of mysterious folktales told by generations of Mexican Americans. Others tell of fateful wedding days, returning ghosts, eavesdropping animals and the most famous, the *Llorona*, the crying woman who kills her own children.

Until the 1960s the most popular Mexican American literary genres have been oral. In the late 1960s and early 1970s Mexican Americans began to produce a hitherto unknown amount of written literature. For the most part, this renaissance of Chicano literature found its readership among the educated, with the possible exception of the one-act plays, *Actos*, directed by the Teatro Campesino, created by Luis Valdez. The majority of these bilingual plays were not written, but created "through improvisation by a group" of farm laborers who were also the performers and constituted the majority of the audience (Valdez 13).

Much of Chicano literature written in the 1960s and 1970s—history, fiction, poetry and literary criticism — was aware of the political ramifications of a unified Mexican American population. In 1959, shortly before this renaissance of Mexican American letters, José Antonio Villarreal published the novel *Pocho* that "has always been somewhat of an embarrassment to Chicanos" (Saldívar, R. 65). It was criticized in the Chicano community for its assimilationist outlook, its *bildungsroman* form that allows a youthful narrator to analyze his elders and for the disintegration of the Mexican American family that it portrayed.

Some Chicano criticism of the 1970s, 1980s and early 1990s was reductionist when it came to the formation of a Chicano literary canon. Perhaps this attitude stemmed from the fact that oral literature is subject to editing by the community it serves. For example: "In the corrido [a ballad] individual goals and communal concerns are one and the same" (Saldívar, R. 62). "Chicano" affiliation was sometimes measured by whether a Mexican American subscribed to the political goals of the Chicano movement. Identification with community values thought to distinguish the Chicano population from the mainstream population and other minority groups tended to be the common thread that unified this literature that was written primarily by men.

Identification, whether in search of Chicano identity or in its affirmation, has been a dominant theme in this literature for these last three decades. The Chicanas tweaked the male-centered identity question by asserting their conflicts with patriarchal viewpoints and thus painting a broader picture of the Mexican American female than was available for the male. However, the early dominance of a patriarchal viewpoint and the appended, rather than embracing, inclusion of female authors in their midst contributed to a somewhat limited canon and identity. For example, lawyer and Chicano activist Oscar Zeta Acosta's novel *Autobiography of a Brown Buffalo* (1972) was lauded by the canon, despite its graphic images, whereas John Rechy's equally graphic *City of Night* (1963) was ignored because its hero's principal dilemma was not his Mexican American ethnicity, but his sexual identity. During the 1970s and 1980s, "[o]vert political expression and the portrayal of a standard Chicano identity became the hallmarks of the preferred texts in the growing Chicano canon" (Barvosa-Carter 267). Although this form of criticism is primarily a tradition of the past, Chicano detective fiction could find itself marginalized by a narrow politically motivated ethnic identity.

All literature is a product of its historical era and its literary antecedents. Much of Chicano detective fiction has the same historical roots as the canonized literature first produced in the 1960s and 1970s, but it is also a product of the demographic changes of the last twenty years that this study explores through the works of individual authors. This chapter takes a look at Romantic nineteenth-century roots that renaissance Chicano literature and current whodunits share.

The authors whose works are considered in the body of this study identify themselves as having a Mexican American heritage, and each has written two or more detective novels. Their novels are influenced by Anglo American and British formulaic mystery and spy fiction. However, for any of them to be without at least a modicum of influence from Mexican or Mexican American oral literatures is virtually impossible. All of the authors included in this book are university educated readers and were or are students of literature. Even though Mexican American literature was primarily an oral literature these authors can claim precursors in the works of a slim number of novels written in the nineteenth century. This chapter discusses a popular oral genre, the *corrido*, a Mexican or Mexican American ballad, and novels of foundational fiction that date from the annexation of northern Mexico by the United States.

By 1853 there were nearly 100,000 new U.S. citizens of Mexican origin living in the United States (Gonzales, M. 79). The Gadsden Purchase of 1853 completed the annexation of northern Mexico that began in Texas in 1836. Their written literature consisted for the most part of memoirs, short fiction and poetry primarily published in Spanish language newspapers. Novels were rare because "the particular economic and cultural circumstances of the nineteenth-century Southwest were not conducive to the production of novels" (Paredes, Raymund 32). Two notable exceptions in the history of Mexican American literature are the Romantic foundational fictions of María Amparo Ruiz de Burton, *The Squatter and the Don* published in English in 1885, and *The Son of the Storm* and *The Calm After the Storm*, first published in Spanish in 1892 by Eusebio Chacón. During and after the Mexican Revolution, from 1910 to 1920, many educated Mexicans fled their country, wrote in Spanish and published more extended fictional narratives, short stories and a few novels. However, during the second half of the nineteenth century and the first half of the twentieth few Mexican Americans were literate, nor did they have either the disposable time or a cultural tradition of reading novels, a consequence of Spain's prohibition of the writing and importation of novels to its colonies that was in force until Mexican independence in 1821.

Traditional oral forms of literature, Spanish medieval *romance* (ballad poems), religious "*alabados* (morning songs), *pastorelas* (Christmas plays), *posadas* (shepherd plays) and [secular] folktales," continued to be popular after the colonial period and to this day (Fernández 253). The *corrido*, a secular ballad sung in Spanish that passed the news of achievements and frustrations from community to community, continues to be sung. Currently its most popular songs, those that tell the stories of drug trafficking,[1] are prohibited in Mexico and largely ignored by Chicano critics and the mainstream media alike in the United States.

In the late nineteenth and early twentieth centuries, Spanish *romancero* (ballad poetry) was transformed in America — Mexico and southwestern United States— into the *corrido*. The *corrido* was the most accessible form of secular literature available to the majority of Mexican Americans. It was primarily a song about men that told of abuse by Anglo Americans and the confrontations between them and the Chicano workingman. During the Mexican Revolution it brought news from home to the Mexican immigrant population of the United States. Some of the *corridos* sung were regional adaptations of specific Medieval Spanish *romances* and others retained many of the literary conventions of *romancero* but told new stories.

The earliest *romances* have been shown to be fragments of Spanish epic poetry of the twelfth century that told the story of Spain's 800-year battle, the *Reconquista* (711 to 1492), to rout the Moors from the Iberian Peninsula. Conflict is the dominant theme of *romancero* and the *corrido*. A discussion of these genres is presented here with the intention of highlighting their social and symbolical roots. When *romancero* was adapted by the Mexican and Mexican American population it was already well suited to their particular nineteenth- and twentieth-century ideological needs. As we shall see in chapters three and four, the *corrido* is not unique in its retention of what Fredric Jameson terms "a socio-symbolic message" (Jameson *Political* 141). "The Shaman Sleuth" discusses the historical circumstances that cultivated the Romantic national tale in Europe while "The Lieutenant and the Chevalier" will examine the emergence of the detective genre as an ideological message.

An ideological message central to an original form can withstand appropriations committed by opposing ideologies[2] even when "reappropriated for new ideological (and nationalizing) purposes" (*Political* 141). When reappropriated by an opposing reality the socio-symbolic message will "be functionally reckoned into the new form," be only superficially apparent, but will not have been lost to the literary form itself (*Political* 141). The Spanish epic ballad originated as a call to arms by a conquered people during the later half of the *Reconquista*, was later enshrined as the national song of the conquering Spanish monarchs and as the song their conquest of America. Its reality as the anthem of a conquered people was buried. However, during its history in America, *romance* continued to live and change. The *corrido* is a prime example of a literary genre whose original ideological message resurfaced. Like the original fragmented epic, the *corrido* sings the song of a conquered people who actively challenge their oppressors.

The first published collections of *romancero* appeared in 1545, but erudite interest began in the Court of Isabella and Ferdinand and coincided with the national consolidation of Spain in 1492. When the battles of the *Reconquista* had ended and the conflict shifted to the ideological front of religious "reality" the Jews (1492) and then the Moslems (1502), some of whom had been allies of the Spanish in the battles of the *Reconquista* and had aided the writing of Spanish history, were deported from Spain or forced to convert to Catholicism. At this point *romancero* is heavily influenced by its written versions and preserves only superficial traces of the historical conflicts of the *Reconquista*. It preserves through exaggeration — by the exclusion of more mundane artifacts associated with the epic hero and through erudite embellishment of his enemy's luxury — the hero's austerity in contrast to the villain's gluttony that later will figure in the characterization of a unified and nationalized Spanish identity in the nineteenth century. A song that tells the story of the exploits of a fiercely independent soldier-leader, whose service is given willingly to an honest monarch or an honest cause, no longer defines *romancero* in 1545.

Historical events of the eighteenth and nineteenth centuries moved Spain even further from its *Reconquista* past. The Borbón dynasty (1701–1808) centralized the administration of government and promoted the *Frenchification* of Spanish culture. In 1808 Napoleon installed his brother as the Spanish monarch. His reign was short lived, but more humiliation was in store for Spain: the loss of the majority of its American colonies in 1821, intermittent civil wars that contested the legitimacy of the crown and native sons who embraced European liberalizing movements. Liberal writers emulated the forms and themes of *Reconquista* literature and its individualistic hero, in order to protest a centralized federal perspective and the loss of traditional regional rights that dated from nearly

1,000 years earlier. *Romancero* as a literary genre made a comeback that reversed the 1492 ideological perspective. However, some of these same Romantic writers later put aside their reformist ideologies and joined other writers and scholars in a return to the *romancero* agenda of 1492: consolidation and origin mythology.

Meanwhile, on the other side of the Atlantic in nineteenth-century Mexico and south Texas, *romancero* that had been around since the conquest of America was emerging as a uniquely American adaptation: the *corrido*.

Murder is the topic of one ballad that brings its point home on the blade of knife in the *romance* and on the barrel of a gun in the American *corrido*. The *romance* "La amiga de Bernal Francés," originally recorded in fifteenth-century Spain, and its American sister "Elena" are two versions of a particularly gruesome murder story. A comparison between them is a good example of the retention of an ideology and the traces of "the historical ground ... in which the original structure was meaningful" (Jameson *Political* 146). "La amiga de Bernal Francés" has been a very popular *romance*, that, according to *romancero* scholar Mercedes Díaz Roig, has at least 76 variations in America alone. Versions of this *romance* continued to be sung as late as 1964 in Spain and 1953 in New Mexico (Alvar 278, Díaz Roig 55). Crime and passion seem to be enduringly popular subjects.

The early twentieth-century *Tejano corrido* "Elena" and the fifteenth-century *romance* narrate the story of a tragic love triangle: a suspicious husband kills his wife's presumed lover, disguises himself as the lover to confirm his suspicion, then reveals his identity, confronts his wife and kills her also. There is a lot of blood.

Bernal Francés is the lover in the *romance*. The chronicles of the Catholic Kings, Isabella and Ferdinand, describe him as a Spanish captain in the war against Granada, the last and decisive battle of the *Reconquista*, who was as valiant as he was greedy (Menéndez-Pidal 156). The "Bernal Francés" of the *romance* collected in 1938 from an oral source in Spain by Ramón Menéndez-Pidal characterizes him as a Frenchman, an obviously ahistorical *Reconquista* villain since the French had no part in this 800-year battle (153). In this twentieth-century version of the *romance*, the Frenchman is a perfect villain, a necessary enemy scapegoat for nineteenth-century Spain still resentful of a couple of centuries of French meddling. The stoicism and the moral superiority of the wronged husband most likely appealed to *Generalísimo* Franco also.

The material props of this *romance* of Spain emphasize exotic luxury: "sábanas de Holanda" ("sheets from Holland"), "silla de plata con respaldo de marfil" ("a silver chair with a marble back"), bath water of "agua de toronjil" ("lemon balm essence"), a bed of roses and a headboard of "alhelí" (a sweet-smelling type of flower) (Menéndez-Pidal 156). When the nameless wronged husband reveals himself, he promises his wife a dress of "fina grana" ("fine woven fabric") lined in "carmesí" ("crimson") and proceeds to cut her throat. This moral tale goes beyond the bedroom; the wife is accused of sleeping with the enemy, a traditional enemy who in this case embodies not only the ostentatious luxury of the ancient Moorish *Reconquista* enemy but also the haughty grandeur of the nineteenth-century French Empire and the greedy materialism of North American imperialism that in 1898 reduced the Spanish Empire to the confines of the Peninsula.

In the Mexican or *Tejano corrido* version the wronged husband, "*don* Benito*" shoots his wife's French lover. Américo Paredes, who published this *corrido* in 1976, states that it was frequently heard circa 1920, a date near the end of the hostilities of the Mexican Revolution. Other American versions of this ballad collected during the twentieth century conserve the luxury of the Spanish Peninsular *romance* (Díaz Roig 55, 62). In the *corrido* collected by Paredes, and in another version collected in Mexico by Vicente Mendoza in 1939, luxury is completely absent (339). This reflects the historical period at the end of the Mexican Revolution after the country had been devastated by ten years of bloodshed and chaos. The choice of weapon, a pistol instead of a knife, is also a reflection of this period of Mexican history. In the *Tejano* version *don* Benito shoots his wife who, unlike the wife of the Peninsular version, is characterized as a mother. The *Tejano* version makes it clear that she not only betrays her husband, but also their children.

The Mexican Revolution left the country and its people in ruin and with little direction. In its literature Mexico has been seen as orphaned by the destruction of this civil war and by the greedy interests of revolutionary leaders. Two examples are Mariano Azuela's *Los de abajo* ("*The Underdogs*") of 1916, and Carlos Fuentes' *La muerte de Artemio Cruz* ("*The Death of Artemio Cruz*") of 1962. In the *corrido* Elena's infidelity, her lack of focused commitment to her marriage, is responsible for her children's orphanhood. She asks that they not be told of her sin; symbolically her children represent Mexico and will be protected from the stigma of adultery. Her husband promises to keep the secret and the shame of their history withheld from them. The history of the atrocities committed by some revolutionaries during the battle and later in postrevolutionary Mexico through the machinations of the Institutional Revolutionary Party (PRI) have not been told until very recently.

In "Elena" it is possible that "*don* Benito" is a reference to Mexican

President Benito Juárez (1861–1872) whose presidency was interrupted by the French puppet Empire of Mexico. Mexican historian Enrique Krauze highlights Juárez's Zapotec[3] characteristics of "natural stoicism," "sobriety" and "industry" (160). If Paredes' date of 1920 accurately reflects the date when this *corrido* began to circulate, the references to the French invasion of the nineteenth century and to Benito Juárez, who ultimately recovered the country for the Mexicans, seem to refer to an earlier historical period. However, in conjunction with the reference to Elena's orphaned children, her French lover can also refer to the Frenchified dictatorship of Porfirio Díaz that the Revolution toppled.

Paredes collected this *corrido* in Texas; its popularity in the 1920s reflects a Mexican American, *Tejano Mexicano* sense of abandonment. The Mexican dictator Díaz ignored the mistreatment of Mexican Americans and Mexican nationals in Texas and gave no quarter to people of these groups who fought North American abuse (see Acuña, Hart and Paredes). Typical of the *corrido*, the song ends with moral advice: "Señoras," it says, must be careful not to let what happened to the "cautelosa" ("crafty") Elena happen to them. Considering the political undertones of the original twelfth-century *romancero* and those mentioned above that are evident in the *corrido* "Elena," it would appear that this *corrido* manifests an ideology similar to that of the conquered Spanish who fought for the unification of their peninsula and their individual rights against a beguiling enemy.

Two exemplary, but not unique, Mexican American *corridos*, "The Ballad of Joaquín Murrieta" and "The Ballad of Gregorio Cortez," describe a wrongly accused Mexican who fights for his rights in the United States. In both of these documented late nineteenth-century, early twentieth-century ballads identifying with the Mexican American community saves the life of hero as he outwits the representatives of North American authorities (see Limón *Mexican* and Paredes *With His*). For Paredes the "Ballad of Gregorio Cortez" is "deadly serious" singing that throws out a "challenge" that represents an earnestness that he describes by the phrase, "I will break before I will bend" (*With His* 33).

Paredes collected *Tejano* versions of the "Ballad of Gregorio Cortez" in the 1950s and his narrator, who tells the story of the *corrido* tradition in *With His Pistol in His Hand*, laments that the song of south Texas and its epic hero has lost out to "these pachucos[4] ... mumbling damn-foolishness into a microphone" (34). His groundbreaking study of this ballad encouraged the scholarship of Chicano poets, songwriters, ethnographers, novelists and literary critics. However, Paredes was wrong about the ballad's staying power and its defiant message being lost. There is no doubt that the *corrido* has continued to influence Chicano literature and popular culture (see Limón, Lomelí et al., Rebolledo, Rivero, Tatum, Pérez-Torres, Saldívar, J. and Saldívar, R). The original Spanish medieval epic continues to change and adapt. A current popular reincarnation is the *narcocorrido*, that has chosen as its hero the border drug traffic king who comes across in this genre as a tragic or successful "pirate" who flouts the law on both sides of the border and in some cases acts as a benevolent Robin Hood providing his community with material assistance and protection.

Since the early nineteenth century, during Romanticism, literary histories have been organized and taught as the work of a particular group of people defined by ethnicity, by political borders or both. Mexican American authors have been engaged in a similar pursuit, but it was not until the 1960s that this became a pan–Mexican American project whose initial objective was not only the writing of history but the recovery of written and oral literature and the production and dissemination of Chicano literature and art. The novels of María Amparo Ruiz de Burton and Eusebio Chacón are among these recently rediscovered works.

In the early nineteenth century the new nations of America, north and south, were writing their identities, genealogies of *patria*. The national tales of the American nations emulated the romance form of their European fathers. Mother authors were in short supply; the Romantic heroine was the embodiment of mother country and was fertile ground either waiting patiently for the plow or open to the desecration of weeds. The authors of these romances, as Doris Sommer notes, "passion[ately]" needed to establish their own non–European, American identity (*Foundational Fictions* 15). Even though they did not want to be identified with Native Americans, they readily assumed the characteristics Jean Jacques Rousseau (1712–1778) had attributed to the "natural man"— primitively pure, materially disinterested, a participant in governance by natural law and unfettered by meaningless dogma — as markers to separate themselves from the old world and connect them with their new land. Among these writers are the U.S. writer James Fenimore Cooper (1789–1851), the Argentine José Mármol (1817–1871) and the Colombian Jorge Isaacs (1837–1895). These authors, and others, were spokesmen or power brokers of the newly independent nations and played a major role in defining new gentilics: "American" (in the United States), "Argentine" and "Colombian" to their fellow citizens. The gentilic "Chicano" would have to wait until the second half of the twentieth century, when a pan–Mexican American identity became a contextual reality.

Doris Sommer notes in *Foundational Fictions; the National Romances of Latin America*, that these tales typically culminate in either the hero's marriage to the heroine, or her tragic death and his continued longing for her, that throughout the course of the novel has been associated with his yearning for an environment that is both stable and confirms his American identity. European Romantics worked to establish an inherent identity that emphasized a homeland nationality or ethnicity, in opposition to those imposed and in affirmation of those discredited by imperial governments. For the Romantic, the historical and artistic inheritance of his homeland or ethnicity were considered crucial in order to define his inherent identity that would in turn support and give meaning to a natural connection to his region. In Germany the Grimm brothers researched folktales and language as the means by which a German ethnicity could claim distinction. In British dominated Scotland, Sir Walter Scott novelized the history of his countrymen. In America, authors of the early nineteenth century created their identity from the raw material of the American landscape, Rousseau's image of the "noble savage," Americanized European language, religion and traditions.

Unlike many of their European counterparts, Romantic American national tales were stories with contemporary settings, and for this, among other reasons, Sommer's term "foundational fictions" describes them well. "In the United States, it has been argued, the country and the novel practically gave birth to each other. And the same can be said of the South [South America], as long as we take consolidation rather than emancipation [from Europe] to be the real moment of birth in both Americas" (*Foundational* 12).

Since their wars for independence, liberal versus conservative conflicts have plagued the former Spanish colonies. Referring to Jameson's genealogy of the origin of the romance genre, Sommer states that these novels "developed a narrative formula for resolving continuing conflicts, a postepic conciliatory genre that consolidated survivors by recognizing former enemies as allies" (*Foundational* 12). Typically the lovers in these novels are from two different political persuasions: one is liberal and the other conservative. In North America and South America these fictions are referred to, if not by name then by content, when national identity is in question (*Foundational* 51). The power they have assumed in the defining of national identity is confirmed by the fact that in Latin America they are required reading in public schools and have been used to consolidate power in times of conflict. Whereas in the United States even though these novels have disappeared from many reading lists, they continue to be a fertile source for epic dramatizations of our history.

María Amparo Ruiz de Burton published a Romantic foundational fiction, *The Squatter and the Don*, in 1885 whose female protagonist was a Mexican American woman born in California. Her novel is one among many works by Mexican Americans that predate the 1960 Chicano literary renaissance, but it is unique because it was written in English in the Romantic national tale genre and attempted to define the new American citizens of Mexican ancestry to mainstream readers.

Even before the forced annexation of northern Mexico by the United States, European and North American "ethnographies" and pulp fiction were describing two, and only two, Mexican populations in this area: the lazy, dark, violent, sexual, poor Mexican and the genteel, polite, intelligent, wealthy, fair complexioned Spaniard (see Acuña, Gonzales, M., Limón, Padilla, Paredes and Ridge). Ruiz de Burton employs the "Spanish card" to cash in on the popularity of Anglo European romanticization of Hispanic southern California and to forcefully voice her opposition to the disenfranchisement, abuse and impoverishment of the Mexican American population of California in 1870. The "Squatters" of her title are characterized as the opposites of the Spanish "*Don*" and therefore they replace "black" in the dominant black/white paradigm of U.S. racism, whereas "Spanish" replaces "white." Ruiz de Burton, as the wife of a northern Civil War officer, had to have been familiar with the racial paradigm of black and white that read, and in too many instances still does read, as bad and good. I am not suggesting that Ruiz de Burton subscribed to this paradigm, but she did use it to her advantage. The "bad" squatters were encouraged by the government to homestead, to settle "unsettled" lands, that were in fact owned by the "good" Mexican Americans, but whose titles of ownership the government questioned along with their use.

As in the case of other former Mexican citizens across the Southwest, *don* Mariano, the "*Don*" and the protagonist Mercedes' father, loses all to Anglo European interests despite his noble "Spanish" sentiments that include heroic civility and fair play. Mercedes eventually marries the son of a squatter who through his connections and money has unsuccessfully tried to defend *don* Mariano's land. Ruiz de Burton's novel features a fair Spanish *señorita* and her romantic involvement with the handsome son of a squatter to sympathetically involve an Anglo European readership in the history of the legalized robbery of the lands of the "*Dons*" in California. Ruiz de Burton takes advantage of a historically documented common practice in the Southwest — European American males married Mexican women — then debunks the "anthropological" and pulp fiction stereotype of the lazy, dark, violent, sexual, poor Mexican with her *Californio* protagonists and unites the Anglo European in a matriarchal line with the Californian Mexican Americans of the nineteenth century. Somewhere in this story the Mexican American patriarchal line is lost.

*The Squatter and the Don* reproduces legal arguments used by the federal government in support of homesteaders who flooded California during the second half of the nineteenth century. *Don* Mariano owns an extensive cattle ranch that is invaded by farmers who claim the right to shoot his cattle when they trespass on their crops. The farmers justify their cause by accusing *don* Mariano of misusing his property because his land is uncultivated. The federal government will not evict the farmers until *don* Mariano has proven that he has title to the land his family has ranched for generations. He defends his case in court for years, but with the loss of his livestock and his mounting court costs in Washington, D.C., he is financially ruined and loses his land. *Don* Mariano's case reflects the plight of too many large and small landowners of Mexican ancestry in the West.

The Treaty of Guadalupe-Hidalgo (1848) guaranteed the former Mexican citizens full rights as U.S. citizens and guaranteed that their language, religion and property would be respected. These guarantees were rarely enforced and this population has continued to be a less than fully enfranchised population of the United States. An initial and continuing criticism leveled against this population, as portrayed in Ruiz de Burton's novel, was that the Mexican Americans were not taking full commercial advantage of their landholdings (see Acuña, Griswald del Castillo, Gonzales, and Pitt). This charge was updated in 2004 with the publication of Samuel P. Huntington's *Who Are We: The Challenges to America's National Identity*. Economic criticism of this type justified the wholesale robbery of Mexican American property and is typical of veiled Anglo European contempt of Hispanic culture that was and is supported by U.S. history and fiction whose heroes work for national goals that are defined in economic terms.

A case in point comes from one in a series of children's novels, which was also a popular television series in the 1970s, that traces a family's westward movement: Laura Ingalls Wilder's *Little House* series. Even though the protagonist Laura shows a sympathetic interest in Indians it is the comment of a neighbor, Mrs. Scott, that underlies the justification for the settlement of the Ingalls family in Indian Territory. Mrs. Scott comments: "Land knows, they'd [Indians] never do anything with this country themselves. All they do is roam around over it like wild animals. Treaties or no treaties, the land belongs to the folks that'll farm it. That's only common sense and justice" (*Little House on the Prairie* 211). Later the child's hero, her father, assures her that the Indians are no threat: "When white settlers come into a country, the Indians have to move on. The government is going to move these Indians farther west, any time now. That's why we're here, Laura. White people are going to settle all this country, and we get the best land because we get here first and take our pick" (237). The Ingalls family does, however, have to move on because the government has yet to dispose of the Indians' rights to their land.

Initially, many new Mexican American citizens embraced the government of the United States perhaps because they had experienced living conditions in the harsh Southwestern environment. In this remote outpost the Mexican federal government rarely provided the support people needed and occasionally intruded in an undemocratic bureaucratic fashion in the affairs of the settlers. Many were confident that the U.S. government would pay attention to their frontier needs and allow them to have a greater voice in their own governance. Beginning in 1821, the first 25 years of independent Mexico were not administratively distinguishable from the colonial period. The governance of Mexico's northern states was dictated by the conservative oligarchy of central Mexico. Some Mexican residents fought alongside their Anglo European neighbors for the independence of Texas. In California, a prominent leader of the Mexican population, Mariano Guadalupe Vallejo, negotiated with the revolutionaries of the Bear Republic. He did not believe that their barbarian tactics were characteristic of the United States, which he believed respected democratic governance. Ultimately, he learned otherwise, losing, like *don* Mariano, the great majority of his land in legal battles (Padilla *My History* 77–108).

Immediately following the annexation of northern Mexico, laws were enacted by the United States to divest Mexican American property owners of their land and to prohibit foreign nationals from mining in California. Arbitrarily these laws were not applied to European or English speaking foreign nationals but did include U.S. citizens of Mexican ancestry. Denied equal access to material well-being, education and communication, the Mexican American population became dependent on insular regional communities for support until after the Second World War. These communities were not passive, but they had relatively little means by which to communicate with each other, much less with the North American social and political establishment (see Acuña, Gonzales, M., Gómez-Quiñones and Pitt).

Romantic nationalism was just so many broken eggs for the Mexican American resident of the Southwest during the second half of the nineteenth century. Mexico had encouraged Anglo European immigration to the Texan homeland of this population; the United States seemed to offer a government by representation; Mexico's defense of this population, nonexistent or sporadic, was initiated by U.S. armed aggression. Mexico's president-dictator, Antonio López de Santa Anna, took payment from the United States for these lands and then went on to sell more Mexican land to the "colossal of the North" with the Gadsden Purchase of 1853. The

United States did not respect the guarantees of the 1848 Treaty of Guadalupe-Hidalgo. Where in all this mess could a "Mexican American" even know what to call herself, establish lines of communication with *Californios, Nuevo Mexicanos, Tejano Mexicanos* or a less populous group of her same background? In all this chaos Ruiz de Burton felt the need to express self-affirmation. Unfortunately, her English language novel was unavailable to the majority of her Mexican American contemporaries, who spoke only Spanish and could not read.

In Ruiz de Burton's novel there is a clear message that conforms to the basic message of Latin American Romantic foundational fictions. She puts her case before her readers as a love story. The lovers are equally noble people, but their families are in conflict. The consummation of their relationship will combine the best of each family and will signify the beginning of a new nation. This conciliatory tale implies that compromise is in order, a stance that would not have been appreciated in the heady 1960s and 1970s of the Chicano movement.

The groundbreaking revelations and the strident tone Rodolfo Acuña's *Occupied America: The Chicano's Struggle toward Liberation* published in 1972 characterized the stance of the Chicano movement and no doubt contributed to significant gains in education, income and political power. With a more consolidated political base the dialogue with mainstream America has become more effective.

Detective fiction seeks to resolve conflict. In the following chapters I will explore how the mysteries of Anaya, Hinojosa, Corpi, Ramos and Nava approach the resolution of conflict.

# 2

## The Shaman Sleuth
### *Rudolfo Anaya's* Shaman Winter

*Shaman Winter* is the third novel in Anaya's cycle of the exploits of private eye Sonny Baca. The recently published *Jemez Spring* (2005) completes the cycle. Baca's career begins as a Chicano *James Bond*. Through the course of the first three novels the detective must commit to an increasingly spiritual outlook in order to solve each mystery. With the successful conclusion of the case in *Shaman Winter*, Baca has evolved into an investigator-priest. As *Zia Summer* (1995), *Rio Grande Fall* (1996) and *Shaman Winter* (1999) move increasingly toward spiritual solutions, it becomes clear that Anaya uses a detective genre framework to introduce the reader to a world view that is not compatible with a spy-thriller's neat resolution of conflict.

The first three novels of the cycle develop distinctive parallel narratives — contemporary, historical and metaphysical — that are not conclusively resolved on any of these planes. *Shaman Winter*, while entertaining in a *James Bond* fashion, undertakes a greater project: to transform the popular British spy-thriller into a regional historical narrative. Anaya's history of New Mexico is a complex foundational tale that extends the images of the *Aztlán* homeland developed during the Chicano movement of the 1960s and 1970s. Anaya updates the 1960 Chicano foundational tale by diminishing its association with the empire of the Aztecs in *Shaman Winter*.

In Anaya's story the Western distinctions between real time and dream time become hazy as do the distinctions between the literary genres of sociopolitical history and mythological history. In many ways, Anaya's narrative recalls the Nahuatl literary traditions of *Itoloca* and *Xiuhámatl* that were indigenous to speakers of Nahuatl, including Aztecs and non–Aztec peoples. Miguel León-Portilla translates the classification

31

*Itoloca* as "what is said about someone or something" and *Xiuhámatl* as "annals or manuscripts of the years" (León-Portilla *Los antiguos* 50).[1]

*Shaman Winter's* contemporary narrative incorporates basic elements of Ian Fleming's *James Bond* formula: an arch villain, beautiful women, high-speed car chases, violent confrontations, the use of modern technology and a handsome detective. *Shaman Winter*, however, outlines the history of New Mexico, and a Native American perspective informs both its contemporary *James Bond* narrative and its historical text. Through shamanistic powers, times of chaos in the past are revisited. On the *James Bond* plane, real and present danger is confronted. The shamanistic powers that the detective learns to respect and utilize stabilize the situation by connecting temporal and rarified planes— the past, present, future and the metaphysical.

Does this sound like romanticized fantasy? Chicano literary critic Ramón Saldívar has classified Anaya's *Bless Me Última* as a "romantic" novel (*Chicano* 103). What does this mean? Romance genre literature is called "romantic." This term has been used in association with popular genres— westerns, romances and mysteries— and has come to have a negative connotation when literature with a capital L is discussed.

"Romance" is a topic for discussion and in order to clarify what the term represents and why Anaya's cycle is romantic I turn to the Marxist Fredric Jameson and the humanist Northrop Frye. Jameson's genealogy of the romance genre begins in the twelfth century when

> Romance in its original strong form may then be understood as an imaginary "solution" to real contradiction, a symbolic answer to the perplexing question of how my enemy can be thought of as *evil* (that is, as other than myself and marked by some absolute difference), when what is responsible for his being so characterized is quite simply the *identity* of his own conduct with mine [*Political* 118].

At this time of trouble in Western European history, chaos and stability vied for power. The *chanson de geste* is the literature of the winners of this confrontation and as such it needs to answer the question: "What do we call our enemy now that we are living with him?" The *chanson de geste* resolves this conflict by figuring the enemy, the other, as a mirror image of the self; both are honorable knights. When the enemy is "defeated and unmasked, he asks for mercy by *telling his name* ... at which point he becomes one more knight among others and loses all his sinister unfamiliarity" (*Political* 119). According to Jameson, an imaginary resolution of conflict is basic to romance genre.

In contrast, Frye finds the origins of romance not in a genealogy of literature per se, but in a universal form of human expression: folktales. For Frye, "romance is the structural core of all fiction: being directly descended from folktale, it brings us closer than any other aspect of literature to the sense of fiction ... man's vision of his own life as a quest" (15). Frye's evaluation tends to emphasize ethical polarities that may be culturally unintelligible for a reader unfamiliar with the social historical context of a particular literature: good and bad, hero and villain, upper and lower worlds (49–53). In my opinion these worlds need to be located within particular social historical contexts.

Both Jameson's Marxist and Frye's universal humanist frameworks for romance rely on hermeneutic analysis. Hermeneutic analysis presupposes that an inherent truth is encoded in all literary expressions. Nineteenth- and twentieth-century hermeneutic literary analysis has followed two paths: "religiously tinged" and "a hermeneutics of suspicion" (Holub 381). "The first type ... attributes to hermeneutics the function of recapturing or recollecting meaning" (381). The second type "tears away masks and reveals false consciousness" (381). Frye's analysis recalls the "religiously tinged" model and Jameson's the "hermeneutics of suspicion." For Frye, all literature is explained as variations of "the maze without a plan" or "the maze with a plan," both of which are "two aspects of the same thing": romance (31). From Jameson's perspective all literature "is to be seen as an ideological act in its own right, with the function of inventing imaginary or formal 'solutions' for unresolvable social contradictions" (*Political* 79). Frye's analysis "recaptures meaning" and Jameson's exposes the "false consciousness" behind the romance story. He and Frye seem to agree that structurally all literature stems from romance; they disagree as to its origin and function. For Jameson, romance literature addresses actual social economical problems of a particular population as in the problem of the twelfth century above. For Frye, it expresses a universal human quest for knowledge of self. For both authors, literature encodes truth, and to arrive at the truth they establish *a priori* a series of steps for an informed reading of the text that will ultimately reveal the encoded truth.

Anaya's mystery cycle is romantic in both a Marxist and a universal sense. For this reason, it is possible to question whether its reading is meant to lead to a singular truth while at the same time, appreciate the complexities of a romantic narrative.

As *Shaman Winter* begins, Sonny Baca, a handsome thirty-something Chicano male, is confined to a wheelchair because of his last exploit as a detective in *Rio Grande Fall*. "'I feel like James Bond getting rescued by two lovely women,' Sonny said, taking a hot tortilla from the plate and slapping butter on it. 'James Bond doesn't hold a candle to you,' Rita said, placing a plate of huevos rancheros in front of him" (Anaya *Shaman* 282–283). In this scene Sonny is in the company of his girlfriend, Rita, and her friend Lorenza, one of his spiritual teachers. James Bond? Indeed, yes!

A first impression of Anaya's cycle of novels recalls Umberto Eco's description of Ian Fleming's spy-thrillers as being "built on a series of oppositions which allow a limited number of permutations and intersections" ("Narrative" 97). These consist of series of relationships between opposing characters or values along with other levels of narrative structure (108). The pairs on this list "do not represent 'vague' elements but 'simple' ones that are immediate and universal" (97). Remember that "universal" is Frye's key to romance. Initially Sonny is a *Bond*-type playboy. Similar to *Bond* villains, the arch villain, Raven uses Rita and Lorenza to entrap Sonny. Lorenza is a *curandera* ("healer") who was enlisted by Rita in *Zia Summer* to help Sonny recover from a personal trauma. Rita represents Sonny's "immediate and universal" need for food and sexual gratification, while Lorenza represents the equally universal needs for spiritual and healing care. Anaya uses two women, Rita and Lorenza, to personify two characteristics of woman: carnal and spiritual. For Sonny this distinction need not limit his relationship with either woman; he lustfully contemplates Lorenza or contemplates his spiritual union with Rita. The female, Rita-Lorenza, is in an oppositional relationship to the male, Sonny as in "Bond-Woman."

Among the oppositional relationships described by Eco is the one between Bond and M, Bond's superior and the Director of Her Majesty's Secret Service. M is seen as having a "global view" and "a superiority" over Bond (98). *Don* Eliseo, Sonny's aged neighbor, introduced in *Zia Summer*, plays the role of Sonny's "M." Like Fleming's M, *don* Eliseo is "always present as a warning" even if he is not a participant in the exploits of the detective (Eco "Narrative" 98). Sonny's nemesis, Raven, performs the same functions as the villains in the Bond-Villain relationship. Even though Raven is a singular protagonist, he takes on various forms, different names and ethnicities in the course of the cycle. Despite his many manifestations his *modus operandi* is consistent as is that of the various *Bond* villains. His crimes, like theirs, threaten the structures of society itself.

Like Bond, Sonny is an "absolutely ordinary person" (Eco "Narrative" 98), "a regular guy, one of la plebe [ordinary people], one of the vatos [guys]" (Anaya *Shaman* 359). Bond does not exercise "superhuman faculties"; it is Bond's "obstinate fidelity" to his superior that allows him to "overcome superhuman ordeals" (Eco 98). Sonny's dogged pursuit of his own "soul," as overseen by *don* Eliseo, allows him to triumph over Raven (Anaya *Shaman* 357).

Eco, however, might consider some of Sonny's exploits as evidence of "superhuman faculties." In *Shaman Winter*, Sonny has learned from *don* Eliseo to physically enter his dreams. When Sonny masters this talent, he nullifies the villain's powers, frees those whom Raven has captured in dream time and real time, and saves New Mexico from a nuclear disaster. Contemporary Western separation of spiritual and physical worlds of action collapses as these spheres penetrate each other, mix, and dissolve the borders between them.

Anaya's structural parallels between Rita/Lorenza and Bond's women, Sonny and Bond, *don* Eliseo and M, and Raven and any one of Fleming's arch villains suggest the possibility of extending this structural conceit in order to connect the metaphysical and the physical as in the case of "soul" and "obstinate fidelity" as represented by the apprenticeship relation the protagonists Sonny and Bond have with *don* Eliseo and M. Following this reasoning, Anaya's structure breaks with a basic tenet of the spy-thriller genre: the supernatural has no place in a *James Bond* fictional world. By questioning Eco's definition of the *Bond* "superhuman," the separation of spiritual and physical worlds, Anaya promotes the unification of the physical and the spiritual and transforms the entire genre.

"The story as a 'game'" is another structural element of Fleming's *James Bond* fiction as outlined by Eco ("Narrative" 108). He describes this device as a challenge familiar to all readers of Fleming, whose basic plot follows an outline that enumerates the rules of the "game." Eco compares reading *Bond* spy-thrillers to watching the Harlem Globetrotters play basketball (113). Their fans know that the Globetrotters will win and Fleming's readers know how his novels will end, but for both, the variables are unknown and pleasurable. "The scheme is invariable in the sense that all the elements are always present in every novel" (Eco 108). The oppositional pairs presented in each *James Bond* narrative function like chess pieces; they are strictly limited in the manner in which they may move, but the ever changing combination of moves gives novelty and risk to the game and the plot. The roles performed by the characters are mere rhetorical devices used to encourage the reader to follow the plot. If, after reading *Zia Summer*, we assume that Sonny Baca will face the same or a similar villain, will be supported by a familiar contingent of helpers and female companions, that his dreams will play an important role in his success as a detective and that he will again be able to nullify his nemesis's power, we will be rewarded for our predictions in our subsequent readings of the cycle.

A "Manichean ideology" underlies Fleming's narrative structure and, according to Eco, his narrative is Manichean "for operative reasons" ("Narrative" 115). Fleming uses the oppositional pairs of "Free World and Soviet Union," Anglo-Saxon racial purity and non–Anglo ("Great Britain and Non-Anglo-Saxon Countries") or racially mixed, in the same manner as the pair that Eco labels "beauty and grotesque monstrosity" (115). Whether Fleming uses Manichean oppositions as purely rhetorical devices, as Eco suggests, or actually subscribes to their ideological content, there is no doubt that they form a key element in his narrative structure. "Fleming is ... building an effective narrative apparatus.... To do so he ... puts into play precisely those archetypal elements that have proved successful in fairy tales" (114).

When Eco uses of the term "Manichean" to describe the relationship between "good and evil" in Fleming's *Bond* fiction, he employs the Occidental usage of the term that is devoid of any nuances ("Narrative" 115). The oppositions in Fleming are Manichean because Bond and those allied with him cannot represent evil and conversely the villain and his cohorts can never have any association with good. The rules of Fleming's game would be obscure without this clear distinction between good and evil (115).

An initial reading of Anaya's narrative cycle, particularly *Zia Summer*, could suggest that Raven is a selfish, militant environmentalist whose project is to destroy the earth in order to save it from humankind and that he stands in direct opposition to Sonny, also an environmentalist, but a humanist. Sonny could be seen as a dedicated guardian of nature, a sort of New Age Native American, in the same way that James Bond is seen as a freewheeling, but dedicated guardian of Western Democracy. The arch villain's militant environmentalism could be seen as representative of a proactive Euro American, or an eco-terrorist approach to conservation whose means are destructive and thus remove, from an Occidental Manichean viewpoint, any association his goals might have with good.

Anaya's oppositional pairs use a different game board. His use of Manichean rhetoric appears to be reminiscent of Fleming and as such serves as rhetorical bait to engage his reader and outline his "game" from a Western perspective. However, the conflict between Raven and Sonny is closer to Asian Manichaeism that views good and evil nuanced by each other respectively. The *Sonny Baca* cycle envisions the oppositional pair as one expression of the union of dualities. Even in conflict two is one. In one of Sonny's dreams, the Coyote, his "guardian animal spirit," or *nagual*, says to him, "The world of the spirits is bound to the world of the flesh.... There are not two worlds. Dream and waking, it's all the same. Raven and the sorcerers separated the worlds. They set themselves up as the priests who could take you into the dreams to interpret them. But the road of symbols is clear to anyone who wills to see" (*Shaman* 261). Combative Raven and Sonny are one.

*Don* Eliseo's life-style and stories link contemporary *Nuevo Mexicano* spirituality, a syncretic Native American and Christian religiosity, with its origins that are to be found, according to Sonny's dreams, in sixteenth century Mexican indigenous and Spanish cultures. In one story, *don* Eliseo tells Sonny about a pair of trickster brothers, a common pair in Hopi, Navajo and Pueblo Indian mythologies as well as in Mexican pre–Columbian lore.

The heroes of *don* Eliseo's story are two brothers, Raven and Coyote, who saved the people, the human race, and returned them to earth's surface. The people with the help of the brothers were able to emerge from their dark and lifeless cave. Raven broke the earth's surface with his sharp bill and Coyote's long tail gave them the means to climb out from their hole. But the people, "in their haste ... had left their dreams behind," and "unfortunately the evil sorcerers also grabbed Coyote's long tail, and so they, too came to live on earth" (*Shaman* 271–273). Coyote and Raven taught the people how to feed themselves and how to respect life. But the "evil sorcerers" were jealous of the respect the people had for Coyote and Raven and initiated a competition between them for the recovery of the dreams of mankind. Coyote and Raven failed to deliver these whole; the dreams were "dropped" by both and "fractured." Like all tricksters, Coyote and Raven are egotistical and continue "arguing and pulling tricks on each other to this day" (271–273).

Coyote and Raven are related in opposition, in origin and purpose, which is not true of the relationship between Bond and his enemies, but is true of the relationship between Sonny and his arch enemy Raven.

The gods of Native American religions are frequently dual deities representative of linked oppositions, such as man and woman. However, "opposition" does not properly express the nature of these relationships within a Native American belief system. For example, the Native Americans of the Southwest and those of the central plateau of Mexico have long had to contend with a tenuous water supply for their agriculture. In these geographies, drought and flood are the norm. The relationship between the gods, in many cases twins, is representative of a constant negotiation for balance between the various forces of nature. This is not precisely a battle between good and evil, but rather a juggling of power. If there is too much water there will be destructive floods, if there is too little water there will be no food. Water itself is not good or bad. The Navajos say there are two kinds of rain: the heavy male rain pours down and carries away the earth itself and the gentle female rain soaks into the parched ground and renews the earth. If the power on one side of the duality is in ascendance this may temporarily stabilize the relationship, but if this power overwhelms its complement, the balance is lost, disaster follows and chaos reigns until the power of the other twin begins its ascendance.

The experience of the Mexican and the *Nuevo Mexicano* has been over time that of a duality: Spanish and Native American. The duality, *mestizo* ("half-caste," of Spanish and indigenous parentage) has variously privileged one or the other of its "twins." Anaya has taken the *Nuevo Mexicano's* experience of the Native American belief system as a theme and organizational tool for his narrative cycle. *Don* Eliseo's convictions represent a balance between Christianity and Southwestern indigenous beliefs. There are clear references in *Shaman Winter* to syncretic religious convictions and practices, the rhythms and rituals of Catholic Christianity and to those of the Navajo, Hopi, Zuni and New Mexican Pueblos as exemplified in *don* Eliseo's story of Raven and Coyote. Furthermore, there are links to pre–Columbian religious practices and literature from central Mexico.

Creation mythologies enact a people's view of themselves in relation to their environment and are reflective of the self-perception of a particular culture. The Judeo-Christian-Islamic myth posits a sole and singular deity through whose will the cosmos is created. "Then God said, 'Let us make human beings in our image, after our likeness, to have dominion over the fish in the sea, the birds of the air, the cattle, all wild animals on land, and everything that creeps on the earth'" (*Oxford Study Bible*, Genesis 1:26). The god of Islam, Christianity and Judaism creates man in his image and gives man dominion over the earth. The singularity of this view and the relationship of man to earth are reiterated in the covenant that the god-creator establishes with man after the flood (*Oxford Study Bible*, Genesis 9:2).

Nahuatl myths of central Mexico describe creation as the joint and often conflictive effort of a group of gods. Furthermore the nature of each god is far from singular and is itself dual. Deific will in Native American belief systems is taught to the faithful. The faithful believe in a plural and often conflictive deific proscription.

For those of us educated by Eurocentric literatures the underlying concepts of polytheistic belief systems are difficult to understand because the literature of our education predisposes us to organizational patterns of thought manifest in our literary genres. Literary structure communicates the framework of thought. A photograph and a painting of the same object are different representations because of the materials used to represent the subject. The two representations can be compared, but in order to do so we must take into account the differences of the two mediums. To approach understanding a polytheistic religion, an exploration of its literature can be helpful.

Principal literary genres in Nahuatl classification of narrative are *Itoloca* and *Xiuhámatl*. Some scholars are averse to the use of the word "literature" to describe the means used by the Nahuas to conserve and distribute their histories and myths, preferring the term "poetics" because it is less likely to imply that pre–Columbian oral and written genres were complete unto themselves. *Itoloca* is an oral genre that recounts sociopolitical history and mythological accounts as simultaneously witnessed occurrences that are ever-present. *Xiuhámatl* is a graphic genre still to be found in a very limited number of Nahuatl artifacts due to the fact that the Spanish conquest in its evangelical zeal destroyed the majority of pre–Columbian documents (Robertson 10). *Xiuhámatl* lists the attire and attributes of the gods, and material and historical data. Both genres integrate the spiritual and the physical. The limitations of the graphic genre *Xiuhámatl* prohibited the transcription of nuances such as motive, but the Nahuas (León-Portilla *Los antiguos* 65–66), like the medieval bards of the Spanish *Reconquista* (Bailey 65–66), and the indigenous people of New Mexico practiced and taught the skills of oral narrative.

In *Shaman Winter* Sonny has come to possess a bowl inscribed with glyphs that purport to unravel the temporal and historical mystery he is investigating. Sonny will be able to "read" the text of the bowl, but only after completing his apprenticeship with *don* Eliseo. He needs to be taught in the interpretation of the symbols inscribed on the bowl. This education is more complex than learning to read because each symbol carries layers of meaning instead of a one to one relationship between symbol and word.

*Xiuhámatl* prompted the "readings" of the oral *Itoloca* in a way that was similar to the "readings" of Christian medieval art by an illiterate layperson. The illiterate laity who had heard the story of Christ retold annually in its entirety at the pulpit would have been able "read" the chapters of this story with all its motivational nuances when in front of the religious paintings of the time. In the twenty-first century only a *literate* specialist with the knowledge of medieval symbolism can replicate this feat.

The "Creation of the Sun and Moon" as read by Patrick Johansson is a superior CliffsNotes version for a course in Nahuatl Poetics 101. His careful analysis of the creation myth of the sun and the moon brings to the forefront the organizational tools of Nahuatl literature. He deconstructs the transcription of this myth recorded in the *Florentine Codex* and is able to present an example that demonstrates not only the organizational characteristics of Nahuatl poetics, but also the relationship of the transcribed myth to the indigenous belief system.

For the Nahuas, as for the medieval layman, graphics were of primary importance. Johansson's analysis of the myth of the sun and the moon refers to five principal groups of Nahuatl glyphs—numbers, dates, objects, ideas, and phonemes—that make up the tools of the written genre, the *Xiuhámatl* (León-Portilla *Los antiguos* 56). The myth of the sun and the moon in the *Florentine Codex* is a postconquest transcription that uses the Spanish alphabet to represent the phonemes of Nahuatl oral narrative, *Itoloca*. The tales of the *Florentine Codex* were communicated verbally to Fray Bernardino de Sahagún in Nahuatl by native informants who referred to "pictures" or *Xiuhámatl* that prompted their faithful reproduction of histories and myths (Robertson 169). Johansson is working with a phonetic transcription, the oral "text" or *Itoloca*. Nevertheless the relationships that he charts between the various elements of the verbal text continue to be shaded by the preconquest glyph register, the *Xiuhámatl*. One example in his analysis is the connection he makes between two passages of the narrative that describes the selection of the two deities who would become the moon and the sun.

These two gods are Tecuciztecatl, *caracol* ("seashell") and Nanahuatzin, *purulento* or *bubosillo* (the "putrid" or "scabby" one). Two lines cited in Johansson's analysis compare and contrast the words spoken by the council of gods at the point when Tecuciztecatl and Nanahuatzin will be sacrificed to become the moon and the sun. Tecuciztecatl volunteers himself: "Teteoe, ca nehuatl niyez" ("Oh gods I will be [the one]"), but does not have the courage to step into the fire. Then Nanahuatzin is chosen by the council, "Tetehuatl tiyez, Nanahuatze" ("Nanahuatzin, you will be [the one]") (Johansson 121). Johansson underscores a multilevel relationship between these two lines of the narrative. First he points out the grammatical alternation between "I" and "you," secondly that of deity/deities and a heavenly body/heavenly bodies, thirdly a vocal alternation between the phonemes "n" and "t," and lastly the semantic alternation between subject and object. Johansson's semiotic analysis brings to mind a visual and positional relationship between these gods/heavenly bodies that is supported by the narrative itself (112–117).

Tecuciztecatl's name "seashell" makes this god representative of beauty and of the intra-uterine state of being that is neither male nor female at this point (Johansson 96). Nanahuatzin is close to death and, as the "putrid" and "scabby" one his disfigurement obscures his gender creating an androgynous figure (León-Portilla *Los antiguos* 26). Tecuciztecatl is afraid of the fire; Nanahuatzin is not. Ugly Nanahuatzin sacrifices himself to the fire to become the sun, while vain Tecuciztecatl makes up his mind. He ultimately sacrifices himself, but neither moves in the heavens so the remaining gods throw a rabbit at Tecuciztecatl the moon. Its indelible impression is left there for all to see and to this day there is a rabbit rather than a man in the moon in Mexico. Only then do the moon Tecuciztecatl and the sun Nanahuatzin move.

The names of these gods conjure vivid and conflicting graphic images. Raven and Coyote, so distinct in their physical characteristics, are both images of god and are both responsible for the people. In order to impart the idea of their deific selves, for Nanahuatzin and Tecuciztecatl, for Raven and Coyote, singular images do not suffice. The graphic images of this and Anaya's myth are multiple, conflictive and interlocked, and are linked to linguistic expression as shown by Johansson's semiotic analysis.

In reference to the concept of duality as demonstrated in the text and linguistic elements Johansson writes the following:

> For man, in ontological terms, the establishment of the duality is the outstanding transcendental occurrence. This widening of the unit separates the subject from the object. The Creation myth clearly distinguishes an undifferentiated duality that precedes a differentiated duality (masculine/feminine, light/darkness, etc.). The second [the differentiated duality] is obtained from the first, mediated by a transcendental act (rabbit becomes moon) that alters identity. Therefore, in mythic terminology, the *two* [my emphasis] is ambivalent; it can express a twin duality very close to a unity or also manifest a dynamic differentiated duality [119–120].[2]

From a Judeo-Christian-Islamic perspective, or a popular Western *James Bond* perspective, the subject/object separation and their inversions, the ambivalent value of "two" and the alteration of identities are all perplexing even after reading the CliffsNotes to Nahuatl Poetics 101. So we're going back to class and to Anaya's *Shaman Winter*.

In *Shaman Winter* a romanticized mythological history frames the narrative and gives equal importance to symbolic and physical evidence. Anaya outlines New Mexico's history by referring to documented historical events and his detective evaluates physical evidence. Furthermore, the glyphic register recorded on a Toltec bowl, called the "Bowl of Dreams of the Americas" or "The Calendar of Dreams" encodes a history whose outline the detective has read in written texts, but only through his dreams will he be able to narrate the complete story recorded on the bowl (159). *Don* Eliseo tells Sonny that in order to read the different "dreams" encoded on the bowl he will "have to go into each one [dream] to understand it" (163).

The glyphs on the Toltec bowl tell the history of the northern American continent. Only after having learned to enter and order his dreams through his spiritual education is the detective able to "read" the bowl (159–163). The register on the Toltec vessel encodes the "Mesoamerican myth of creation," the creation of four different "suns" that "bring ... us to the present age" of "the fifth sun" (162). According to Nahuatl, Mayan and many Southwestern Native American mythologies during each of the "suns" or eras that preceded the present, the creation of "man" was imperfect and for this reason life has been destroyed. In Anaya's tale, during the fifth sun, life is again threatened — the life of the sun itself. Raven is amassing the necessary spiritual tools to stop the sun's movement and plunge the world into darkness thereby destroying life as we know it.

In his cycle of detective fiction, Anaya incorporates "*Xiuhámatl*" images reminiscent of Southwestern indigenous and pre–Columbian graphic traditions that include colors, numbers, cardinal points, calendrical information based on celestial observation and *atavíos* ("physical attributes, distinguishing props or costumes"). He has titled each volume in the series for a season of the year: summer, fall, winter and finally spring.

In *Shaman Winter* and *Zia Summer,* the solstice is the villain's and the hero's date of triumph or defeat. Each of Sonny's dreams in *Shaman Winter* associate a period in New Mexican history to one of the cardinal points of the compass. Numbers in all the novels organize the actions of Raven. The names of the two principal actors, "Raven" and "Sonny," suggest their colors and the association these colors had for the Nahua with basic materials in their lives: black — ash, smoke, obsidian —for Raven, and yellow —corn, sun, gold —for Sonny. Coyotes and ravens are animals native to the New Mexican landscape and are the *naguals*, the spiritual embodiments of the protagonists. As the former they contribute to Anaya's descriptions of nature and as the later function as actors in the novels both united with and separate from the protagonists. When either a raven or a coyote appears in the real time of the novel the reader knows that either Raven's or Sonny's shamanistic powers are active and that soon real time may be obscured as the protagonists meet in dream time. The gold medallion of the Zia sun passes back and forth between them in real and dream time and is representative of their common spiritual origin, their connection with the beginning of history of man, with the life-giving sun and New Mexico. A Native American image, the Zia sun is the central image of the New Mexican state flag.

The periods of New Mexican history that Sonny returns to in his dreams are those of crisis, confrontation and chaos. These periods also represent the four cardinal points that were of mythological significance for the Nahua and continue to be of significance for Native American populations of the Southwest and Mexico. South, then north, then east, then the west and finally again to the south, Sonny moves to different points on the compass.

Sonny's first dream returns him to 1598 on the southern border of New Mexico along the Rio Grande and to the Spanish conquest and subjugation of the Native American populations of what is now the state of New Mexico. In 1680 he is present to witness the Pueblo Revolt in the north that initiated and then completely routed the Spanish from his New Mexican home. U.S. Col. Stephen Kearny invaded from the east, and Sonny is again in the thick of the action as the United States conquers and subjugates the people of this area in 1846. Two decades later he is on the western plains in the north of the state where wandering landless veterans of the Civil War violently displace *Nuevo Mexicanos*. In his second-to-last dream Sonny returns to 1916, goes south and is involved in a U.S.-Mexican border conflict suggestive of twenty-first century border conditions that have exacerbated cultural and racial intolerance faced by Mexican Americans today. In this dream Sonny returns with his great-grandfather, Elfego Baca, to a now armed and deadly U.S.-Mexican border.

Sonny is not the only dream traveler. At each of these critical points in New Mexican history Raven appears as a participant and it is his presence that muddies the water and pushes the forces of history into chaos. In his dream travels Raven brings death to the *Nuevo Mexicano* population, but his violent disruption is not limited to historical events. He also disrupts the thread of Sonny's history in the present as he kidnaps the past. In the space of dreams Raven kidnaps four of Sonny's ancestral grandmothers starting with Owl Woman, a Native American he abducts along the northern bank of the Rio Grande.

Anaya tells us that the "Bowl of Dreams of America" is "Toltec" and traveled from Tula, a pre–Columbian city, north of what is now Mexico City to Sonny's New Mexico. "The Toltec empire collapsed 250 years before the rise of the Aztec state, yet Tula was still remembered as a center of power and civilization, whose cultural legacy held much prestige among the urban populations: to be a 'Toltec' was synonymous with being 'civilized' [in Aztec society]" (Townsend 44). Anaya suggests that parallels can be drawn between the character of Raven and the Toltec magician-god Tezcatlipoca and between Sonny and the Toltec prince-priest-god Quetzacóatl. Because of the prestigious place "Toltec" held in the Aztec culture, this suggestion could be extended to pre–Columbian *Aztlán*, the birthplace of the Aztecs, and Chicano movement *Aztlán*, the homeland of Chicanos. Anaya connects contemporary Chicanos and twelfth century Toltecs.

"Whoa, stop the horses, this story is out of control," might have been the comment of Kearny or one of his soldiers in 1846. But the story is not out of control. The structures and artifacts of Chaco Canyon, a National Park in northern New Mexico, continue to be seen by visitors from a Kearny perspective as mysterious. The park attempts to educate its visitors by debunking the "mystery" in the display cases of the museum's orientation center, and clearly documents the commercial and spiritual connections between this Native American civilization and central Mexico. Do stop the horses and visit Chaco Canyon.

The writing of history, historiography, is a soft science. The museum at Chaco Canyon, like the majority of our modern museums, has a wealth of material from which they select to create their displays. In this third millennium there is an abundance of available historical artifacts and documents; choices must be made, and organizational schemes aid us as well as the museum curators of Chaco Canyon. "Third millennium" is an expression of an organizational scheme that predisposes the reader to count the years of human existence by a system that is based on the Christian calendar. Likewise the "Calendar of Dreams" in Anaya's cycle selects information with the aid of a cultural organizational scheme.

The Christian calendar influences how America and the Occidental world organize the details and the information that constitute the history we call our own. Without this or another scheme history is a random collection of facts. Throughout the ages historians have had agendas that have dictated their preference of organizational tools. Some have been subtle and some have been more obvious.

Rudolfo Anaya, historian of *Nuevo Mexicanos*, initiates his history in 1598, but he also refers to an era that predates the introduction of the Christian calendar. 1598 is the "birth year" so to speak of the *mestizo* population and the syncretic culture of New Mexico. To support his calendrical perspective Anaya must introduce more than actions and dates; he must culturally educate his reader regarding the significance the facts held in his organizational scheme. For this reason he refers to preconquest Tula. What he has done is a practice of all historians to a lesser or greater extent and is particularly characteristic of writers whose cultural histories are not well known.

Fictional and nonfictional accounts of the Romantic period offer some insight into Anaya's historical perspective. In a teleological history, a popular historiography during the Romantic period, facts are organized by an underlying religious or spiritual narrative. Another perspective, the Formist, is characterized by an abundance of detail with an almost absent narrative and organized by important categories of information. Together or apart these viewpoints are very successful in presenting the cultural foundation of regional histories. In whatever era, current events will shape historical perspectives. The Romantic Era is characterized by independence movements, some successful, others miserable failures. Large empires were subject to the demands of their ethnic minorities and met these demands with either insignificant favors or brutal repression. Anaya's history of the Chicanos of New Mexico is also a story of violent conflicts between a subjugated population and the forces of empire: Native American, Spanish and those of the United States.

In his history of the Romantic era, *Holy Madness: Romantics, Patriots and Revolutionaries, 1776–1871*, Adam Zamoyski establishes as his thesis the importance of Judeo-Christian religious vocabulary as the era's tool of narrative organization. The Romantics' revolutionary zeal for sociopolitical change was couched not in secular terms but in Judeo-Christian religious vocabulary and as such is a teleological narrative. Zamoyski traces not only the rhetoric of the European nations, but also that of ethnic groups that did not gain independence during the Romantic Period exemplified by the Polish, Hungarian, Slovak, Croat, Rumanian, Czech, Irish, Scottish, Welsh, Belgian, Dutch and Greek peoples. The Zionist Movement also dates from this era and shared the goals of the populations mentioned above.

The "national tale" (Zamoyski's term), a fiction genre, was more widespread than its detective sister in eighteenth- and nineteenth-century Europe. Many national tales, and I include mysteries, have in common two characteristics that Frye defines as basic to romance: the "quest" and a "disconnected" or "coincidental" episodic narrative (15, 46–47). These stories search for or question an ethnic or regional identity; they answer this query through the narration of a series of loosely related events.

Initially the dominant linguistic majority of each European "nation" had no need for this quest; "nation" was neither an ethnic nor a linguistic concept, but rather a bureaucratic organization controlled by the hereditary ruling families of Europe. In other words "nation" was a secular concept devoid of cultural definitions.

The national tale's episodic, coincidental nature is also evident in the nonfictionalized histories written during the era that Hayden White describes as "Formist":

> The Formist mode of explanation is to be found ... in the Roman-
> tic historians and the great historical narrators ... — in any histori-
> ography in which the depiction of the variety, color, and vividness
> of the historical field is taken as the central aim of the historian's
> work. To be sure, a Formist historian may be inclined to make gen-
> eralizations about the nature of the historical process as a whole....
> But, in Formist conceptions of historical explanation, the unique-
> ness of the different agents, agencies, and acts which make up the
> "events" to be explained is central to one's inquiries, not the
> "ground" or "scene" against which these entities arise [14].

White might have been describing Anaya's history of the *Nuevo Mexicanos*.
Anaya is a master of details; his "depiction of the variety, color, and vivid-
ness of the historical field" cannot be denied. However, Anaya also writes
a teleological history.

For many literary critics and historians the tremendous social
upheaval and terror of the French Revolution marks Romantic literature
of the eighteenth and nineteenth centuries (see Brown, Duff and
Zamoyski). Upheavals and terror are the "acts which make up the 'events'"
that Anaya explains in his *Nuevo Mexicano* history. At the initiation of the
nineteenth century, the French Revolution's promise of social justice had
been subsumed by Napoleonic French imperialistic goals. In Mexico after
independence in 1821, the Mexican born Spanish or *criollo* composed the
wealthy minority that dominated the Native American and *mestizo* populations. New Mexico, previously part of colonial Spain and in the year
of independence a part of Mexico, was not an exception. The majority
population was *mestizo* and did not receive any benefits from the independence from Spain.

In Europe, the populations conquered and forcibly assimilated into
the French Empire, the Austro-Hungarian Empire, the British Empire
(Scottish, Welsh, Irish), the Ottoman Empire and the Spanish Hapsburg
dynasty (Galician, Catalan, Basque and ethnic Spanish liberals) all voiced
their desire for what Alexis de Tocqueville, citing the French Revolution's
rhetoric, called the "regeneration of the human race" (Zamoyski 71).

"Regeneration" of a particular ethnicity or, in contemporary jargon
dating from the Cold War, "self-determination" was pursued by this generation either militarily or through their writing, or both. Many Romantic authors were also activists. These poets and scholars searched the past
of their cultural and geographical inheritance for characteristics which
would define a regional or ethnic character in opposition to enlightened
despotism's and French imperialism's universalism that distinguished
between class, but repressed cultural distinctions of language, social practices and folklore.

Romantic nationalism failed in its utopian project of creating a brotherhood of self-determined nations. This project was frustrated by the traditional alliances of European monarchies, militant imperialism, growing materialism, higher standards of living, a growing apathy of the masses for war and a few crumbs of constitutional reform (Zamoyski 341–363). Romantic literature with its wealth of ethnic and regional detail was either suppressed by the privileged population within the political boundaries of a nation or, conversely, was used to justify the dominance of this population. The French, English, German, Spanish and Austrian nations were now reconstructed by teleological and Formist histories as *patria*, or fatherland. In other words, the imperial nations co-opted the rhetoric of the Romantic individualist for the purpose of personifying nationalization projects.

Formist and teleological histories are the fundamental building blocks of the concept of *patria*. From their base in Tenochtitlan, the Aztecs, originally a small northern nomadic group, militarily established their dominance over practically all of Mexico and Central America. Without the connection they drew between themselves and the Toltecs, this relatively new "nation" would have lacked a cultural history typical of that of a "*patria*." Their history was so bound to the cultural history of the Toltecs that when news of Cortés and his Spanish invasion reached the Aztec capital it was rumored that he was the Toltec prince Quetzacóatl venerated as a god throughout Mexico and Central America. Nahuatl texts of the Aztec Empire identified Quetzacóatl as a priest and ruler of Tula who was visited and tricked by Tezcatlipoca ("Smoky Mirror") into drunkenness. In a drunken sleep Quetzacóatl committed incest with his sister and then in shame abandoned the city of Tula, but for many peoples subjugated by the Aztecs his triumphal return was expected. *Shaman Winter* refers to the symbiotic relationship between the Aztecs and the Toltecs.

The "Bowl of Dreams of America" in *Shaman Winter* is an actual bowl. It is shiny black like the color of a raven's feathers and of the same material, obsidian, as the "smoky" mirror used by pre–Columbian peoples. In Anaya's story Quetzacóatl's "Plumed Serpent" glyph appears on the obsidian bowl of dreams and along with the glyphs of the Zia Sun and the horns of a cow that represent Sonny Baca. The Zia Sun refers to the Native Americans of New Mexico and refers to Sonny's first name: "sunny." *Vaca*, "cow" was Sonny's Spanish ancestor's last name and, with a change in spelling, is Sonny's last name, "Baca." Quetzacóatl was recognized as the priest of Ometéotl, the supreme dual deity, the "Señora de nuestra carne, Señor de nuestra carne" ("Lady of our flesh, Gentleman of our flesh") who gave light to the earth (León-Portilla *Literatura* 39). Each morning Sonny witnesses *don* Eliseo as he addresses "Los Señores y las Señoras de la Luz" ("The Gentlemen and Ladies of the Light") (*Shaman* 162). Sonny's connection with Quetzacóatl is further enhanced because he is being tutored by *don* Eliseo as a "priest" of *los Señores y las Señoras de la Luz.*

Chronicles of the Spanish conquest based on Nahuatl myth describe Quetzacóatl as a ruler of Tula who forbade human sacrifice, a position that historically puts him in sharp contrast to rulers of the Aztec Empire. These same histories assert that human sacrifice only began in Tula after Quetzacóatl had fled from his own sinful image as reflected in a mirror held up to him by Tezcatlipoca. As Quetzacóatl was tempted with alcohol and incest by Tezcatlipoca, Raven tempts Sonny with the power of the Zia Sun and his "priestess" in the first novel of the cycle. Similar to the Navajo perspective toward rain, among their many incarnations Quetzacóatl and Tezcatlipoca embody two manifestations of the wind: the gentle wind that brings rain and the brutal wind that causes destruction (Martí 94, 109). They are twins. This distinction and parentage is not unknown to Sonny and is reflected in his relationship with Raven: "Sonny mused. Raven was his alter ego, his other self, the dream of chaos" (*Shaman* 377).

Aztec history was written from a teleological perspective to discredit the myth of Quetzacóatl and enshrine Huitzilopochtli as the dominant godhead of Mesoamerica. After having established themselves for a little more than a century in the Valley of Mexico, the Aztecs were still treated as newcomers. In 1426 an "extraordinary" figure became the advisor to Aztec emperors; Tlacaélel was the power behind the throne until his death in 1481 (Townsend 67). His political, economic and judicial reorganization, along with his administrative changes paved the way for, and sustained, the powerful Aztec military theocracy until the Spanish conquest in 1521. In order to support his administrative changes Tlacaélel destroyed previous documents and supplanted them with a new teleological history of the Aztec nation. Quetzacóatl became a minor deity displaced by the Aztec sun-god Huitzilopochtli. With this change the number of human sacrifices, primarily drawn from non–Aztec populations, was significantly increased (León-Portilla *Los antiguos* 47–49, 92–93). The supremacy of the sun in nature and its importance relative to human existence was stressed by the Aztec theocracy. The sun needed to be fed by humanity.

Under Tlacaélel's direction a party of explorers was sent to find Aztlán, the legendary place of Aztec origin, and establish the superiority of an Aztec genealogy. When they returned from the north, a successful journey was recorded. They observed Coatlicue, Huitzilopochtli's mother, gave her presents and confirmed the legitimacy of their cosmic inheritance of the Valley of Mexico (Townsend 55, 56). The Aztecs had acquired such power that they were able to write their own history and rewrite the history of the Valley of Mexico.

The connection between written history and power is not lost on Sonny. While musing over the textual histories of New Mexico and computer records from the Los Alamos nuclear facility, he comes to the conclusion that "history glorifies those who write it. We need to arm ourselves with computers and write our history, our punto de vista ["view point"]. Why not curanderas ["healers"] armed with computers? They would explain the healing process don Eliseo knew so well" (*Shaman* 381). Here Anaya, through his protagonist's words, lists sources for and goals of his historical-mythological cycle of detective novels.

The tales of *Nuevo Mexicanos* that Sonny has heard from *don* Eliseo and those of his generation, along with the books and newspapers he consults in Albuquerque's libraries have provided sufficient information for a successful nullification of Raven's powers in *Zia Summer* and *Rio Grande Fall*. However in *Shaman Winter*, Sonny decides that if he is going to be able to find Raven and learn how he gained access to the Los Alamos nuclear facility he will need to enlist a computer hacker. The data found by the hacker — telephone, travel and surveillance records — is used by Sonny to successfully link Raven with a powerful national conspiracy. The conspirators call themselves the Avengers and are led by prominent government officials. The computer data in and of itself does not provide the narrative framework that, for example, *don* Eliseo's stories do, but is a listing of a mixed bag of raw data that can be seen either as a listing of material properties or as a listing of personality characteristics from a *James Bond* perspective. The data can also be interpreted as *Nuevo Mexicano* twentieth century *Xiuhámatl* glyph that lists the material and spiritual components of Raven's plan. Anaya is to Sonny what Frey Sahagún was to his sixteenth-century Nahuatl informants. Sahagún wrote using the letters of the Spanish alphabet and Anaya writes *Shaman Winter* using the characters of the English and Spanish alphabets. Sonny, his informant, like Sahagún's informants, relies on glyphs to prompt his organization and verbal communication of *Nuevo Mexicano* history.

In real time during the course of the novel, Raven has kidnapped three young Chicanas. Shortly before the climactic scene of the novel, Sonny's last dream, and with the help of a youthful computer hacker, Sonny is able to discover the identity of Raven's fourth victim and learn when and where Raven will attempt to kidnap her. The hacker provides Sonny with data and because Sonny recognizes a victim profile, or in other words a *Xiuhámatl* glyph of characteristics, he is able to identify and locate the next victim. The data consists of a date, the victim's *atavíos* and the initial letter of her name, C. The date refers to Raven's plan that must be completed before the winter solstice. The three victims have been young Chicanas who would have dressed to play the female lead in a Christmas pageant. The costumes required by their roles are their *atavíos*, their "distinctive dress." The C "glyph" refers to the fourth victim's name, Celeste, which is consistent with the initial letter of the first three girls' names: Consuelo, Catalina, and Carmen. Using this list of characteristics Sonny is able to complete the last "paragraph" of the "*Itoloca*," the narrative that began with the first kidnapping, and go to the scene of the fourth and last abduction.

The data that Sonny collects describes Celeste's pending kidnapping and completes a pattern that was outlined by the three previous abductions. Preceding each girl's disappearance Sonny's dreams have returned him to a specific date and place in New Mexico's history where he witnesses the abduction, or attempted abduction, of one of his ancestral grandmothers by Raven. It is never clear from a "logical" *James Bond* perspective why Raven needs the young women or the grandmothers. However, in the case of Sonny's grandmothers and following the "logic" of Sonny's dreams we realize that Raven consolidates his power over the present and the past with each kidnapping. His geographical reach extends as he snatches the women from distinctive and far-reaching areas. The waning sun of the approaching solstice decreases Sonny's influence over historical and contemporary events while increasing Raven's influence. The combination of terrestrial and celestial dominance works in Raven's favor. As Raven abducts a grandmother the chance that Sonny himself will cease to exist increases. Shortly before Celeste's abduction, Rita, who has only just learned that she is pregnant, must be rushed to the hospital; she has suffered a miscarriage losing her and Sonny's child. The implication is that Raven has consolidated his power over Sonny's future (*Shaman* 400) and soon Sonny himself will cease to exist.

After Sonny's first dream where Owl Woman, his first ancestral grandmother, was captured by Raven, Sonny asks *don* Eliseo, "But if he captured Owl Woman, if he took her away from Andres Vaca, and thus kept their child from being born, why am I still here?" *Don* Eliseo answers, "There are four roots to a man's history ... as there are four sacred directions from the Center. Four quadrants of the universe. He needs to take four grandmothers in order to kill your spirit" (*Shaman* 43).

Sonny is unable to stop the fourth kidnapping; Celeste is abducted. To rescue her, the other women and his own "spirit," he must enter still another dream. His physical and metaphysical powers combine for this final confrontation. Sonny has regained the use of his legs after his van overturned while pursuing Raven and Celeste. He stands and practices with the only weapon capable of nullifying Raven's power: a New Mexican Native American dream-catcher that *don* Eliseo has made for him. In the sequence that follows Sonny confronts Raven with the help of *don* Eliseo and Chica his dog.

Sonny constructs a sixth dream and commands Raven's presence; in his joy at seeing the kidnapped girls and his grandmothers, Sonny finds himself tricked into Raven's circle of power. Chica and *don* Eliseo enter the circle to protect Sonny; *don* Eliseo is killed by Raven and Chica is wounded by Raven's ravens. Sonny and Chica are able to move out of the circle, and Sonny is able to trick Raven into his own sphere of power and pass him through the dream catcher. Thus, Sonny captures Raven's dream and nullifies his power. All elements — the computer information, the high speed chase, the accident, the loss of paralysis, the ordering of the dream, the physical battle and Sonny's success with the dream catcher — create a sequence of events that follow the organizational logic of Anaya's novel. The past and the projected future, acted upon in present dreams, surround and penetrate the contemporary physical world. All — past, present, future and dream — are but permeable levels of one interacting space. It is this underlying logic that organizes Anaya's history of New Mexican Chicanos.

Though Anaya's historical perspective may be resistant to Western logic, Anaya's readers, their curiosity piqued by the *James Bond* narrative, will be confronted by Anaya's alternative perspective. At the very least the reader is obligated, paraphrasing León-Portilla, to look for and take into account, the writer's own specific concepts of his cultural institutions. The reader should look further than any apparent similarity these cultural institutions may have to our own[3] (*Los antiguos* 50).

At the beginning of *Shaman Winter*, Sonny dreams of his ancestor, Andres Vaca, an experienced Spanish soldier with Juan de Oñate's party of soldiers and settlers, who in 1598 have crossed the Rio Grande to settle and Christianize what will become New Mexico. Andres is chosen by a young Native American shaman, Owl Woman, as her mate. She initiates their marriage of cultures by bathing him with water from the Rio Grande that she pours from an obsidian bowl she received from the priests of Tula. This same bowl turns up in the hands of Raven and is the vessel he uses to transport a plutonium core. The bowl is recovered by the authorities at Los Alamos nuclear laboratory, lost again to Raven and recovered from him by Sonny. In his dreams Sonny reads the glyphs on the bowl that combine with his conscious reading of published New Mexican history. The bowl physically takes him into the last dream of the book where he rescues his past, his grandmothers, and the kidnapped young women from Raven's power.

Anaya has written a *Nuevo Mexicano* Chicano history by undertaking the rewriting of pre–Columbian history in order to adjust the Chicano mythological inheritance of Nahuatl Aztlán to a pre–Tlacaélel Toltec-Aztec inheritance. Tula was abandoned sometime during the twelfth century and the Toltecs were dispersed. Even though the myths and artifacts of the Toltec culture were held in esteem by the Aztecs, the Toltecs themselves were indistinguishable from various other indigenous populations at the time of Aztec immigration to the Valley of Mexico (Townsend 44). In the passage that follows, Sonny's historical dream of 1568, Anaya rewrites the Toltec archeological record:

> The elders told Andres Owl Woman's story. When she was only a girl, Owl Woman had journeyed south with a shaman to the land of the Aztecs. She had visited Tula, the ancestral holy place. When she returned, she brought with her the bowl the ancients called the Calendar of Dreams [also called the "Bowl of Dreams of America" in Anaya's text].
> The priests of Tula knew their time on earth was coming to an end and that their way of life would be ruthlessly obliterated. Their temples were desecrated, their ceremonies abolished by the Spanish friars.
> The dream of peace was dying, but the elders of Tula knew a new dream could be born. Owl Woman was chosen to carry the Calendar of Dreams north. She was instructed to wait for the man who could take her north to old pueblos. There among the descendants of the Anasazis a new dream was to flourish. There she would give birth to a new people, and she would deliver the bowl to the priests of the pueblos [*Shaman* 17].

Even though Anaya has rewritten the historical time line and sixteenth-century Owl Woman's interaction with the priests of Tula is an historical impossibility, this passage does, however, refer to actual connections between contemporary civilizations—the Toltec civilization and Native Americans of the Southwest.

Recently it has been argued that the Toltecs had at least a limited presence at Pueblo Bonito in Chaco Canyon, a large Anasazi ceremonial center in northern New Mexico (see Rayman) and it has been shown that an extensive trade network between Southwestern indigenous peoples and the central Mexican plateau, the home of the Toltecs, existed during the twelfth century (see McGuire).

Furthermore the possibility of resurrecting the dying "dream of peace" referred to by "the elders of Tula" bears an unmistakable resemblance to the legend of the return of Quetzacóatl who was supposed to return from the east to reclaim his title. Townsend notes that this legend may have been initiated by the Spanish or may have been written by the Aztecs themselves to explain their defeat as having been pre-ordained (18–19). Even if the legend did not exist before the Spanish landing in 1519 it has been part of the story of Mexico for the last 500 years and as such is representative of a syncretic and *mestizo* history. Through the inheritance of his ancestors, Owl Woman and Andrés Vaca, Sonny, the *mestizo* revisits his southern roots in order to claim his northern homeland, Aztlán, and reestablish the dream of peace.

During the Chicano movement of the late 1960s and 1970s, activists and writers researched Chicano history and some took on the project of creating an origin myth that would address their Native American heritage. "Aztlán," first introduced in 1969 as part of "El Plan Espiritual de Aztlán" (Alurista et al. 58–63) was formulated as the spiritual and geographical home of the Chicanos and fixed in the Southwest of the United States. Since 1969 "Aztlán" as the rallying cry of activism has undergone many transformations, but none of them have displaced the Aztec association with Chicano "Aztlán" (Pérez-Torres 56–96). Anaya's history of New Mexico as the Chicano "Aztlán," a spiritual and geographical home, omits the totalitarian, military past of the Aztecs along with their practice of human sacrifice. By focusing on the Aztec's Toltec cultural inheritance, the story of Quetzacóatl and its connections of with the Native American populations of New Mexico, Anaya rewrites Chicano origin myth, as did the Aztecs before him did with their history. He removes the Aztec totalitarian agenda from the tale and introduces Southwestern Native American culture in conjunction with central Mexican indigenous culture, and then consecrates their "marriage" with the Spanish in a new *Nuevo Mexicano* Chicano foundational tale. This new history is focused on the inclusion of both halves of *mestizo* in contrast to the original Chicano myth that privileged the indigenous half and the early twentieth-century *Nuevo Mexicano* literature that privileged the Spanish half.

The importance of Sonny and Rita's romance in Anaya's *Nuevo Mexicano* foundational tale is underscored by the following statement from Doris Sommer:

> From those ... books [Latin American foundational fictions] I could (correctly) assume that readers were being invited in as participant observers in the love affairs that generated countries. Identification with the frustrated lovers whose union could produce the modern state was precisely the desired effect on the tenuous citizenry of newly consolidated countries. It was a mirror effect that survived

mass distribution to required readers ... that their differences from
the elite lovers did not really matter [151–152].

Anaya uses the *James Bond* model of detective fiction to invite a "mass"
audience to witness the "elite lovers," Sonny and Rita, who are capable of
knowing so much more than those of us who have been taught to value a
*James Bond* perspective. With each subsequent volume, Anaya abandons
a bit more of the good guys–bad guys, materialist logic typical of the spy-
thriller and adopts the logic of a foundational tale told from a perspective
heavily indebted to Native American cultural institutions.

     Imbued by the experience of many worlds and temporarily free from
the chaos created by Raven, his cosmic twin, Sonny is finally able to make
a serious proposal of marriage to Rita. Anaya concludes *Shaman Winter*
when, in Rita's company, Sonny "looked into her eyes, and she saw the wis-
dom that had settled into his soul. She drew him to her and whispered,
'Yes, a new dream'" (442). Through his dreams Sonny has explored the
chaos that has continually disturbed the peace of his ancestors. He made
this journey through his dreams, applied the knowledge gained in his
dreams to the real world, the knowledge gained in the real world to his
dreams, and constructed a mutually harmonious, but conflictive whole. A
"new dream" is on the horizon, but because it is part of a mutually harmonious *and* conflictive whole it will always be inconclusive.

# 3

## The Lieutenant and the Chevalier, Buenrostro and Dupin

### *Rolando Hinojosa's* Partners in Crime

Rolando Hinojosa's first detective novel, *Partners in Crime: A Rafe Buenrostro Mystery* (1985) is the eighth volume of his *Klail City Death Trip*.[1] The series takes place in the twentieth century but tells the story of generations of U.S. and Mexican residents along the Lower Rio Grande. Their history is told by multiple narrators: some individual, some communal, some anonymous. From the series' initiation Rafe Buenrostro has been one of the many participants in this macrotext. *Partners in Crime* is the first lineal novel in the series and appears to be told by a single anonymous third person. The novel focuses on Rafe, a homicide detective, and it is this character who organizes the multiple narratives into a forward moving plot. Narration, as in previous works by Hinojosa, includes testimony, hearsay and media clips. This analysis of *Partners in Crime* looks at two Romantic literary traditions, *costumbrismo* ("Customs and Manners") and detective fiction, that this eighth text recalls.

Lieutenant Buenrostro of the Belken County Homicide Squad and Chevalier Dupin, Edgar Allan Poe's citizen of nineteenth-century Paris, share an investigative style that stresses the importance of impartial observation. These detectives are talented observers who avoid assuming that all that they observe will necessarily fit into a singular preordained pattern. In *Partners in Crime*, the dialogue with Poe's detective narratives adds another dimension to the history and identification of community that is the underlying theme of the *Klail City Death Trip*.

Hinojosa is acutely aware of his choice of genre for the separate volumes of the series; "'The critic is always present,'" he commented to José David Saldívar in 1984 ("Our Southwest" 184). His epic poem *Korean Love Songs* posits Rafe as the narrator of a genre in "the tradition of British World War I poetry" (J.D. Saldívar "Introduction" 47). This volume combines the *corrido* tradition (R. Saldívar "*Korean Love Songs*" 143) with a European tradition that together are able to come to some understanding of a war that took Mexican American males from the valley and exposed them to alien traditions, but also gave them educational opportunities they may not have found if they had had the option of staying at home.

In *Partners in Crime* the *costumbrista* genre, prevalent in much of the series, combines with the detective genre to illuminate a particular period in the history of Hinojosa's border valley. Intimate knowledge of the minutia of the whole community now becomes a valued investigative tool. The protagonist, a person with the particular skills necessary to order the chaos of crime, has an added advantage over his fellow detectives. He is a *Tejano Mexicano* and knows his community well, but because of his experience outside the Lower Rio Grande Valley, his knowledge of its history and his education, he also knows the various other populations of the valley. He recognizes change in his environment because, like Dupin, he is intimately familiar with his surroundings.

By including Poe's detective genre in the repertoire of the literary forms that make up the *Klail City Death Trip*, Hinojosa opens literally and symbolically another chapter in his story and extends the teleology[2] of its literary history. The year 1972, when the novel begins, coincides with an invasion of the valley by outside forces. For valley residents it has now become necessary to intimately know the background of the people around you, neighbors and invaders, as well as one's own.

Charles Tatum, in his review of *Partners in Crime*, concludes that "Hinojosa has learned well from the masters of detection," and that "[w]hat moves *Partners in Crime* are the essential ingredients of good detective fiction, whose main interest consists in finding out, from circumstances largely physical, the true order and meaning of events that have been partly disclosed and partly concealed" (470). Antonio Prieto Taboada, in his analysis of *Partners in Crime*, suggests that the detective genre focus has been a part of the structural organization of Hinojosa's previous works in the *Klail City Death Trip* series, because to reconstruct the events the reader must commit himself to a "textual investigation" of these fragmented narratives (119).

José David Saldívar's "Critical Introduction" to the *Klail City Death Trip* series describes *Partners in Crime* as part of this series and as such is the continuation of a major project. "[W]ith the same effect as the traditional historical novel, Hinojosa's *Klail City Death Trip* invents a body of characters and discourses in which we see reflected the ways of a South Texas society and the people who constitute it" (60). *Partners in Crime*, a segment of the "historical novel," contains some of the same textual references typical of the previous works along with initiating a dialogue within the detective genre.

For Saldívar the structure of the historical novel *Klail City Death Trip* narrates an "ascent" and then a "descent" (J.D. Saldívar "Critical" 49). The "ascent" is from the *Nuevo Santander*[3] past when in 1749 the first settlers from colonial Mexico, among them protagonist Rafe Buenrostro's family, began to live and work north and south along the Rio Grande. The "descent" commenced in 1803 when large numbers of Anglo Americans, including the ancestors of the protagonists of the Klail-Blanchard-Cooke family, arrived to settle in this area of colonial Spain. Later in 1865 Mexican nationals, represented by the Leguizamón family, crossed the Rio Grande and left Mexico for Texas and then profitably allied themselves with the Anglo Texans (51). Initially the series presents the "ascent" and "descent" in the form of a dialogue between the past and present recorded in the contemporary time of the novel. Old-timer *Tejano Mexicanos* look back nostalgically to the past while the current generation views its life marginalized by the political, social and economic structures assembled and controlled by the Anglo American population (57).

Spanish, English and Tex-Mex border variations of each, along with code switching, are all languages of the *Klail City Death Trip*. But as the series develops, in a progression that coincides with the chronology of each volume's original publication, Spanish recedes and English becomes the dominant language (with the exception of *Korean Love Songs* where the use of English reflects the environment of the U.S. military). The first bilingual text, *Mi querido Rafa* presents a rupture in the series for José David Saldívar and Rosaura Sánchez. For critic Sánchez, the events in *Mi querido Rafa* are organized on a "horizontal time axis" that is more commonly associated with detective fiction, rather than on a "vertical axis" with references to the *costumbrista* tradition (93). Sánchez also notes that narrator Galindo's series of interviews in the second half of *Mi querido Rafa* configures Galindo as "a detective of sorts" who attempts to piece together, with the help of various individuals' comments, the events that took Jehú Malacara (Rafa's cousin) from the Klail City First National Bank (93). The English language and the plot, investigative if not actually lineal, of *Mi querido Rafa* anticipate the references to English language literature that are found in *Partners in Crime*.

José David Saldívar notes that there is a shift in the position of the

*Tejano Mexicano* relative to his relationship with the present that begins with *Mi querido Rafa*. Rafa Buenrostro and Jehú Malacara more fully participate in the Anglo Texan world. "For the first time in the *KCDT* series, we are taken to the very source of financial power in South Texas" (57). From first-hand observation, Jehú Malacara communicates in his letters to Rafa Buenrostro the working details, formerly unknown in the series, of the financial power structure commanded by the Klail-Blanchard-Cooke family. *Partners in Crime* is written in English. This is no idle choice; Hinojosa has two native tongues. His selection of English for this volume of the series reflects the fact that Jehú and Rafe[4] are now presented as full participants "in the Texas Anglo world" (58). The camaraderie of the Korean War and the subsequent access to education provided by the G.I. Bill, not an attitude change on the part of the Anglo Texan, has precipitated this shift in the positions of Rafe and Jehú, the two main characters in the series.

In *Partners in Crime*, the world of the nostalgic old-time *Tejano Mexicano*, that of contemporary Texans, Mexicans and Anglos and that of the Klail-Blanchard-Cooke power structure have "been displaced by the world-market" of the drug traffickers (J.D. Saldívar 59). This situation in *Partners in Crime* calls for a negotiated truce among the inhabitants of Belken County (Hinojosa's fictional Texas county where Klail City is located). *Partners in Crime* suggests that in the future Anglo Texans and *Tejano Mexicanos* will have to work together to protect their valley from global drug trafficking.

Rosaura Sánchez, in her article "From Heterogeneity to Contradiction: Hinojosa's Novel," explores intertextuality in the "macrotext," *Klail City Death Trip*.[5] The series carries on a dialogue with particular peninsular Spanish fifteenth- and sixteenth-century publications, and Spanish language literature of the Romantic period as well as the Mexican and Mexican American oral traditions of the Rio Grande Valley. Intertextuality in a work of fiction is a dialogue with literary history. The author of fiction, like the author of a literary history, selects the textual references or the actual texts to include in his history, and by including them in the literary work creates a secular teleology (Brown 3).

The intertextuality described by Sánchez in Hinojosa's macrotext informally outlines a literary history that includes a nonfiction genre, the chronicles and biographical sketches of fifteenth-century Spain,[6] Renaissance picaresque,[7] a genre that approaches in its form the modern novel with its lineal organization, and Romantic *costumbrismo*. The resulting "literary history" combines biographical historical narrative, picaresque confrontations with the "other," and *costumbrista* nostalgic and ironic explorations of traditions. All of these genres have served to define national character in Spain.

Intersecting with this peninsular literary history are the oral literatures of the Hispanic Rio Grande Valley that include folklore, gossip and *corridos*. The *corrido* identified the *Tejano Mexicano* in contrast to the Anglo Texan, serving a similar function to peninsular *costumbrismo* that lamented and criticized the *Frenchified* peninsula in contrast with the Spanish characteristics it highlighted.[8] The "literary history" of the *Klail City Death Trip* before *Partners in Crime* outlines a body of literature primarily episodic in nature that develops a cultural and historical identity by recalling the accomplishments and characteristics of a group of people as distinguishing, positive and valuable in contrast to those of the "other."

The narrator of *costumbrismo* puts himself in a position of intimacy with his readership by assuming that they are aware of the general circumstances that he narrates and, seriously or ironically, his description is only to fill in details that may have escaped their knowledge. Hinojosa, like the Spaniard Mariano José de Larra (1809–1837) before him, establishes a compliant relationship with his readers, or, using Doris Sommer's term, an "authorial community" ("Textual" 149). The detective genre also assumes that it is on intimate terms with its readers.[9]

Hinojosa's *Klail City Death Trip* does not tell its story from a solo point of view. There is no single narrator in any of the novels including *Partners in Crime*. Hinojosa's voices have a timeless quality. Even though they are characters in the contemporary world of the novel, their telling of the past is also a narration of their present experience (Sánchez 77). Frequently the story-teller protagonist effaces his presence and a contemporary or historical document functions as the narrator — a literary convention that was not uncommon in the work of *costumbrista* Larra or in the detective stories of Poe. Sánchez points out that Hinojosa's fictional narrative dialogues with various nonfiction genres: the interview, the letter and other documents that include newspaper articles, official documents and "Radio Talk" (83).

*Partners in Crime* is told by an unnamed third person narrator. He does not assume a singular perspective, but refers to a "source" of information. He does not describe the thoughts of the characters, but instead transcribes them. These thoughts are presented as if the narrator had a direct line to the sound bites, the clear one-liners, of the characters' thought processes and had recorded what he heard. This is not a stream of consciousness narration. We are only privy to thoughts that can be projected as simple statements, summations of the feelings we do not "hear." Nor does the narrator observe the characters physically; their physical descriptions are very infrequent and usually occur only when the characters describe themselves while looking at their own reflections or at each other. Descriptions of the setting are almost exclusively limited to material articles and their surroundings that will be recorded in a detective report. Unlike most third person narratives, Hinojosa's narrator in *Partners in Crime* assumes neither an omniscient stance nor a reduced close-up perspective. Each character speaks for himself or is described by an anonymous communal voice.

The introduction of the five detectives provides an example of the narrative perspective of the novel. These are the first paragraphs of *Partners in Crime*:

> A note, folded and scotch-taped to the telephone dial; he could hardly miss it, and it contained no surprise, either: "Oakland 3, Reds 1. I now owe you $20." It was signed *C*.
> The *C* stood for Culley Donovan, his partner and chief of detectives for the Belken County Homicide Squad.
> Rafe Buenrostro smiled, opened a side drawer on his desk, and slid that IOU along with the others signed by Donovan during that October 1972 World Series [5].

From these initial paragraphs we learn nothing about the perspective of the narrator. This short introduction sketches the relationship of Rafe and Donovan who, by his name and title, we assume is Rafe's Anglo boss. But he is also Rafe's "partner," and theirs seems to be an easy relationship based on mutual trust as shown by the drawer full of IOUs. Rafe knows more about baseball than Donovan does, but doesn't rub it in or the IOUs would have been cashed. There appears to be no animosity between them. Other than the bare bones of an office — "telephone," "Homicide Squad" and "desk"— and a date, the narrator provides no context for what he reports. Superficially this is a straightforward listing of facts and is representative of the narrative stance of the novel as a whole.

The introduction of the Homicide Squad continues with a brief transcription of Rafe's thoughts: "It had been a stupid murder.... Fell on his lap, as it were. An idiotic murder, he thought. And then, not for the first time in the last eleven years, 'Most of them are'" (5). It is as if Rafe was voicing out loud the conclusions of his thought process that is hidden from the reader. These statements are brief, and other than the reference to a period of time, the narrator provides little context.

After a conversation between Donovan and Buenrostro, Detective Sam Dorson is introduced: "Sam Dorson was another member of the Belken County Homicide Squad. Of what Harvey Bollinger, the District

Attorney, was pleased to call *his* Homicide Squad" (6). The use of the words "of what" and "pleased," and the emphasized "*his*" inform the reader that Harvey Bollinger is resented by the Homicide Squad and that Sam, as a "member" is also a "partner" in the relationship of trust established between Rafe and Donovan. This passage is representative of the community sound bites Hinojosa employs: the words appear to have popped into the heads of the Homicide Squad as a group.

A description of the organization of the Homicide Squad and its material resources is presented by quoting directly, or as hearsay, from the following bureaucratic sources: "accounting and inventory," "Bollinger's and Parkinson's budgets," "the state's Attorney General" and the "*obvious logic*" of "his Opinion Committee" (6–7). The reader learns that these bureaucracies organize the Homicide Squad, but their "*obvious logic*" shows them to be out of touch with the day-to-day operations and needs of the detectives. The phrase "five men, five desks" is repeated in this description and the last two detectives, Joe Molden and Peter Hauer, are introduced like extensions of the furnishings provided by the "*obvious logic*" bureaucracy.

Molden and Hauer, like the furnishings, are just two more material properties that are listed. They "rounded out the five-man unit" (7). The narrator makes a sarcastic comment about them without ever having to commit himself to anything more than providing a list. The classical genre did not allow the narrator to overtly direct the reader in regards to the criminal's motivation. The first few pages of Hinojosa's novel establish the necessary semblance of an impartial narrative voice. It is covertly implied that Molden and Hauer are not respected members of the squad because they are associated with the bureaucratic furnishings. Our suspicions of Hauer's incompetence, and by association of Molden's, are confirmed by a bit of hearsay: "Hauer was called Young Mr. Hauer by Sam Dorson, for reasons best known to Dorson, and if there was resentment on the part of Hauer, he didn't show it. At least not in public" (7).

As shown in the examples above, the narrator of *Partners in Crime* claims impartiality by framing the narrative with the characters' dialogue, abbreviated thoughts and office hearsay. The *Klail City Death Trip* series, including *Partners in Crime*, is written from polyphonic perspective. This narrative perspective is enhanced, as Sánchez notes, by the contribution of "various styles, modes and language varieties" that include popular Spanish sayings (78, 83). In *Partners in Crime*, English colloquial interjections dominate. These are unmarked by quotation marks, but are offset from the text and precede or follow actions, dialogue or the reported thoughts of the characters. These establish a bond between the reader of English and the characters, and also serve as shorthand for the thoughts of the characters that presume a common "language" of mind. Some are: "Fell in his lap" (5), "And that was that" (5), "but there it was" (7), "Nothing fancy about it" (7), "Assholes" (12), "Bless you!" (24), "Easy as pie, to coin yet another phrase" (47), "A signal honor" (69), "It was in the bag." (74), "Too much excitement" (75), "That kind of a day" (108), "It was a start." (127), "A running joke" (181), "Tools of the trade" (230), "They were in business." (235) and "Bullshit" (242). The language of *Partners in Crime* functions as it does in the whole series as a dialogized "heteroglossia"[10] (Sánchez 78).

Among the new "languages" added to the dialogue is that of "typical male-bonding" observed by Samples (154) included in the colloquial North American English expressions noted above. The various "languages" refer to specific circumstances in ethnic or social groups. Furthermore, the "reproduction" of nonfiction documents testifies to the fact that Hinojosa writes a polyphonic novel. He relinquishes the "authority" of the narrator to the community, in Belken County and across the border in Barrones, Mexico, to encompass the various populations of the Rio Grande Valley. This communal voice is reinforced by a literary history—*costumbrismo* and the *corrido*—that was initiated in the earlier volumes of the *Klail City Death Trip*. In *Partners in Crime* this voice is extended to include English language expressions and texts.

Keeping in mind that Rolando Hinojosa is an author of fiction whose texts are rich in references to Spanish language literature, that he is a literary critic and has been a professor of English, Spanish and American literature, the inclusion of English language literary references in *Partners in Crime* is not surprising. The literary interests of his detectives are not "attempts to break down some of the stereotypes for law enforcement personnel" as Susann Samples suggests in her review of the novel (154). Detective Donovan is reading Charles Dickens, a nineteenth-century realist who had not severed his Romantic roots, who published his novels in episodic chapters and who had an "ear" for the various lexicons of his time. Dickens is the contemporary of Benito Pérez Galdós (1843–1920) who transformed the *costumbrista* minutiae of Madrid into lengthy realist novels and shared Dickens' ability to reproduce various sociolinguistic registers. Both are contemporaries of Emilia Pardo Bazán (1852–1921), a realist novelist who is recognized as the originator of the peninsular Spanish detective story. Pardo Bazán combined the didactic tradition of some *costumbrista* writing with the investigation of crime to produce morality mystery tales.

Rafe is well versed in the writings of Charles Lamb (1775–1834), an English author recognized for his "humor, whimsy, and faint overtones of pathos" (Siepmann 547), whose best known writings are a body of letters, some of whose lines Rafe has committed to memory (*Partners* 42). A superficial comparison between Lamb and the Spanish *costumbrista*, Larra might highlight their "humor and pathos," the epistolary form of many of their texts, the dates of their deaths and their participation in the Romantic literary movement of their respective countries. Detective Sam Dorson reads and quotes from Johann Wolfgang von Goethe (1749–1832), a founder of European Romanticism. Dorson also knows all the songs from the Gilbert and Sullivan operettas (1871–1896) that satirized Victorian society and the plots of their favorite Romantic era operas.

There is an intersection of textual references from the earlier volumes of the *Klail City Death Trip* and those of *Partners in Crime* and its meeting point is eighteenth- and nineteenth-century Romanticism. The series eschews a "pragmatic, strategic appropriation of the national model of literary history" criticized by Stephen Greenblatt (54), while at the same time constructs a communal history, a "teleology," that does refer to "progress" (Greenblatt 54), but whose agenda is not progress driven.[11] Therefore, *Klail City Death Trip* is reminiscent of Romanticism's ethnic and national fictions but, due to the polyphonic perspective of the author and the richness of its linguistic registers, avoids being didactic.

Because *Partners in Crime* is both a lineal and a detective novel, it is structurally different from the preceding texts of the *Klail City Death Trip*, and, in my opinion, refers to another Romantic era author: Edgar Allan Poe. In *Partners in Crime* the relative isolation of Belken County has completely eroded, and the values and traditions of the population there and in neighboring Barones are being undermined. Crime works as a metaphor for these unpleasant changes.

The majority of detective stories are urban romances. There are exceptions of course, but an established parameter that can be breached must define the community where the intrusion, a crime, takes place. The urban environment describes an area with distinct geographical and social boundaries, but it is also an area accessible to outsiders. Miss Marple would have had nothing to investigate and Eco's monastery would not have admitted his detective, if it were not for the fact that the environments they describe were permeable.

As mentioned before, the detective genre is a romance genre and as such adapts itself to a succession of contemporary environments. As times change so does the mystery story. Eco and Christie limit the physical extension of their settings in order to highlight the intrusion of an alien character. The very British world of Miss Marple during World War I and II was suspicious of outsiders and protected its traditional cultural values, which is what the detective novels of Agatha Christie also strived to accomplish. The protagonist of Umberto Eco's late twentieth-century detective novel *The Name of the Rose* is an investigator and friar who is an informed outsider in a thirteenth-century monastery. He is a man from the Middle Ages, but has been created from the perspective of the late twentieth century. He could perhaps be compared to world diplomats or international businessmen of today who understand global politics and economics and are not deterred by regional traditional values. In *The Name of the Rose* the moving masses of pilgrims, teaching and traveling clerics and conquering religions of the Middle Ages parallel the migrations of twentieth-century peoples and ideas.

Both Christie and Eco retain basic elements of the genre, but their adaptations are reflective of their particular environments. For Jameson their transformations of the genre are typical of romance literature:

> [T]he problem raised by the persistence of romance as a mode is that of substitutions, adaptations, and appropriations, raise the question of what, under wholly altered historical circumstances, can have been found to replace the raw materials of magic and Otherness which medieval romance found ready to hand in its socioeconomic environment [*Political* 131].

The different configurations of the detective genre and the emergence of the genre itself represent "wholly altered historical" circumstances. Poe's detective fiction coincides with the emergence of an urban police force that was in turn a response to whole scale emigration from rural areas to industrialized cities. Hinojosa's selection of detective fiction to continue the saga of Klail City is in response to demographic change in the Rio Grande Valley.

The detective genre has undergone many transformations from its romance roots, but what the nineteenth century expected of its newly founded police force and what twenty-first-century citizens would also want from their police has not changed. We want security. The success rate of fictional (and actual) police officers has never lived up to the success rate of the Romantic or contemporary fictional detective. To be caught up in a detective novel is to dream the dream of salvation, but in order to dream this dream a capable protagonist needs to lead the way.

A favorite hero of Romanticism was the pirate or highwayman, an outcast who had no choice but to turn to crime. A lovely young maid could tragically recognize his inner goodness. The conflict between socioeconomic forces and regional traditions, as represented by the dashing pirate and his swooning maid, concludes with their heroic deaths at the hands of the king's men. To paraphrase Jameson, this "imaginary" solution to the conflict posits a "nostalgic" utopia, a "salvational logic" where metaphysical transcendence has not lost its position in face of "nascent capitalism" (*Political* 128, 148).

At the beginning of the eighteenth century the Industrial Revolution had swollen urban populations and crime had increased in England and in France. The social problems of debt and vagrancy were widespread, and were criminalized. Crime and punishment were very visible; actual criminals were sung about in ballads, written up on broadsides and executions were held in public. It was during the nineteenth century that city police forces were established in London, Paris and New York (see Holquist and Porter).

The detective story of the early nineteenth century took advantage of the popular fixation on crime. Pirate poetry and narrative and its likes had titillated the imagination of the reading public. Detective fiction flowed from this stimulating narrative of "other" and adventure, but it was a genre that attempted to calm the fears of its middle class readership who didn't have any personal knowledge of pirates, but were all too aware of crime. In the detective genre, the criminal was caught and stability was restored. Christie and Eco's detective fiction accomplish the same goal relative to the time and place of their writing.

According to Michael Holquist the "historical" creation of a police force, still a tentative and untrustworthy organizer of chaos, confronts Poe's quintessential nineteenth-century Romantic poet personality. Enjoying a relatively stable period, having secured the editorship of *Graham's* under the condition that he stay on the straight and narrow, the poet put aside the Romantic horrors of chaos in his personal life, invented tales of ratiocination, puzzles to be solved (see Haycraft). Perhaps in order to rationalize his own demons, Poe found a model for the organization and restriction of chaos— the police — that he seized upon as a tool to stem his personal pathos. Haycraft quotes what he terms as Joseph Wood Krutch's "brilliant over-simplification": "Poe invented the detective story that he might not go mad" (164). Fictionalizing the police was not sufficient. Poe improved the nonfiction model by adding an amateur detective with a superior rational intellect who surpassed his professional colleagues in the investigation and resolution of crime.

The detective genre has not been as developed by writers nor is it as popular among readers in the Spanish speaking world as in the English speaking countries of Great Britain and the United States. For some critics this is because capitalism has not been as strong in these countries; for others it is because democratic institutions have not been as strong in the

Spanish speaking world (see Alewyn, Kaemmel and Simpson). In my opinion the lack of interest stems from the fact that these populations have been subject to mercurial economic and ideological fluctuations. Both Cuba and Argentina, during periods of infatuation with, or under the undue influence of Anglo culture, read mystery novels in translation, and in Argentina produced volumes of Anglo-imitative detective fiction (Simpson 44, 97). Relatively speaking these were periods of domestic tranquillity and powerful dictatorships (Fulgencio Batista, 1952–1958, Juan Domingo Perón 1946–1955) with close ties to the United States and Great Britain.

The Chicano detective genre first appeared in the fictional year of 1972 when *Partners in Crime* takes place and responds to demographic changes in the United States that became quite obvious by 1985 when it was published. During World War II, Mexican Americans began to move to the cities and since the 1960s this group has been a predominantly urban population. In the 1960s and 1970s, increased drug use and drug-related border crime affected the population as a whole and in particular those along the U.S.-Mexico border. In the 1980s there was a dramatic increase in the policing of the border that has continued to escalate.

The central character in detective fiction is the detective, and Rafe Buenrostro is no exception. However, Hinojosa's polyphonic narrative and his detective's methods seem to function as disclaimers to both the author's and the detective's authority. In her review, Samples was disappointed that the subtitle *A Rafe Buenrostro Mystery* had mislead her to assume that Rafe would control the criminal investigation with the same all-knowing aplomb as Christie's Hercule Poirot. (154). Typically the narrator of detective fiction assumes an authoritative stance and the story privileges the utterances and summations of action that have a direct bearing on the development of plot — the investigation of the crime. However, in *Partners in Crime* and in Poe's "The Murders in the Rue Morgue," crime itself is not the central focal point of the narrative. The methods of the detectives, the *chevalier* and the lieutenant, are of more importance than the crimes they investigate.

Lieutenant Rafe Buenrostro and Chevalier Auguste Dupin do not actively collect the majority of the evidence in the cases they investigate. However, each detective is ultimately responsible for putting the pieces of the puzzle together. Hinojosa's characterization of a detective, of his methods, of his way of life and background recall many of the characteristics of Poe's detective who is recognized as the original model for the genre, but whose position was overtaken by Conan Doyle's Sherlock Holmes. Sir Arthur Conan Doyle formalized the Romantic personality of the detective hero and he, not Poe, established the "salvational logic" of this new romance (Jameson *Political* 128). His supposedly morally ambiguous and intellectually aloof detective was a specialist in hunting out evil. The crimes Holmes investigated were motivated by diabolical greed and passion.

Dupin and Buenrostro are each from an "illustrious family" that has been reduced to lesser circumstances, and no longer wields any measurable economic or political power (Poe "The Murders" 339). The previous volumes of the *Klail City Death Trip* recount that over generations the Buenrostro family has lost the majority of its land in the valley and with it economic authority to the nineteenth-century late comers, the Klail-Blanchard-Cooke and the Leguizamón families. Dupin's "sole luxuries" were books. His North American chronicler and companion is "astonished ... at the vast extent of his reading" even though he is a reader himself (Poe "The Murders" 339). An elderly gentleman Rafe encounters in his investigations, Mr. Woodall, is impressed with Rafe's knowledge of Charles Lamb (42). The three readers on the Homicide Squad of five are all senior members: Donovan, Dorson and Buenrostro. Their "sole luxuries" include more than books, but not much more. In the case of Rafe, there is a fishing trip he does not take and his secret relationship with Sammie Jo Perkins of the Klail-Blanchard-Cooke family. In contrast, the two younger members watch sports on television, drink beer and barbecue together while their wives either look on in disgust or escape for shopping trips.

Both Francisco Lomelí and Antonio Prieto Taboada contrast the lack of community ties and social commitment of the loner detective of the Anglo American and British genre with the close family ties and social commitment of the Chicano detective (Lomelí et al. 299; Taboada 120). From previous volumes of the *Klail City Death Trip,* it is known that Rafe Buenrostro maintains family ties and his closest relative is his cousin Jehú Malacara. Rafe, like Dupin (Poe "The Murders" 339), does not hide these ties, but in *Partners in Crime* he sees his family only infrequently. He, not unlike Dupin, spends time sequestered with an intimate companion. "Our seclusion was perfect. We admitted no visitors. Indeed the locality of our retirement had been carefully kept a secret from my own former associates," writes Dupin's chronicler (Poe "The Murders" 339). Dupin's time is spent reading; Rafe passes his weekends in seclusion with Sammie Jo. Sam Donovan wonders what Rafe, his partner and fellow widower, does on the weekends: "Well, he loved to fish and hunt, but was that all he did? Donovan didn't know" (169). Not even Rafe's partners, like Dupin's chronicler's former associates, know what he is doing on his off hours.

The personal lives of Buenrostro and Dupin are closely guarded private affairs. However, each leaves his retreat for "that infinity of mental excitement which quiet observation can afford" (Poe "The Murders" 340). Dupin has no need to wander the streets of Paris, but he can afford to do so because he is not frightened by their disarray. His reclusive life style has educated him in "quiet observation" that allows him to establish a logical order to the chaos he observes, and which provides him with "mental excitement." Throughout the *KCDT* series the picaresque adventures are primarily left to Jehú, whereas "quiet observation" has been Rafe's sphere. "To everyone's surprise" after having completed a law degree, Rafe returned to the valley and became a patrolman (*Partners* 110). Already homicide detectives at the time, Donovan and Dorson recognized the "methodical, logical mind" that Rafe had cultivated in law school and observed how he put it to work on the roads of Belken County (*Partners* 110). Rafe is not a nineteenth-century Romantic recluse, but he has never been characterized as particularly forthcoming about his personal life or as an overtly gregarious social guy. He is a poet, the "author" of *Korean Love Songs.*

Dupin and Buenrostro are careful observers. They observe without a scheme to be filled in and then, from the evidence they collect and reject, create a logical organization of the material. Their logic, unlike the "*obvious logic*" of the bureaucrats referred to in the introduction of the Homicide Squad or the facile conclusions of the newspaper reporters read by Dupin, includes the probability of coincidence as a factor in the events that they eventually explain. Motive does not have the importance in their investigations that it assumed as the genre developed — for example in the stories of Sir Arthur Conan Doyle.

In the introductory paragraphs to "The Murders in the Rue Morgue," Dupin's chronicler makes a comparison between a chess player and a checker player to illustrate "the higher powers of the reflective intellect" (337). In chess, an oversight will result in "injury or defeat" because it is magnified by the already proscribed moves of the pieces and because the "possible moves are ... involute ... the chances of such oversights are multiplied" (337). However, in the game of "draughts" or checkers, if both players are equally experienced in the game, a lapse of attention will not lose the game, and "only by some *recherché* movement, the result of some strong exertion of the intellect" will the game be won (337). This serves as part of the introduction to Dupin's methods that will be illustrated by the murder story itself and is in sharp contrast to the "game" that author Ian Fleming plays in his *James Bond* narratives.

The "mental excitement" that pushes Dupin to leave his sanctuary and keeps Buenrostro typing out police reports is not a spectator sport; it's like observing a game of checkers. Samples's criticism of *Partners in Crime* confirms that Dupin's and Rafe's investigative and crime solving style is not familiar to contemporary readers of the genre more accustomed to a formulaic plot, the thrill of physical confrontation or a last-minute dramatic resolution. Samples notes that "[e]ven the actual arrest of the murderers is without fanfare — ordinary and anti-climatic [sic]" (154).

In the "Murders in the Rue Morgue," Dupin invites the owner of the murdering orangutan to his apartments. Dupin is prepared for violence, but his calm summary of what he has learned convinces the orangutan's owner that he will not be prosecuted and physical confrontation is avoided. Dupin has drawn him to his apartment by placing a false notice in the newspaper requesting the owner of a lost orangutan to visit him and claim it. In *Partners in Crime* the assassins are caught completely off-guard, still trying to communicate with their contractor, the "murderer" who hired them. Like the unsuspecting owner of the murdering orangutan, they are caught unawares because they did not realize they were under suspicion. Their capture could have resulted in a dramatic confrontation, but they were too preoccupied with their relationship to their contractor to suspect that the police have cornered them. Both *Partners in Crime* and "The Murders in the Rue Morgue" conclude without the fanfare of violence.

The secondary narratives of *Partners in Crime*, dismissed by Samples, and labeled by Klaus Zilles as "false starts" serve the same purpose as Poe's introduction to his detective's methods in "The Murders in the Rue Morgue" (Samples 154, Zilles 41). After defining "the higher powers of the reflective intellect" and before the initiation of the murder investigation, Dupin's chronicler describes a walk taken with his friend where he observes this intellect in action. In *Partners in Crime*, the first two cases introduce the methods, successful and unsuccessful, of the Belken County Homicide Squad.

The first murder in *Partners in Crime* involves a case of mistaken identity: the murderer shoots the wrong man as the hapless victim exits the intended victim's apartment. This was a domestic dispute gone awry. A man learns of his wife's infidelity and in a blind rage goes to the apartment of her supposed lover and shoots the building superintendent who has been fixing a leak in the bathroom.

In the second case investigated in *Partners in Crime*, a man's body is found in a car abandoned in an agricultural field. The victim's residence is searched and this leads off on various trails, all of which are false. However, we learn that sometimes the most commonplace method of investigation is the most productive: Rafe finds the address of the mysterious Woodalls, who are linked by a paper trail to the victim, in the phone book on his desk, while the other detectives have been laboriously searching criminal records. The victim was gay and this is assumed to be the motive for his murder. However, like the first case, and the majority of murder cases according to Rafe, this is a "stupid murder" (*Partners* 5). The victim's sexual orientation had nothing to do with his untimely death; he had the bad luck to give a ride to a mentally unstable hitchhiker who, for reasons impossible to know, murdered him. Period.

The history of the hitchhiker, McKinlow, adds another dimension to this prologue of investigative methods. McKinlow has been interred in the Flora N. Klail Institution for the Insane for many years. By blackmailing the director of the asylum, a petty but constant thief of state property, the patient was allowed to leave the premises at will. This case points out that corruption in government agencies is to be expected and that the most obvious motive, the one handed to you — homosexuality in this case — should always be questioned.

The murder of Belken County prosecutor Dutch Elder that dominates *Partners in Crime* is the result of mistaken identity and was committed by hired assassins in the employ of a Mexican government official. This same official, trusted by the Homicide Squad, hands the detectives a plausible solution to the murders at the Kum Bak Inn. He explains that Dutch Elder inadvertently stepped into a gangland assassination of Mexican nationals that came about because of a power struggle between known old-time valley smugglers. Fortunately, Rafe knew the valley's inhabitants, criminal and straight, too well to accept this solution.

The first case introduced the nonmotive of mistaken identity. The second case demonstrated how valuable knowledge of the familiar is in an investigation, the complicity of authority and a material motivation for this complicity, and the danger of presupposing any fixed sequence of events in combination with the assumption of a particular motivation. The contractor, the "murderer" of the Kum Bak Inn victims, is the chief of police of Barrones who has used his position to take over small scale drug smuggling operations and to initiate a big time illegal traffic in cocaine. Two of the three men killed at the Kum Bak Inn were his competitors and the last of the old-time smugglers. The third was Dutch Elder who stepped out of the restroom in the Kum Bak Inn and was mistaken for the missing Mexican kingpin of the gang on the assassins' hit list.

Hinojosa uses chapters one through thirteen of the thirty-seven chapters as an introduction to the "main murder" that will illustrate what the first two murder investigations have outlined. Poe uses the first third of "The Murders in the Rue Morgue" to define "analytic ability" and to introduce the detective and his methods. Only the last two-thirds of the story recount the murders in the Rue Morgue and the investigation of this crime. At the conclusion of his definition of analytic ability, Poe advises his reader that, "[t]he narrative which follows will appear to the reader somewhat in the light of a commentary upon the propositions just advanced" (339). Hinojosa's advice to his reader is presented in the first two cases investigated by the Homicide Squad. Rafe told us on page one that most murders are "idiotic" and it should not surprise the reader that Hinojosa sees a need to define "idiotic" before addressing the main case (5).

The *chevalier* and the lieutenant rely primarily on documents collected by others. For Dupin the collection of evidence is the task of the Paris police and its publication is the privilege of the Paris newspapers. For Rafe the Belken County Homicide Squad and forensic laboratory does this job. As a member of the Homicide Squad, Buenrostro does gather evidence, but his part in this activity is no greater than that of the other detectives or the lab technicians. Dupin and Buenrostro follow up the documented evidence — newspaper accounts and police reports — with a minimum number of interviews and first hand observations. Poe's and Hinojosa's tales partially reproduce the "documents" of the investigations as either a fictional chronicle or a police report. The narratives combine these with the detectives' methods. Both detectives are careful observers of their communities, and the routine, the mundane, the plodding are what each pursue as they search for the exception.

Before initiating the investigation of the "Murders in the Rue Morgue," Dupin demonstrates to his chronicler that his knowledge of routine events is precisely the knowledge necessary for the recreation of unseen events. Antonio Prieto Taboada in his reading of *Partners in Crime* accurately states that Rafe follows "*pistas culturales*" ("cultural clues"). Because he knows his community well, he is able to see more meaning in any given clue than the other detectives (Taboada 122). He is the only detective able to identify the man who hired the Kum Bak Inn assassins. Only Rafe realizes that the Barrones police chief's explanation of treason among the ranks of the old-time smugglers rings false.

Hermeneutic closure, assumed to be basic to the detective genre, is not part of *Partners in Crime* or the detective stories of Edgar Allan Poe. Critic Richard Alweyn and many of Poe's contemporary critics have criticized him for the lack of a satisfying ending to some of his fiction. Poe's contemporary American critics admired his work but criticized his lack of maturity; their criticism veiled their distrust of his morality. His works were seen as immature and incomplete, because they did not work toward the construction of a hermeneutic truth. In other words, they were morally unsatisfactory (Carlson 35–56). Alweyn points out that in "The Murders in the Rue Morgue" there is no "murderer" to be found. "E.A. Poe did not create a single complete detective story.... For a wild orangutan cannot commit murder, only manslaughter. To say this is not to split hairs. For a murder presupposes a motive and a plan, the most important factors in the detective story" (78).

Commenting on *Partners in Crime*, Klaus Zilles "venture[s] to say that this is probably the only whodunit in the history of the crime mystery genre whose principal plot line is based on an absurd mix-up" (41). Of the five murders referred to in *Partners in Crime*, three were not planned any more than the murders of the women in their home on the Rue Morgue. Dutch Elder and the victims of the two auxiliary narratives happened to be in the wrong place at the wrong time; they were not consciously singled out as victims. "Not to split hairs," but their deaths were manslaughter, not murder. The orangutan goes free, as does the "murderer" who hired the assassins at the Kum Bak Inn. In Poe's "The Mystery of Marie Rogêt" the murderer is never named and never apprehended. In *Partners in Crime*, Rafe is able to recreate the circumstances that led up to the murder and those that followed and even name the "murderer," the man who hired the killers, but he is not able to apprehend this man, or even witness his just death as is the norm in most detective novels. We only learn in Hinojosa's second *Rafe Buenrostro* mystery, *Ask a Policeman* (1998) that the "murderer" was finally apprehended only to escape again. Because of the absence of motive, neither Poe nor Hinojosa fashion a morality tale out of a murder mystery. In Poe's tales cited above and in *Partners in Crime* it is possible to get away with murder.

Hinojosa and Poe have very little interest in the particular motives of individual criminals, but are interested, Hinojosa more so than Poe, in showing the complicity between public opinion and bureaucratic authority. Both authors are very aware of the role assumed by the media as a chronicler and judge of criminal activity and its power to form public opinion. In "The Mystery of Marie Rogêt," Poe argues with actual newspaper accounts of the murder of a young woman in New York, a scenario that he fictionalizes and transposes to Paris (Poe "The Mystery" 198). In "The Murders in the Rue Morgue," Dupin argues with the conclusions the fictional newspapers have drawn from the same facts that he has read in their pages. In both cases, Dupin does not accept the motives that have been suggested for these crimes by the newspapers.

In "The Murders in the Rue Morgue," a young bank employee, known to Dupin, is arrested because the newspapers have implied that money may have been the motivation for the crime and the employee was once seen leaving the home of the victims. This upsets Dupin and he vows to discover the murderer and clear the name of this humble bank employee. In "The Mystery of Marie Rogêt," the newspapers suggest that the murdered young woman had loose morals and met with her just fate because she was out at the wrong time of night. This was not the case; she was from a humble background and she innocently believed that a handsome naval officer would marry her. Instead he kills her.

In *Partners in Crime*, the media works against the Homicide Squad and serves the purposes of the politically ambitious good ol' boy, Belken County District Attorney Harvey Bollinger. In a case previous to the investigations narrated in the novel, Bollinger invited the press to witness the arrest of a notorious murderer as a means of furthering his political ambitions. His goal was foiled by a long wait. The reporters all got drunk in the airport lounge, fought among themselves and nearly impeded the arrest. They were ultimately duped and deprived of witnessing the arrest and singing the praises of Bollinger by a clever move on the part of the Homicide Squad that successfully apprehended the suspect.

The "main murder" investigated in *Partners in Crime* is the outcome of socioeconomic forces that have recently invaded the valley and the good ol' boy bureaucracy of Klail City and Belken County. Harvey Bollinger and Dutch had repeatedly argued about Bollinger's self-serving and media grandstanding management of the D.A.'s office. An exasperated Dutch punched Bollinger and was forced to take a leave of absence. He went fishing. On his way to his favorite fishing spot, he stopped at the Kum Bak Inn for some take-out beer. He was blown to pieces by the fire of two automatic weapons and a shotgun.

Parallel to the killing of two Mexican nationals that caught Dutch Elder in the crossfire at the Kum Bak Inn is the drug related crime committed by 12 bank employees, tellers and managers in Klail City that could affect more than 200 people, the families and friends of the employees, and the community as a whole (*Partners* 155). The "underpaid" tellers have been supplementing their income by laundering the money of drug traffickers (115, 151–152). Jehú, who is the first to know about this criminal activity, is careful to protect the accused bank employees from the press and thus diminish any repercussions that could have been suffered by the community.

If Poe has imbedded any "moral" in "The Murders in the Rue Morgue" or "The Mystery of Marie Rogêt," it is one that he and Hinojosa share: the complicity between bureaucracy and the press is not in the interest of the people both purport to serve. The Anglo American and British detective is in general a self-employed private investigator. Poe's C. Auguste Dupin established this trend that also included an anti-bureaucratic stance during an era that initiated invasive bureaucratic control — the urban police force to begin with — over the daily lives of Western populations. Poe's life history shows he did not know how to live with authority either as a student or as an army officer, or ultimately as the editor of *Graham's*. Even though the police may be bunglers in the British classical genre, as exemplified in Agatha Christie's work, there is no anti-bureaucratic stance. However, in the United States during the Great Depression when the federal bureaucracy became by far the largest single employer, the hard-boiled genre reestablished an anti-bureaucratic attitude.

*Partners in Crime* recounts the history of crime in the valley. The traditional economic base, oil and agriculture, has never given a decent living to the majority of its residents and is now being undermined by the intrusion of big time drug trafficking that is accompanied by a long list of invading federal bureaucratic agencies: the FBI; Department of Agriculture; U.S. Department of State; Mexico's *Relaciones Exteriores*; the United States-Mexican Consultative Mechanism; the Southwest Border Regional Committee; Immigration and Naturalization Service; the U.S. Treasury Department's Bank Enforcement and Operation; the Department of Alcohol, Tobacco and Firearms; the International Boundary Commission; the General Services Administration; Department of the Interior; Department of Commerce; Department of Housing and Urban Development; Department of Labor and the Department of Transportation and the Mexican *Secretaría de Asentamiento Humano y Obras Públicas* (*Partners* 159–161). This amounts to a full scale bureaucratic invasion.

Jehú's boss Noddy Perkins, the principal owner of the one bank not affected by the money laundering scheme, is not thinking of the finances of the general populace when he says to Jehú, "Someone's trying to fiddle with our money" (117). But he is, like the rest of the residents, wary of bureaucratic intrusion. J.D. Saldívar and Taboada note that criminal activity in *Partners in Crime* is the result of too few economic opportunities for the majority in conjunction with the invasion of large scale drug trafficking. The intrusion of drug trafficking in the valley threatens not only what has been good about this community, peace and relatively little crime, but also is disrupting what has been wrong, the bureaucratic monopoly of the good ol' boy network.

Before *Partners in Crime*, illegal opportunities in the valley were unequally divided. The Klail-Blanchard-Cooke family with their allies, the Leguizamóns, practiced very profitable full scale legitimized robbery of the original *Tejano Mexicano* land for generations, while the illegal activities of the *Tejano Mexicanos* and their Mexican border town neighbors in Barrones were limited to smuggling and petty thievery. The prior texts of the

*Klail City Death Trip* traced the crimes of the ruling families; *Partners in Crime* presents a brief history of the crime that was not legally sanctioned.

Nieves Hernández and Mariano Reséndez, two "legendary *contrabandistas* ["smugglers"]," whose history might have been sung in one of the many *corridos* of the *tequileros* ("liquor smugglers") of the Prohibition years, are used as code names by the hired killers and their contractor. The distance in scale — technical, economical and geographical — between the operations of the *tequileros* and the drug traffickers is laughable, and Rafe voices his appreciation of the "sense of humor, and history" that inspired this choice of code names (238). The early twentieth-century *tequileros* were followed by marijuana traffickers who began their careers in crime in the brothels and bars of Barrones. Goméz-Solís, chief of police in Barrones describes their history prior to and during World War II and recounts that these criminals would "roll all manner of G.I.s ... strong-arm local merchants, too, when necessary, and bought off or paid some cops here and there." Then after the Second World War, "they branched out ... they began to hire out as *guns* [and] by the Sixties, they could all look back to over thirty years of friendship" (179). Goméz-Solís concludes that these aging smugglers are now engaged in a war between themselves. Rafe sees beyond this false conclusion, and realizes that a network of international cocaine cartels is eliminating the small time smugglers of Barrones.

Meanwhile on the north side of the border, in addition to the relatively small scale thievery of the bank employees of various ethnic and racial backgrounds, *Tejano Mexicano* auto thief Packy Esdudillo is hard at work. Packy, along with an Anglo buddy, stole his first car as a minor just before World War II. Both were sent to a juvenile facility. When they stole another automobile, they were conscripted into the army. After the war, Packy returned to Klail City and continued to steal cars and smuggle them across the border into Mexico his whole life without a conviction. But in 1972, at the time the novel takes place, he is so afraid of the powerful new bosses of the cocaine cartel in the valley who hired him to steal the getaway car used by the Kum Bak gunmen, that he calls the Belken County Homicide Squad. He's looking for the safety of jail so he gives himself up and confesses to auto theft. He realizes that a good lawyer could probably get him off yet again, but instead he seeks the protection of the police and conviction as preferable to being a target for the global drug trafficking thugs.

*Partners in Crime* in its dialogue with Poe's detective genre suggests a correlation between the nineteenth-century creation of urban police forces and the twentieth-century bureaucratic intrusion into the Rio Grande Valley. Populations have grown, crime has become more widespread, and both Poe's fictional Paris and Hinojosa's valley are no longer as isolated from outside influences as they were prior to the stirrings of the French Revolution and the Korean War. The Anglo Texan power base has been eroded by the intrusion of global drug trafficking and the bureaucratic agencies of the Federal government sent to conduct a War on Drugs.

*Ask a Policeman: A Rafe Buenrostro Mystery* (1998) is a much more conventional detective novel than *Partners in Crime* and demonstrates a close dialogue with contemporary Anglo American detective and crime fiction. In *Ask a Policeman* the pace of the narrative picks up, the secondary narratives are closely related to drug trafficking and violence increases. All of which suggests that the intrusion of outsiders, both Anglo American bureaucrats and multi-national drug smugglers, into the valley is in full swing.

There is no consummation of a foundational romance in *Partners in Crime*, but a romantic cohesion of sorts between Rafe and Sammie Jo has blossomed before the beginning of the next chapter in the *Klail City Death Trip, Becky and Her Friends*. In this volume, the Mexican American protagonist, a wannabe paragon of Anglo society, divorces her husband to marry Jehú. Even though traditional pressures from both sides of the cultural divide condemn her infidelity, she does not back away from her decision. This is a union of Leguizamón and Malacara-Buenrostro that favors the original *Tejano Mexicano* perspective. In the next novel, *Ask a Policeman*, Rafe and Sammie Jo Perkins have been married for four years. This is a reversal of the marriage between Anglos and Mexicans as documented in the history of the Southwest and fictionalized in Mexican American Ruiz de Burton's nineteenth-century foundational tale, *The Squatter and the Don*. With *Ask a Policeman* the Mexican American male, instead of the Mexican American female, marries the Anglo. Sammie Jo, Noddy Perkins' daughter, is part of the Klail-Blanchard-Cooke ruling Anglo family of the valley. From the perspective of a foundational fiction, the joining of the powerful Leguizamón and Perkins' clans with the Malacara-Buenrostro families recognizes the need to establish an alliance between traditionally antagonistic groups.

In *Partners in Crime*: Sammy Jo's father Noddy Perkins sensed that the family's power was being assaulted from outside forces, bureaucratic and criminal, but the coin turns in the sequel, *Ask a Policeman*. The now frail old man feels he must project a tolerance he has never practiced and confesses to Rafe, his son-in-law, that he was never prejudiced (18). With this most likely false confession, Noddy appears to realize that in order to conserve the integrity of the community in face of the outside onslaughts it will be necessary to integrate the community and establish a more equitable working relationship. In *Ask a Policeman*, a local man from a centuries old *Tejano Mexicano* valley family, Rafe Buenrostro, is the head of the Homicide Squad and occupies a position of authority and power that outsiders had denied to his ancestors. Rafe has the responsibility to defend the community, including his feeble father-in-law Noddy Perkins, and thus, with nary a nostalgic backward glance, the valley has changed again.

# 4

## Poetry in Action
### *Lucha Corpi's* Cactus Blood

Poet and novelist Lucha Corpi has written three *Gloria Damasco* mysteries, *Eulogy for a Brown Angel* (1992), *Cactus Blood* (1995) and *Black Widow's Wardrobe* (1999), and one *Brown Angel* whodunit, *Crimson Moon* (2004). Of this group *Cactus Blood* best represents Corpi's talents as a poet, as well as her commitment to the sociopolitical goals of Chicano/a activism and feminism.

In *Cactus Blood*, the poet works with metaphor and the novelist incorporates Chicano history and elements of the classical whodunit. Corpi explores the activism of the 1960s and 1970s, the role of Chicanas as leaders, poets, laborers, and the double marginalization of women of color in the United States by racism and patriarchal privilege. Among topics addressed are the exploitation and endangerment of Mexican and Mexican American farm workers, the problems undocumented women face and the prejudicial treatment of lesbians.

Despite the serious nature of its topics, *Cactus Blood* is an entertaining mystery. However, some readers of mainstream detection might find it a confusing tale because this narrative trespasses and transforms many conventions of the formulaic genre. *Cactus Blood* raises many questions seldom addressed in popular mystery novels and prominently employs the use of metaphoric language. My analysis addresses these characteristics of Corpi's novel by showing how they can be integrated into what I call a "Chicana Foundational Tale."

One transformation of the formulaic genre performed by *Cactus Blood* and other minority detective fiction is the use of the mystery novel to communicate an alternative ideology. Tim Libretti's analysis of Corpi's *Gloria Damasco* mysteries points out that the detective genre undermines and openly contests hegemonic ideologies.

Critics have recognized the "conservative" nature of classical detective stories. Libretti refers to Dennis Porter's reader-centered criticism that posits that the popularity of the whodunit is based on its affirmation of membership in a shared cultural community. This community is viewed as "conservative" because its goal is to preserve and conserve its hegemonic unity. Libretti shows that Porter's configuration of "cultural community" describes a compliant relationship between the mystery and its readers. This same relationship can be descriptive of "Third World" mysteries because these also presume the reader and the novel share some cultural values that both want to preserve.[1] Because detective fiction explains past events, it is an excellent genre for minority inquiry "and critique of dominant social forms" (Libretti 68).

The primary difference noted by Libretti between the recognized "canonical" genre and Corpi's detective opus is that there is no return to the "beginning but a recognition that the conditions of internal colonization persist" (80). Furthermore, in the *Damasco* mysteries "the quest for justice is just beginning" (80). "Third World" adaptations do not return to "historical endings" typical of the "generic form of the detective novel" (80). Instead the historical and social circumstances that surround these works demand that the cyclical form — the "historical endings"— of the genre be transformed. Anaya's detective series and Hinojosa's *Klail City Death Trip* return to the past but do not make this trip in order to remove a criminal. They are not out to catch the crook and reestablish the status quo. Their forays into the past are to inform the present of the possibility of future change.

That "the detective fiction formula [can] easily serve a politically radical and social transformative function" is not a stumbling block for an inquisitive and open-minded reader (Libretti 67). Michael Nava is adept at couching his off center views in his commercially successful hard-boiled novels. Corpi, however, takes liberties with the genre that Nava does not. Amalia Gladhart's review of *Cactus Blood* points out some of the obstacles a reader may face if she is also a consummate reader of mainstream detection.

Gladhart laments that "the novel's resolution does not live up to the intricacy of the set-up" (254). So true: the novel's first chapters present a set-up similar to those that are acted upon in the classical genre. However, in *Cactus Blood* we are not led to a traditional follow-up, resolution and return to status quo. Following the leader, the reader finds himself in what appears to be a typical whodunit expecting that the focus of the narrative will be the investigation of the death presented at the outset, but this mysterious death only serves as a catalyst for a much broader, unresolvable and ongoing investigation. Gladhart's short review does not address the fact that Corpi uses the formulaic set-up to pique reader interest and to question the "truth" of the genre itself.

Whodunits are popular because they are predictable. Chicano detective fiction is not an exception if readers can, like Gladhart, first recognize where these novels depart from the formula. Then the reader needs to compare what they conserve and what they discard from the models they transform. Chicano mysteries preserve the assumption of compliance between the reader and the story and the narrative outline of romance.

In Romantic literature of the eighteenth and nineteenth century "truth" was the object of desire; irony was not part of Romantic fiction, nor is it a part of a formulaic detective novel. A reliable narrator is paramount, and pleasure, not frustration, is what readers of the detective genre expect. "Ironic realism" is the term used by Northrop Frye to describe the most prestigious fictional narratives of the second half of the twentieth century. According to Frye, contemporary realism is taken to such a point that in order to proceed with an analysis of the text, the critic is forced to decode the central query of the text to find the "reality" or the "truth" behind the narrative, and then propose the question and the answer embedded in the text.

Frye suggests that the reader return to the romance genre, its underlying structure, in order to understand contemporary literature. For a reading of these same texts that he terms "modernist," Fredric Jameson asks that the reader recognize the "absent presence" of "fantasy" as if it were "a word on the tip of your tongue or a dream not quite remembered" (*Political* 134–135). Ambiguity for Frye and Jameson can be understood by returning either to the folktale or medieval romance.

Frye and Jameson describe contemporary detective fiction as a form of romance. What is lost in their "translation" from romance is more easily recovered than that of prestigious or modernist fictions. What is missing from most detective fiction is the transformation that was worked on folk heroes or epic protagonists as they followed their quests. Detectives are notoriously static characters. Contrary to this norm the Chicano detectives, Sonny Baca, Rafe Buenrostro, Gloria Damasco, Luis Montez and Henry Rios, grow and change.

Mainstream detective fiction does conserve other recognizable romance forms and rhetoric. Its framework follows a clear hermeneutic organization; it immediately announces a "question" that must be answered by the plot. The whodunit is a story whose "principal object" is for the reader "to discover, by an interpretation of clues, the answer to a problem posed at the outset" (Kermode 179). More than any other genre the detective story requires "the disposition, in a consecutive narrative, of information which requires us to ask both how it 'fits in,' and also how it will all 'come out'" (Kermode 180).

The formulaic text emphasizes the initial question and the conclusive answer that constitute its structural framework. Within this basic framework each text progresses towards resolution and as it precedess it must digress and prolong the mystery. The detective genre conforms to a basic definition of literature. It is more than a list, less than a poem and tells a story that puts the reader at a distance from his own reality. At the same time, with little effort, it requires him to evaluate, look at and contemplate his environment by alternating slow motion and fast forward to hold his attention (see Eagleton ).

There are, of course, an infinite variety of digressive and progressive narratives within each tale and the genre as a whole. These may satisfy the reader's curiosity about some picturesque contemporary reality, give him an insider's view of a lifestyle or occupation, transport him with travelogue detail to an exotic place and culture, or even affirm his affection for cats or jazz. However, many critics of the genre agree that those digressions that affirm the cultural norms of the reader's community seem to dominate the genre (see Eco, Jameson "On Raymond," Grossvogel, Kaemmel, Kermode and Porter).

These stalling narratives are exemplars of those that define Formist histories; they are the facts—"clues"—of a culture. The information that will reveal the final solution to the mystery is presented explicitly in the clues couched in these narratives or encoded implicitly by the communal values shared by the reader and the narrator of the authorial community. When reading the works of Anaya, Corpi, Hinojosa, Nava and Ramos it is important to recognize that the authorial community is not homogeneous— Mexican American is Mexican and American — and the "clues," whether the forward or backward moving ones, will not conform to a singular cultural viewpoint.

A first reading of a formulaic novel answers the question "Who *done* it?" It is assumed by critics that the second reading will answer the question "Why did he do it?" The simple answer — the perpetrator of the crime was "evil"— is unsatisfactory because it only partially answers the question. In the classic genre and the spy-thriller, the detective and the villain are seen as representatives of the polarization between good and evil. In the contemporary British and Anglo American genres motivation is more easily understood by reassessing the romance form of narrative.

Jameson's analysis of romance genre removes the qualifications of "good" and "evil." First, as mentioned in regard to Anaya's cycle, "evil" is a label for *other*, the unknown, "alien, different, strange, unclean, and unfamiliar," that when unmasked is identified as the self (*Political* 115). Secondly, "good and evil" is an "ethical binary" of any ideology that labels the outsider as "evil" and reinforces the "hold of ethical categories on our mental habits" (*Political* 115, 116).

Jameson follows Nietzsche's thought on the concept of ethics: "it is ethics itself which is the ideological vehicle and the legitimation of concrete structures of power and domination" (*Political* 114). Therefore, to answer, "Why did he do it?" it is necessary to investigate the ideological context of "good" and "evil" when these qualifiers are used or implied as labels in a particular text. (Anaya, as noted earlier, explores an ideological context of good and evil.)

The contemporary mystery's detective is usually the "everyman" of his community, whose distinction is that he or she is more sensitive than average, similar but not the same as the defiantly independent Romantic hero. Chicano detectives and their Anglo cousins do not differ in this respect. This sleuth is not the reclusive intellectual who dominated early detective fiction and the "classic" British genre of the early twentieth century; rather he is similar to the hard-boiled detective of Depression-era U.S. crime fiction. The contemporary villain tends to be associated with some insidious social ill, as he was in hard-boiled fiction. The classical genre's villain is an aberration, the sole representative of a social or moral evil whose removal returns the community to a peaceful status quo. The contemporary genre's victim of crime is rarely entirely innocent or too blatantly guilty, at least not until the end of the novel, of trespassing the norms of society. Chicano detective fiction is consistent with the contemporary mainstream whodunit in regards to this initial ambiguity between "good and evil."

Even if the clues and the investigative techniques of the detective challenge credulity, the reader follows them because he has agreed to believe the narrator. A reliable narrator is central to the structure of the formulaic detective genre. No matter how implausible the answers to the questions of "Who?" and "Why?" may seem, they are given from the narrator's organizational perspective and are supported by the content of the novel (Holquist 157–158). Chicano detective fiction also conforms to this rule of the formulaic genre.

On one level there are realistic elements in the narrative that connect the reader with an actual observable world, usually contemporary but sometimes historical, and on another level there are traces of an earlier romance genre. Both ensure detective fiction's popularity and respectively confirm the reader's knowledge of his *real* world and his universally *inher-*

*ent*— if we follow Frye and Jameson — knowledge of romance genre. In other words, readers are comforted by a familiar genre and the affirmation of their communal ideology (or a learned ideology when they are not a member of the authorial community) and its material representations.

Umberto Eco shows how ideology is expressed overtly in Ian Fleming's James Bond series where capitalist Britain repeatedly saves the world from communism. Critic David Grossvogel notes Agatha Christie's covert use of ideology when she employs ethnic identities to either lead or mislead her reader toward the resolution of the mystery. During the Depression, North American readers confirmed their interpretation of corruption as the dominant problem of the time and comfortably affirmed their moral superiority over the super wealthy, the down and out and minorities by reading Raymond Chandler's detective novels. Poe's popular detective, an impoverished aristocrat living in self-imposed idleness that allowed for close and careful observation had to be *French*, otherwise his U.S. chronicler might have noticed that his hero did not embody the American ideals of a classless society and industry.[2]

The promise of resolution, of "full hermeneutic closure" is perhaps the one element that most distinguishes the detective genre from other forms of contemporary literature and is the factor that most directly contributes to its enduring popularity (Kermode 185, Porter 87). The plot of a mystery novel is circular. The story ends where it started either centered on the resolution of the crime, the murder itself, or the resolution of "Why are things the way they are?" as in Chandler's novels (Jameson "On Raymond" 145–146). In either case there is no projection into the future. The "present" of the novel is a trail of clues that lead to the "past" of the crime. Detective fiction guarantees closure and this comforting pleasure can be easily found again in yet another whodunit. Mystery fans, in my opinion, are notoriously addicted to the genre for precisely this reason. The story conclusively ends with the reading. There is little or no opportunity to project a future for the protagonist so our imagination is frustrated and we pick up our next novel.

It should be remembered that the genre as initiated by Poe was a puzzle in ratiocination, whereas in the classical genre the set-up is presented as part of a game designed to lead the reader toward an unavoidable solution that will be revealed at the end of the novel. In the opinion of Frank Kermode, reading the twentieth-century mystery is a "hermeneutic activity"(179). In the twentieth century the detective story prefers a teleological narrative that prepares the reader for the disposition of the plot and its outcome.[3] In other words the entire novel is set up to present a particular truth.

We could classify classical detective novels as "teleological histories" because the outline of the narrative is primary. The author clearly states the problem to be solved at the outset and relies on the compliance of his reader. This is how mysteries consciously imitate hermeneutic thought. They demand that the reader *play* detective by the *rules* outlined by the fictional detective, otherwise the resolution will not ring true. For this reason hermeneutic analysis is a particularly useful tool for the description of literary constructs and conversely as an indicator of the transformation of the genre when its perspective cannot penetrate or explain a mystery's form.

Hermeneutic analyses of literature, stemming from Hans-Georg Gadamer's *Truth and Method* that built on Heidegger's hermeneutic thought, expressed doubt in the "experimental method hailed by the natural sciences since the seventeenth century" as the "sole path to truth" (Holub 379). This scientific method posits a formula as a guide in progress, free to be continually revised during the path of execution. The "truths" claimed by experiment are constantly open to revision. A hermeneutic path towards "truth" differs because the viewer/reader of art subsumes his position as viewer and integrates himself with an artistic text. From this perspective to participate in the enjoyment of art the viewer is obligated to make himself one with the principles that dictate its form otherwise its "truth" will not be available to him. The subject/object dichotomy disappears. The viewer or reader gives himself over to the rules of the game dictated by the art and participates in the game outlined by a particular work of art.[4]

In the case of Chicano whodunits one cannot assume that the rules of twentieth-century detective fiction will be observed. Gladhart analyzes *Cactus Blood* as an artistic rendition of truth, a hermeneutic of Chicano experience and finds it lacking. She makes the mistake that Libretti does not make by assuming that Corpi's authorial community is analogous to that of British and Anglo American mysteries. An "experimental" reading, the positing of a "formula" and its continual revision, is a more productive path toward the enjoyment of Corpi's mystery.

Anaya, Corpi, Hinojosa, Nava and Ramos transform the genre precisely because they refuse to return to the status quo. A restoration of the past, even the recent past that initiates their whodunits, is a step backward. These novels are about learning from the past in order to project a future where historical abuse will be an impossibility. To pick up the next volume in any of their series is to continue not only the history of a favorite detective but to see if any changes in his or her perspective have occurred, or if the investigator's environment has been transformed since the last novel. These departures from the formula constitute the primary distortions Chicanos have worked on the whodunit.

An Agatha Christie fan may not immediately recognize that Gloria Damasco is not Miss Marple. That is not surprising. Akin to Christie, Corpi initiates *Cactus Blood* with the discovery of a body in the first chapter. Chicano poet Sonny Mares is found dead. Near the beginning of the novel, following the classical formula, all the principal characters are introduced by name, or described, and their connections with the victim through a past event are established. This event was the United Farm Workers' march and strike in Delano, California, in 1973.[5] Playing on victim Sonny Mares' VCR at the time of his death is a video of striking workers being taunted by the Teamsters that concludes with the explosion of a pesticide storage tank.

Authors of the classic whodunit are careful to situate the scene of the crime in time and place. Corpi follows this convention in *Cactus Blood*. Sonny's body is discovered in Oakland, California, on October 13, 1989, the day before the start of the World Series between the Oakland Athletics and the San Francisco Giants, "The Battle of the Bay," and four days before the Bay Area's catastrophic Loma Prieta earthquake that ends the novel. The actions that follow the discovery of Sonny's body are also carefully connected to specific times and locales. This convention chronologically and physically limits the opportunities for the criminal to have acted and encourages the reader to add or eliminate suspects.

Immediately following the discovery of the body, Art Bello, Sonny's best friend, needs to be notified but cannot be found. A search is initiated for Art that leads indirectly to the autobiographical narrative of Carlota Navarro that we read in the fourth chapter of the novel. At the conclusion of this chapter, the list of characters, presumably all suspects in the investigation of Sonny's death, is complete. They include the Chicano poet-activists, Art Bello and Myra Miranda. Also included are an unnamed male (Ramón) with long hair wearing an "Indian hat" who was shown running from the pesticide tank that he has just sabotaged in the 1973 video, Carlota's Anglo American employer and his family (Dr. and Mrs. Stephens, their two daughters Sandy and Remmi, and their son Randolph), Carlota's friend and teacher Josie Baldomar Hazlitt and her husband Phillipe Hazlitt, an Englishman, and finally Carlota herself.

Whew ... this list is as long as any of Ms. Christie's.

As is the case in many tales of the classical genre, the cause of death itself is mysterious. Sonny has died from an "unknown substance orally introduced" (15). In the first four chapters the set-up provides clues that suggest that a person or persons might have had a motive for killing Sonny.

An anonymous note written with lipstick and signed "always" is found, and the perforations in this note match two small but deep cuts in Sonny's mattress. In the fourth chapter we learn that this same note, or a similar one, is linked to Dr. Stephens' rape of Carlota. Perhaps Sonny also raped Carlota and in circumstances similar to Dr. Stephens, was almost stabbed when she left him a note on the blades of a pair of scissors.

More clues come our way when Sonny's brother recalls the bundles of herbs tied with snake skin that had mysteriously appeared at Sonny's home causing him to worry about "some dark force ... at work around him" (28). As the narrative progresses the herb bundles are connected to a Mexican American *curandero* ("healer") and it is learned that this man is Ramón Caballos who was wearing the "Indian hat" in the video. What is his sinister connection to Sonny?

Then we realize that we should be keeping notes because a bowl of grapes is found in Sonny's refrigerator. He bought grapes? Never! Sonny piously supported the continuing UFW grape boycott. All of those involved in the Delano strike (Phillipe, Art, Josie, Ramón and Carlota) become suspects because they all know that the mere presence of grapes would have deeply disturbed Sonny. Did Sonny betray the UFW? Were the grapes left as a warning? Was he killed by a conspiracy of enemies like the millionaire American businessman in Christie's *The Orient Express*?

Because Gloria has observed signs on Sonny's bed that he had intercourse before his death, she suggests that the woman who had been with him left the grapes. She would have been someone familiar with Sonny's commitment to the UFW. Myra, a Chicana activist and an acquaintance of Sonny's, who has not had an easy relationship with him and is a possible link to the missing Art Bello, is added to the list of suspects. Perhaps Sonny's aggressive and unwanted affections finally pushed Myra too far. Or maybe the poets, Sonny and Bello, were in cahoots against the Chicana poet and she has gone on to become a serial killer ... of Chicano poets?

It is obvious that Miss Marple is incapable of handling this case. Only Gloria Damasco can solve this mystery. The fourth chapter, that suggests many of the connections listed above, is the "reproduction" of the autobiographical narrative of the undocumented Mexican woman, Carlota. It is part of a volume of women's autobiography, "Chicana Experiences," that Gloria is editing. This narrative is central to the story of *Cactus Blood*, not so much as a part of the set-up for the resolution of the mystery of Sonny's death — it confuses this investigation — but as an introduction to the clues that Gloria uncovers that are completely unrelated to Sonny's death.

Corpi has spiced her whodunit with the usual ingredients: a body, a mysterious substance, a victim with a number of estranged acquaintances and many suspects with access to the murder weapon, some of whom have a crime hidden in their past. The unexplained disappearances of witnesses and the suspicious demise of one, an attempt to rob information from or kill the detective and the detective's confrontation of the "murderer," followed by "his" confession and suicide, complete the package. So why isn't this a typical whodunit?

Even though *Cactus Blood* eventually tells us *how* Sonny died, we feel cheated. Sonny Mares committed suicide. A few hints early in the narrative suggest that Sonny was despondent but the detectives never look for his psychologist, and instead blame his poor mental health on the mysterious bundles left at his home. Unlike the classical genre, further information regarding Sonny's death is not presented to the reader until the last chapters of the novel when Josie confesses. She admits to having contributed to her husband's accidental death, her cover-up of that crime, her intention to implicate Ramón in her husband's death, of having left Carlota's medication at Sonny's house and the fact that she witnessed Sonny's suicide and neglected to call the authorities. The fact is Sonny's demise conveniently worked with her nefarious plans to cover up her part in the accidental death of her husband, take their savings and live happily ever after with her lover Carlota.

Josie left the grapes and herb bundles at Sonny's home and also at Bello's intending to implicate the *curandero* Ramón in the "murder" of her husband, Phillipe. Ramón might have had a good motive for murdering Phillipe along with Art and Sonny because they had witnessed him destroy the pesticide storage tank where a man was accidentally killed and they later testified against him. After her confession, Josie commits suicide, as well she should for having contorted the formula of the classical whodunit.

The cause of Sonny's death is the revealed truth of a hermeneutic analysis, but the novel has not developed an argument consistent with the rules of the genre so this analysis falls flat, unable to support the novel's conclusion. We don't know why Sonny has committed suicide. It was not premeditated; he himself had not procured the means he used to inflict his death. At the end of the novel it is conclusively shown that these, the foreign substance (Carlota's medicine) and the *menudo* (a Mexican soup famous for curing hangovers) he ate to administer it, had not been left in his home with malicious intent. The medicine and *menudo* happened to be on hand when Sonny felt the urge to end his life.

Corpi abandons the classical genre in Chapter Five by losing sight of Sonny's death and favoring a search for Bello. Fortunately Corpi's detective does not have Miss Marple's single-minded intuition. For Gloria, veering off the path is fruitful because she uncovers "crimes" far worse than Sonny or Phillipe's death.

The detectives, Gloria and her professional partner, Justin Escobar, initially search for Bello, Sonny's missing poet friend. They start on his trail, but then coincidence seems to prevail. Carlota's narrative connects her with Sonny, but she is nowhere to be found. Josie disappears just when the detectives are about to get some information from her, or appears just when they are trying to avoid arousing her suspicions. We are led to believe that Ramón is a prime suspect. Looking for him the detectives learn that he is in prison, or has been released, is suffering from cancer or died of the disease a few years ago. They can't find him. Phillipe Hazlitt's death is believed to have been either a suicide or a disappearance, and Escobar and Damasco do not actively investigate. The police suspect that Josie murdered him, but any reader of detective fiction knows the police are bunglers. Furthermore, this policeman is working in conjunction with *la migra* (U.S. Immigration and Naturalization), so is naturally distrusted by the Chicano investigators.

Mysterious Carlota's life seems to have intersected not only with the lives of all the various suspects and victims in the novel, but also with the lives of Gloria's deceased husband and the homeless of Oakland. Her whereabouts at the time of Sonny's death are in question because of the memory lapses she suffers that were caused by exposure to pesticides. This makes both her testimony and herself suspect, but Gloria instinctively trusts her, and even though he does not, Justin does not actively inquire into what her motivation might have been for having murdered Sonny. From her autobiography, Gloria learned that Carlota penned a note in lipstick to Dr. Stephens more than a decade ago. But if Carlota is innocent, then who left the note written in lipstick on Sonny's bed? To discover this, another series of misleading clues points toward some member of the Stephens family who might have kept Carlota's note all these years. It is never clear what motivation any of them may have had for murdering Sonny.

In each chapter that follows Carlota's autobiographical narrative, the structure of the novel moves further away from the formulaic genre. However, if we base our expectations on the clues contained in the epigraph and in the foreword, entitled "Foreshadows," instead of on the set-up of the first four chapters, it is not difficult to see that we have been forewarned that this mystery will be framed in terms much broader than Sonny's death. He was not the most charismatic of guys, but with each chapter as we get to know the suspects it is revealed that no one seems to have liked or disliked him enough to have wanted him dead.

Sonny Mares' death is unimportant. *Cactus Blood* investigates the social, political and economic ills that restrict a Chicana's self-fulfillment and by extension that of the Chicano community in general as well as the larger community of socially and economically marginalized populations.

Instead of focusing on the hermeneutics of Sonny's death, or Philippe's, or the danger that is presumed to threaten Bello, an experimental analysis is in order. This would start at the beginning of the text itself with the epigraph and "Foreshadows" which precede the first chapter of the novel. This poem and poetic statement frame the novel to a much greater degree than the conventions of the formulaic genre. These introductions and the poetic content of the novel that follows, trespass, contort and transform the classical whodunit, expand the relatively sparse historical data presented in the novel, direct our attention to a feminist perspective and suggest a Chicana foundational tale.

Preceding the first chapter of the detective narrative the author presents an epigraph, a poem by Delia Treviño. Not an active character in the mystery, she is a Chicana poet and novelist whose story is included in the volume of women's autobiography, "Chicana Experiences," mentioned above, that contains Carlota's narrative. Delia Treviño also was the protagonist of Corpi's earlier nondetective novel, *Delia's Song* (1989), set in the early 1970s. Delia was a college student, a Chicana activist relegated to a less active role by the male leadership of MEChA (Movimiento Estudiantil Chicano de Aztlán) when her capabilities could have handled more. She ultimately escaped the silence imposed by Chicano patriarchal society through her writing.

The epigraph frames the poetic content and imagery that intersects with, but deconstructs, the formulaic structure of the detective novel. It refers to unity among Chicanas. Without this unity, Gloria would never have discovered how Sonny Mares died. The poetic images in the epigraph, however, do not lead us to expect that we will be reading a murder mystery. The epigraph from *Cactus Blood* reads as follows:

> We have been the foreshadows of your dream
> guided at times
>           by nothing more than instinct
> Still
>           without our collective voice
>           yours would have remained
>                 a soft cry
>                 a whisper
> in some indifferent stranger's ear.

I
for one
lay claim to have done only this:
provided the soil where your dream took roots.
Nothing else [*Cactus Blood*].

*We* is the Chicana community. In the context of *Cactus Blood* the *we* is represented by a community of Chicana poets: Delia Treviño, Luisa (who died protecting Gloria in *Eulogy for a Brown Angel* and initiated the Chicana autobiographical project), Myra (the poet-activist who asked Gloria to edit "Chicana Experiences" after Luisa's death), Carlota (one contributor to the autobiographical project) and the detective-protagonist, Gloria Damasco. It is through the efforts of this community that women's voices and those of many voiceless others will be heard. Through this collective, that embraces all Chicanas, the *dreams* of the marginalized will take *root*. *Root* and *soil* are connected to the cactus of the title, which is in turn connected to a cactus that accompanies Carlota and her dreams. Gloria's dreams of crime, not common sense intuition, characterize her detective instincts.

In the epigraph, the collective *we, the foreshadows of your dream*, recognizes and encourages an instinctive need to cultivate imagination. *I*, the first person voice of the poet recognizes the great importance of the dream itself and also the need for an environment, a *soil* where the dream can take *root* and flourish. The environment of the dream is a place where women are not harassed or manipulated, where Chicana leadership sustains itself and grows, eventually making significant contributions to the community as a whole.

*Cactus Blood* gives voice to women, and men, in situations similar to those of the characters who do not have access to public forums. It addresses sexual harassment and abuse, poor working conditions, forced assimilation (simulation) and underemployment. Many of the homeless in Oakland who befriend Carlota are veterans who were trained by the U.S. government, but as civilians have no access to gainful employment. Josie's father spent the money he, his wife and Josie earned on drink, and in one instance he tried to prostitute Josie for more money. For this reason, Josie abandons her Chicano roots and warns Carlota never to marry a Mexican. Sonny, who financially neglected his ex-wife and children, sexually harassed Myra. These are situations all too familiar to the female population of the United States. Carlota was raped by her Anglo American employer and poisoned by pesticides. The novel's focus on farm labor reminds the reader of the tenuous and sometimes dangerous position occupied by undocumented workers in our country and that the poor working conditions suffered by this segment of the labor force have not abated.

When heard by the collective *we*, all these characters' voices are transformed from *soft voices* and *whispers* that are heard by *indifferent strangers* into an audible broadcast voice. In one scene Gloria is hurriedly pushing Carlota through a restaurant in Sonoma, California, trying to avoid being seen by Josie. Carlota stops abruptly when she spots a woman eating grapes. She berates the woman vocally and tosses her grapes on the floor, stomps on them and loudly informs the ogling patrons that pesticides are poisoning farm laborers and their families. Attempting to move her along, Gloria promises to return to the restaurant, talk with the management and, if unsuccessful, picket the establishment (177–178). Carlota's *cry* was not *soft*, but it was a lone cry and would have had limited effectiveness. It shocked the woman it was directed toward, but only annoyed the restaurant patrons and employees. If Gloria keeps her promise, however, grapes will no longer be served there. Furthermore, the novel itself accomplishes Carlota's goal: "It's important [that] people know we're still boycotting grapes and why" (178).

The epigraph is followed by the title of the novel, then "Foreshadows" precedes the first chapter of the novel itself. "Foreshadows" narrates Gloria's original, recurring and guiding vision. It introduces the poetic imagery of the novel (cactus, blood, snakes, entrapment, sacrifice and woman), functions as a metaphorical outline for the sociopolitical "investigation" that Gloria will undertake and as a preview of the foundational tale's narrative.

Gloria comments in "Foreshadows": "That's when I saw her.... A slumping female Christ with a prickly-pear cactus cross on her back.... I know I will not rest until I learn for whose sins she was sacrificed." Keeping in mind the novel's subtitle, "A Mystery Novel," we are led to believe that the death to be investigated is that of a woman and not a male. This is a sure clue that *Cactus Blood* will not be the story of the investigation of Sonny Mares' death, nor should we expect to find what motivated his demise, but rather what motivated the sacrifice of this "female Christ."

Gloria's vision narrated in "Foreshadows" occurs before Sonny's death and the initiation of the detective novel per se. She sees herself in a thicket of prickly pear cactus at twilight and face to face with a rattlesnake, backs away, is stuck by the cactus and her blood marks its leaves. At the same time she senses someone behind her, a menacing presence, but cannot turn because of the snake. Her dream continues:

> I saw a clearing in the thorny thicket. Like the snake, I recoiled to gather strength. I jumped through the clearing an instant before the

rattler lunged forward. I shivered at the thought that its fangs had passed a fraction of an inch from my ankle and stabbed the leaf at precisely the spot where my blood was still present. Rubbing my shoulder and leg, I worked my way carefully around a huge, old cactus.

That's when I saw her. The woman. Naked. Her arms stretched up, tied to the fleshy leaves. Her legs together, bound to the stem. A slumping female Christ with a prickly-pear cactus cross on her back, shrouded in blood, bathed in amber moonlight.

Ever since, she haunts my vigil and dreams. I know I will not rest until I learn for whose sins she was sacrificed ["Foreshadows"].

Gloria does not ask, "Who tortured this woman?" but rather "For whose sins was she sacrificed?" Near the novel's end, in the chapter "Dreamshadows and Rattlers," she encounters the female Christ figure on a remote hill top and realizes that "I had just walked into my recurring vision" (198).

Chicano detective fiction transforms the formulaic genre by deemphasizing its hermeneutic logic. Each author puts forth, through literary histories familiar to her or him, a framework dependent on a generic model, but each is independent of the obligation to conform to the formulaic conventions of his chosen model. In the novels of Anaya, Hinojosa, Nava and Ramos, the British or Anglo American genre's formulaic outline takes precedence over other elements of the narrative as both a form to be followed and a form to be manipulated. By rejecting hermeneutic closure, by concluding at a new starting point and abandoning the circular plot they transform their models. Corpi's mystery tale also transforms its Anglo antecedent, but does so by imposing a poetic, metaphoric outline on its narrative model and using this outline as the primary organizational tool for the development of plot.

In the *Gloria Damasco* mysteries, the detective is always guided by her visions. These are sleeping or waking dreams devoid of any content capable of announcing actual clues or suspects. Gloria connects the content of her visions with the ongoing investigation. She sidesteps the leads that would have been obvious to Miss Marple and follows the message that she hears in her dreams. The sociopolitical content of *Cactus Blood* does not fit the set-up, the primary organizational tool of a classical detective novel. It does not move the investigation of the deaths forward, explain them or even distract the progression of the novel with immaterial fluff. The social injustice portrayed is integral to the plot of the novel. The plot is outlined by Gloria's vision of the sacrifice of the *female Christ figure* and for this reason the sociopolitical content functions as "clues" that led toward the resolution of the mystery. Lives have been *sacrificed* for the *sins* of contemporary U.S.A.; Gloria wants to know who committed these sins and why.

Gloria investigates the sins and sinners of our time and place. Among these is a patriarchal Chicano attitude toward the Chicana. In the novel, the dismissal or belittling of the skills of women by male activists is brought to task. As a writer and activist, Myra has labored to denounce the particular abuses suffered by Chicanas, but is only recognized as a sexual object by Sonny, her fellow poet and activist. His policeman brother dismisses Gloria's talents as a detective despite having never observed her on the job. These self-serving actions that promote male dominance also include Ramón's heroic, but misguided, sabotage of the pesticide storage tank. His refusal to work in conjunction with the UFW put the group and its goals in jeopardy. Josie's father's behavior led her to reject her Mexican American heritage and her *curandera* ("healer") mother. She simulates negative aspects of North American materialism; she disobeys the law because she wants more money and less responsibility. Anglo patriarchal privilege proves itself also to be a sinner. Carlota's rapist, a scion of the Anglo community, destroys her life and adversely affects the lives of his wife and children.

Global capitalism as practiced in the United States is a big sinner. Carlota's experience with pesticides is the prime example. Beyond her personal experience, this continuing manifestation of greed affects the health of thousands of farm workers and reminds us of the threat that pesticides hold for the general U.S. population. Pesticides continue to be used in agriculture to generate profits for multinational corporations. Outrageously low wages and non-existent benefits for workers further extend their profit margins. Another indictment of capitalism is seen when Gloria observes the poor and the homeless, many veterans of the Vietnam War, unsupported by the U.S. government and left to cope with life by selling their blood to a private plasma center in Oakland. She concludes, "If there was ever a metaphor for a decadent capitalist system, that plasma center was it" (155).

The novel begins with a video that portrays a bloody example of North American racism: white Teamsters supporting white growers attacked Mexican and Philippine laborers and their families. Racism, whether active or passive, is seen as a sin that is ingrained and promoted by ignorance. The detectives are in a wealthy suburban neighborhood near Sacramento and are trying to question an elderly Anglo couple about the Stephens family. Reluctant to answer, the Anglo couple has mistaken Gloria and Justin for a maid and gardener, Mexican of course, looking for employment. Gloria informs them that she and Justin are Argentinean and with this change in ethnicity their questions are answered and they are invited to have a glass of lemonade with the couple (104, 106). Corpi does not dwell on the topic of racism, but the examples she uses are well chosen. The most poignant and hard-hitting of these is when Gloria witnesses an intoxicated African American Vietnam veteran attack a young Chinese immigrant whose features recall the men he was sent to kill.

U.S. racist practices have limited the opportunities of blacks, Chicanos, Native Americans and, though less in the public eye, those of Asians also. Blacks, Chicanos, and Native Americans are, now and in the past, over represented in our armed forces in proportion to their numbers in the general population. During the Vietnam War, college students were given deferments. At this time there were very few minority students who could take advantage of the educational deferments that so many white students received. Patriots yes, but African Americans, Mexican Americans and Native Americans have also gone to war for the United States hoping that their actions would mitigate racist marginalization and improve their quality of life through education, medical care, economic and political opportunities. Because of this history of racism and war in the United States, the reaction of the African American veteran is doubly painful. His anger is misdirected by the same racism that allowed the government to disproportionately conscript men of his race. He was taught that the men he was sent to fight were lesser human beings.

Gloria accepts no excuses for complacency toward the loss of cultural tradition and political activism. Libretti's analysis of *Cactus Blood* describes Gloria's perspective on the lack of Chicano activism in the late 1980s: "what she longs for is to recapture in the present the political enthusiasm and commitment of the past in order to revitalize and redirect the Chicano movement" (71). With the exceptions of Carlota and Ramón, the Chicano activists of yesteryear have become complacent and now quietly enjoy improvements they fought for in the 1960s and 1970s. Furthermore, traditional *curandera* perspectives are less valued or, in the case of Josie, vilified. She uses her mother's *curandera* knowledge to transform curative herb bundles into black-magic packages that cast suspicion on the healer, *curandero* Ramón.

In touch with signs recognized by cultural tradition, Gloria's mother, Josie's mother and Carlota know that an earthquake is imminent when they observe a change in the sky and numerous posted notices seeking missing pets. This danger, obvious to *curanderas* and their patients, is invisible to Gloria and Justin and other Bay Area residents. "Conservation" in Corpi's detective fiction recognizes traditional practices and environmental concerns. Throughout the Bay Area, Gloria observes with annoyance and disgust as the comfortable majority wastes a precious natural resource to water their gardens during the second year of a severe drought.

It is significant that it is a female who is sacrificed for these sins. Institutions of power in the United States have consistently favored political and commercial expedience over social and environmental concerns and have looked askance at non-traditional science. Men, not women, dominate these institutions. Corpi's parable of sacrifice and resurrection posits a woman as the central figure of redemption.

After the first chapter's initial investigation of Sonny's death, the reader may have forgotten that Gloria has promised to find the sinners whose transgressions have prompted the sacrifice of the *female Christ*. She may also seem to have forgotten this in her pursuit of Sonny's supposed murderer, but her recurring vision reminds her and the reader throughout the novel that the sins for which the crucified female was sacrificed are the objects of her investigation.

If we initially found ourselves concentrating on the mystery surrounding Sonny Mares' death, the question of "for whose sins" resurfaces after Carlota's autobiographical narrative is presented in the fourth chapter. The convoluted whodunit spins off from Carlota's life story, but more importantly her story returns the reader to the thesis question the novel posited in the poetic imagery of the epigraph and "Foreshadows."

The epigraph's *soft cry* becomes a *collective voice* that is *foreshadowed* by Carlota's *dreams* that were heard by the detective and ignored by the *indifferent stranger*. The images in "Foreshadows" of cactus, blood, snakes, entrapment and female sacrifice are repeated in Carlota's narrative. But the metaphorical significance they carry is not fully revealed until the conclusion of the novel. These same images were used by writer Gloria Anzaldúa in her construction of the *New Mestiza* and her borderland environment.

Anzaldúa, Chicana poet, editor, essayist and lecturer, shared Corpi's feminist perspective. She grew up in south Texas in an impoverished Mexican American family. A lesbian and a daughter of a traditional family with well defined masculine and feminine roles, she had to formulate a personal tradition. Carlota, Corpi's central figure in *Cactus Blood*, is an illegal immigrant, an abused domestic, a vessel of Mexican cultural traditions, a lesbian and the author of a poetic narrative of her life.

Anzaldúa's work as an editor of *This Bridge Called My Back, Writings by Radical Women of Color* and her own autobiographical essay and collection of poetry, *Borderlands/La Frontera, the New Mestiza*, offers insights into the characterization of Carlota, Corpi's poetic images and the construction of a Chicana feminist foundational tale.

*Borderlands/La Frontera* as a "fundamental contribution" is "deservedly well known" in Latin America, the United States and Britain for its radical and insightful perspective regarding bordering lands and lives (Mignolo 54, Singh and Schmidt 13). This text is part of the founding canon of postcolonial and border studies. Anzaldúa configures the Mexican American border as a physical space defined geographically and as a cultural space unrestricted by political borders. In 1981, she and Cherríe Moraga edited *This Bridge Called My Back*, now a standard text for many women's studies courses. Anzaldúa was instrumental in exposing the voices of women of color to a greater population. She constructed poetic images that visually portray the liminal space occupied by these women that is situated between the province of community pariahs and mainstream patriarchal and feminist communities. Gloria Damasco's job as editor of "Chicana Experiences" parallels Anzaldúa's in *This Bridge Called My Back* and the metaphors of her dreams recall Anzaldúa's poetic border autobiography. Carlota's narrative and her character function as the glue between the sociopolitical, autobiographical and poetic narratives in *Cactus Blood*.

Carlota initiates her story by explaining the circumstances that led her to emigrate. Before she begins her journey both of her parents have died and this 14 year old has no means of support. A neighbor arranges for her to be smuggled across the border to work as a domestic. After entering California, Carlota travels in the trunk of her future employer's car where she is confined in a crouched position with her small bag of possessions and her "tiny, one-leaf Mexican cactus" (45). Her tears of fear and discomfort water the cactus. We learn from her narrative that the cactus only blooms every five years and its blooming cycles parallel the life cycles that her grandmother predicted would be hers. It is as if she and the cactus are one. Carlota is so uncomfortable in the trunk of the car that she thinks she must be dead, but "[a]s though to remind me that I was still alive, the cactus pricked my chin" (46). Metaphorically the cactus keeps her alive and forces the sacrifice of her blood to dreams of a better future.

The car finally stops and the trunk is opened: "Every muscle in my arms, legs, and belly tensed up, aching for release. Still hugging the potted cactus, I got ready to leap out of the trunk" (46). Carlota is not able to jump out of the trunk, as Gloria is able to quickly remove herself from her cactus enclosure in her recurring vision. However, Carlota, akin to Gloria in "Foreshadows," has *recoiled* and taken the stance of a snake to gather *strength*. The space of the trunk was for a time, in Anzaldúa's words, a "fecund cave," albeit an uncomfortable one. In the darkness of this cave, Carlota was able to revisit the few pleasant memories of her childhood and dream of her future. She reflected on her grandmother's prediction that in the "seventh cycle" of her life she would find "happiness" (46). Like the blooming cycles of her cactus, her life will be punctuated by dormant and active periods. Akin to Anzaldúa's *New Mestiza*, she will need to periodically retire to gather physical and mental strength.

Carlota's narrative tells how much she enjoyed her tenure as Dr. Stephens' daughters' caregiver, how Mrs. Stephens encouraged her to take English classes and how she was befriended by Josie, a teacher's aid, who also encouraged her to get an education. This great year in her life cycle ended two days before her fifteenth birthday. For many Chicanos and Mexicans this birthday is a traditional marker of a woman's emergence from childhood. But Carlota is robbed of this joy and, like Gloria in her vision of herself in the cactus thicket, feels the disturbing presence of someone observing her.

Perhaps for weeks or months, Dr. Stephens had watched her sleep, while she dreamt the innocent dreams typical of adolescent love. One afternoon, two days before her birthday, as Carlota contemplates the shadows cast by her cactus, now grown, and intertwined with those of a saguaro and an agave, she recognizes the eyes she has only felt until this moment. Dr. Stephens approaches her. Carlota is in a dangerous trap. Akin to Gloria, a cactus surrounds her and menacing eyes watch her. From the perspective of Anzaldúa's *New Mestiza* their cactus barricades, "fecund caves," can be seen as equally deadly and empowering.

Dr. Stephens makes a comparison between Carlota's mature body and that of her cactus just before he brutally rapes her. Corpi abandons poetic imagery when Carlota describes the most devastating moment of her life. Having satisfied his lust, Dr. Stephens leaves the house. In his absence Carlota showers and in her humiliation, scrubs herself raw.

Dr. Stephens is still absent after Carlota showers. Fueled by her rage, but afraid to be confronted again, she hastily pens a note in Mrs. Stephens' lipstick, impales it on the blades of a pair of scissors and leaves it on Dr. Stephens' bed where she was raped. She collects her few belongings, digs up her cactus, tosses out one of the doctor's prize gardenias, plants her cactus in its pot and is ready to set off when the doctor returns. He looks for her, sees his destroyed gardenia, but does not see her.

Carlota narrates, "I waited in the shadows, my belongings and my potted cactus in the burlap bag beside me. I recoiled deeper into the [dark ... ness]" (52). Again, she mimics the posture of a snake, but this time, unlike her experience in the car's trunk, she gains physical strength in her confined space. She flees the Stephens' house and the financial security it represents, completely, utterly alone.

Carlota runs, blindly racing across a field of onions recently treated with pesticides. Her skin, scrubbed raw and particularly susceptible, is poisoned. Later, she feels the effects of the pesticide. Her speech and memory are impaired and eventually her whole body ingests the poisons that weaken her and will ultimately kill her.

Debilitated in more ways than one, Carlota concludes her narrative of this night: "I was the violated sister, the dark face of the moon. But I would regather myself" (53). Carlota's description of this night connects her with Coyolxauhqui, the deified moon of the Nahuas and daughter of Coatlicue, who was mutilated and murdered by her brother the Aztec sun god Huitzilopochtli.

It is no wonder that the reader fears Carlota will become the woman Gloria has seen in her vision. She certainly would be an innocent victim. However, Carlota, who at such a tender age has already sacrificed so much, regathers herself. She flourishes, despite bouts of debilitating sickness, without recourse to proper medical care, living by her wits or with the help of friends and the homeless of Oakland and in constant fear of *la migra*. Carlota gets some education, speaks out against the use of pesticides and, as she gains expert knowledge of the multiple problems that arise from their use, is able to earn fees lecturing on this subject. She is a fighter who will not be a sacrificial lamb.

Carlota's story projects a woman who, in a less hostile environment, could have made significant contributions. Her life is tragic, but she does not allow a victimization perspective to rob her of her strength. Her characterization as the "violated sister" and "the dark face of the moon" puts her in a pivotal position reminiscent of the *New Mestiza*. Anzaldúa's *New Mestiza* relies on what she terms the "Coatlicue State." Coatlicue is the mother of the moon goddess Coyolxauhqui that Carlota relates to when she flees the Stephens' home.

Anzaldúa posits that the female characteristics of the pre–Columbian godhead were deformed first by the Aztecs and then by the Spanish. Her view is not inconsistent with current scholarship on pre–Columbian art (Miller 78) or with critics of Chicano literature (Rebolledo and Rivero 189–192).

Impregnated by a feather, Coatlicue, the mother goddess, gave birth to the sun, Huitzilopochtli. At birth, Huitzilopochtli fights his siblings— the moon, Coyolxauhqui, and the stars— who have accused their mother of adultery. He beheads and quarters his sister Coyolxauhqui and scatters his brothers, the stars in the heavens (León-Portilla *Literatura* 13–17).

Anzaldúa suggests that all Aztec female deities may have only been representations of different aspects of an original mother goddess, whom she identifies as Coatlicue. A complex balance of dark and light attributes described these goddesses. However, following Tlacaélel's reconstruction of the Aztec theocracy (1426–1481), the dark or light aspects of the female deities were emphasized. The Aztec patriarchy split the goddesses, renamed them and their original balance was destroyed (*Borderlands* 27). The powerful, complex and contradictory characterization of Huitzilopochtli, the male sun god, was maintained.

The syncretic relationship between Spanish Catholicism and native beliefs further distorted pre–Columbian female icons. These either became saintly figures sanctioned by the Church or dark figures of popular folklore and history. The goddess Tonantsi (also spelled "Tonantzín") became the Virgin of Guadalupe, the positive symbol of Mexican motherhood and nation (*Borderlands* 27), whereas her sister goddess Cihoacoatl (also spelled Coyolxauhqui) became the *Llorona* ("Crying Woman") whose origin in Mexican folklore is both Spanish and Nahuatl (Rebolledo and Rivero 192). Coatlicue became Malinche. This is the contemptuous name given to the native woman baptized as Marina who acted as translator and guide to Hernán Cortés, and who in the Mexican vernacular is called a *puta* ("whore"): the woman who allowed herself to be raped by the Spanish conquistador and who is the mother of the *mestizo* Mexican population.

Anzaldúa recovers the complex characterization of Coatlicue that the patriarchal societies destroyed (*Borderlands* 47). By exploring her interpretation of Coatlicue, we get an introduction to the complexity of Corpi's images of cactus, blood, snakes, entrapment and female sacrifice. The best known representation of Coatlicue, a statue over six feet tall, was "a depiction so fearsome that it was systematically re-interred at various times after its accidental discovery in 1790 in excavations near the Cathedral [in Mexico City]" (Miller 207). The statue is now in Mexico's National Museum of Anthropology. Anzaldúa describes its symbols graphically and insightfully. When given a contextual meaning the statue festooned with human hearts and hands and dressed in a skirt of snakes is a moving image of female power and compassion.[6]

In Anzaldúa's "Coatlicue State," the conscious mind releases itself to the will of the unconscious or Coatlicue herself. The physical, rational body cannot remain in the Coatlicue state; to do so would be to relinquish life. Coatlicue is the unknown. To meet her the conscious self must surrender control. When the mind/body emerges it is armed with increased self-knowledge that obligates the *New Mestiza* to action (48).

The vulnerable *New Mestiza* imagines a *fecund cave* where she retreats to reach the Coatlicue State and renew her self-resolve. Her action is like that of a rattlesnake that has just shed its skin. The snake retreats to its den where it stays until its new skin is tough enough to protect its movement over the rough surface of the earth. While in hiding it is extremely vigilant and will immediately strike any invader. Anzaldúa reminds us that the Olmecs, the oldest civilization of Mesoamerica (c.1500 B.C.), "associated womanhood with ... the serpent's mouth, a sort of vagina dentate" (sic) (*Borderlands* 34). The Olmecs "considered it [the snake's den] the most sacred place on earth, a place of refuge, the creative womb from which all things are born and to which all things returned" (34). The snake's den is the *fecund cave* of Anzaldúa's Coatlicue State. In this confined space the snake is at its most vulnerable, but its strike is least likely to miss its mark. It emerges from the den hungry and protected by its new skin. Anzaldúa's Coatlicue State will not allow vulnerability to be equated with a lack of defense. Moreover, she destroys the dichotomy between vulnerability and aggressive defense.

Cactus functions as a metaphor for Anzaldúa's active self. Before her discovery of the Coatlicue State she refers herself as a "nopal de castilla," a "spineless" variety of cactus that has no "protection" (*Borderlands* 45). She feels the need to "cultivate" an image of herself as a cactus with "needles, nettles, razor-sharp spikes" to "protect" herself (45). The thorny cactus protects itself and gives to the people of the goddess Tonantsi: "[T]he cactus plant ... provide[d] her people with milk and *pulque* [an alcoholic beverage]" and fiber for clothing and other uses (27).

Carlota's cactus is alternately called a "nopal" or a "prickly pear." In contemporary practice the prickly pear is cultivated for food, as a living fence for protection against human and animal invasion and to enclose wandering children and domesticated animals. In the Mesoamerican tradition, documented by Mayan representational art and Nahuatl poetics, cactus thorns were used by rulers to extract their own blood in rituals of penitence in order to ensure cosmic order. Corpi's title recalls mundane images of desert living and extraordinary religious sacrifice; in either space cactus thorns draw blood.

The cactus that accompanies Carlota on her life journey symbolizes giving life and sacrificing life. Corpi's use of cactus can be associated with Anzaldúa's concept of a *fecund cave*: a living fence that restricts and enhances perception. The cactus traps Gloria, but protects her from being discovered by Josie (*Cactus Blood* 199). Metaphorically Carlota's maturing body and its association with her growing cactus calls her to Dr. Stephens' attention and later shields her from him before her escape. The cactus is dangerous and life-giving; it is indigenous to Mexico and southwestern United States and is of symbolic significance as a native plant of pre–Columbian and Chicano Aztlán.

Exiting and entering the *fecund cave* of Coatlicue is a process akin to crossing borders. In the passage below Anzaldúa combines the imagery of the rattlesnake and the physical restrictions of the U.S.-Mexican border to describe how she arrives at the Coatlicue State, is energized there, but is obligated to leave:

> Every time she makes "sense" of something, she has to "cross over" kicking a hole out of the old boundaries of the self and slipping under or over, dragging the old skin along, stumbling over it.... It is only when she is on the other side and the shell cracks open and the lid from her eyes lifts that she sees things in a different perspective. It is only then that she makes the connection, formulates the insights. It is only then that her consciousness expands a tiny notch, another rattle appears on the rattlesnake tail and the added growth slightly alters the sounds she makes. Suddenly the repressed energy rises, makes a decision, connects with conscious energy and a new life begins. It is her reluctance to cross over, to make a hole in the fence and walk across, to cross the river, to take that flying leap into the dark, that drives her to escape, that forces her into the fecund cave of her imagination where she is cradled in the arms of Coatlicue, who will never let her go. If she doesn't change her ways, she will remain a stone forever. No hay más que cambiar [49].

She concludes, "the only thing to do is to change." This is what she and the border crosser must do to live a fulfilling life.

The images *cross over, hole in the fence, walk across* and *cross the river* recall the border crossings of Mexican migrants. As soon as the border is crossed in either direction the migrant becomes the alien, the other who could at this point *remain a rock forever*, by finding solace in tradition and conforming to docile subjugation on either side of the border. Tradition taken from a new perspective will not allow the migrant *New Mestiza* to comfortably remain a rock. She must change in order to live. Contrary to static portraits from within and without, Mexican Americans and Mexicans do change in order to survive and make these changes by adapting cultural perspectives to new environments.

The *New Mestiza* rewrites the metaphysical tenants of both Nahuatl and contemporary Mexican culture, and through an ongoing process of revision is able to find and define herself in a constantly threatening and changing environment. Her imagination in conjunction with her cultural inheritance constructs the *fecund cave* of Coatlicue.

The cave, imposed or circumstantial in Carlota's and Gloria's experiences, is in Anzaldúa's perspective a necessary self imposition. Reinvigorated by having reconnected with her fecund imagination, the *New Mestiza* is able to learn from her crossings. While confined in the trunk of Dr. Stephens' car Carlota recalls her past and looks forward to her future; the confined darkness of the space pushes her to focus on her dreams.

When she gets out of the trunk she expands and enriches her life learning English and caring for her charges. Soon after Gloria makes her way out of the cactus thicket she takes the female Christ down from her cross and the mystery of her crucifixion, of Sonny's and Phillipe's deaths is solved. Hope and agency are restored in the cave.

Anzaldúa's border images and those that parallel them in *Cactus Blood* can be of interest to all readers, not only "wetback" and minority populations of the United States. Everyone who is forced to leave or is ostracized within a community has had this experience. It is one of degrees; borders that separate people can be erected on the ground where politicians draw the lines or on a table, or a floor, where cultural eating habits draw the lines. Humans distinguish members of their group by numerous observable habits that erect borders between them and the "other." Borders are crossed daily even within a community. The appeal of Anzaldúa's crossings is that they are not debilitating; to the contrary she gains strength from them.

Carlota's "border crossings" are traced throughout the novel as she moves from one place to another. The Mexican cactus she so deeply identifies with is planted, uprooted, planted again, regenerates itself from cuttings and leaves new plants in California. Its journey and plantings are symbolic of Carlota's movements and the influence she has on those around her that grows over time from a "single pad" to "multiple plants" firmly rooted in the United States.

"Woman" is the catalyst for the action; women's contributions to the Chicano movement are revived and women's poetry frames *Cactus Blood*. Corpi's characterization of Carlota, like the *New Mestiza*, incorporates historical and metaphysical perspectives that project a feminist worldview. This view is not exclusive. As Cherríe Moraga states in the preface to the second edition of *This Bridge Called My Back*, the collected writings of radical women of color "are for all the women in it and all whose lives our lives will touch" (xix). Moraga uses the word "dream" as a metaphor for a shared feminist sociopolitical agenda in the same way Corpi's fictitious poet, Delia Treviño, uses it in the epigraph to *Cactus Blood*. Moraga writes: "We are a family who first only knew each other in our dreams" (*Bridge* xix). She and the "author" Delia Treviño project a future where this communal unity of dreams has the potential to "make faith a reality and to bring all of our selves to bear down hard on that reality" (*Bridge* xix).

Gloria Anzaldúa's study of the origin and characteristics of Coatlicue offers a feminist spiritual basis for Corpi's foundational tale. Corpi's poetry and her characterization of Carlota work to create a figure that reunites the three characterizations of the Chicana mother. "La gente Chicana tiene tres madres" ("The Chicano people have three mothers") (*Borderlands* 30). These are the Virgin of Guadalupe (the young virgin mother), *La Llorona* ("the mother who never ceases to cry") and Malinche (the violated Native-American woman, mother of the *mestizo* and the conquistador's translator). Carlota is all three.

Acting as Remmi Stephens' nanny for a year, Carlota was the only person to give Remmi a love that was coupled with care and disinterested self-sacrifice. For Remmi, the virgin adolescent Carlota acted as a mother. The *Llorona* represents the "Mexican and Chicana woman's feeble protest when she has no other recourse" (*Borderlands* 33). In a feminist version of the folktale, the *Llorona*— who drowns her own children — takes this extreme action because she cannot feed them and will not see them suffer starvation. Carlota howls like the *Llorona*, protesting pesticides that are killing the children born and unborn she is incapable of saving. Her cry is feeble because she is "illegal" and has no recourse to a broad audience. She is Malinche raped by Dr. Stephens, a "conquistador" in Aztlán. But she, unlike the patriarchal, *malinchista* ("anti–Marina/Malinche") construction of this figure, is a new feminist version. She does not cooperate with the conqueror in the debasing of Native American tradition. That Malinche is Josie, the materialistic *simulationist*. But both are Malinche, the *puta*, a "whore" or "slut" and also a catch-all name for women who are not sufficiently appreciative of male affection. Josie and Carlota love each other more than they love any man.

The three central Chicana protagonists of the novel, Gloria, Carlota and Josie, represent three "incarnations," so to speak, of the Chicana. In a foundational tale, Josie the wannabe Anglo would be representative of a situation and a perspective soon to be relegated to the past. There will be no need for Chicanas to deny their heritage in the future where border crossings between cultures will present opportunities for self-renewal. Carlota is the present; she fights the battle daily by confronting and subverting socioeconomic authority. She is dying, however, and decides to return home to Mexico. She abandons her battle, but initiates a painful journey rather than abandon her culture. The future is left to Gloria. She must bridge the gap between Josie and Carlota reinitiating activism that supports the highest values of U.S. justice and Chicano tradition.

Gloria's visions have predicted the climactic scene of the novel, the crucified female figure. As she becomes more aware of present and past injustices, she realizes that she will have to play a more active role if sociopolitical change is to be realized. Gloria is not only responsible for the publication of "Chicana Experiences," representing the past, but has also been responsible for the discovery of the present and will be responsible for planting the last "tiny" cutting from Carlota's cactus and with it the growth of future Chicana activism.

Anzaldúa expressed in *Borderlands/La Frontera* how she survives and grows on the Texas-Mexico border, on the actual border and the shifting borders erected by both racist and gender-based prejudice. Anzaldúa's construction of self in relation to community addresses the impact that a globalized U.S. economy has on women of color and the problems faced by them, heterosexual and lesbian, within their communities. Anzaldúa tells how people of Mexican heritage have been "taught to believe they are inferior" (48–49) and therefore have been made to "work twice as hard as others" (49). In order to do this it is absolutely necessary to spend some time in inactivity, not as a "lazy" Mexican (49), but as part of a process of self-renewal. If the *New Mestiza* is to work twice as hard, and has accepted that she must "meet the standards of the dominant culture which have, in part, become her standards," then she must renew herself spiritually and intellectually (49).

Near the end of the novel, in the chapter "Dreamshadows and Rattlesnakes," Gloria finds herself face to face with a crucified woman. She takes her down from her cactus cross, works to revive her, and in the process discovers that "Christ" is pregnant. Gloria saves the lives of the mother and child. The woman is Remmi Stephens. It is possible that Spanish speaking author Corpi has invented for her female Christ figure an English sounding name that could be construed as another name for a common Spanish first name, "Remedios" ("Remedies"). Remmi is the remedy to the mystery and the redeemer who is sacrificed for the sins of others.

Remmi is a very minor character who hasn't put in an appearance in the novel until this point. The detective narrative ignores her central role, that has been the focus of Gloria's dreams, and therefore the dramatic revelations of her affair, crucifixion and pregnancy produce a forced ending for this narrative. She may not be the whodunit victim we have come to expect, but she is sufficiently "innocent."

Remmi's innocence, a necessary characteristic for a Christ figure, is central to the foundational tale, because it is through her relationship to Carlota that her innocence it is revealed. Remmi was the neglected child of the Stephens family, whose one year of happiness was when Carlota cared for her. She was kept ignorant of her father's crime of rape until her mother's death almost fifteen years later. When she learns of her father's sin, she is full of remorse for having thought for so many years that Carlota had abandoned her. Looking for Carlota, she comes in contact with the militant *curandero* Ramón while he is in prison. For the same reason she stumbles into Phillipe Hazlitt who is tired of years of silently putting up with Josie's extra-marital affairs and begins to pursue Remmi. Finally she visits Sonny on the night of his death to get information from him about Carlota's whereabouts. In order to get in his good graces she has brought him two gifts: the video of 1973, a present from Hazlitt, and a serving of *menudo*.

Remmi knows that Josie killed Phillipe, that she should fear for her own life, but she goes to the lonely site where Josie will "crucify" her, in order to keep her appointment with Ramón who has promised to reintroduce her to Carlota at last.

Remmi's role seems like a last minute resolution of this mystery novel. However, her role clearly represents a reevaluation of history fundamental to foundational fiction. She needs to pay homage to Carlota and cleanse herself of the false perspective she held for so many years after her one year with her Mexican nanny.

In the hospital recovering from her injuries, Remmi asks Gloria if she can name her yet-to-be-born daughter "Gloria" because Gloria has saved both of their lives. This would have been a fitting name for the daughter of the protagonist of a "Crucifixion" story that should end with a "Glorious" resurrection of the female "Christ." However, this is a Chicana foundational tale. Patriarchal Catholicism, like the patriarchal religious beliefs of the Aztecs, is a vulnerable target.

Gloria requests that the baby be named "Luisa" after Gloria's poet friend from *Eulogy for a Brown Angel* and the original editor of "Chicana Experiences." Keeping this in mind, the fact that Remmi does not die on her cross and Gloria's plans to plant Carlota's cactus, not a cross, on Luisa's grave, it is obvious that the "Crucifixion" story has been re-written.

The epigraph, written by a Chicana poet, suggested the need for women to support each other, to encourage each other's creativity. Gloria has done this by rescuing Remmi's child and naming her after the Chicana poet who gave voice to Carlota's history. In the near future Gloria will plant Carlota's cactus — Carlota's love and care, activism and sustenance — on Luisa's grave. Poetry and action will fertilize each other and take *root* like a *dream* planted in the *soil* of the Chicana community. In the Chicana foundational tale, "Resurrection" is a communal effort, led not by one but by many.

In *Borderlands/La Frontera*, Gloria Anzaldúa describes the collision between the U.S. border and the Mexican border as "una herida abierta ["open wound"] where the Third World grates against the first and bleeds. And before a scab forms it hemorrhages again, the lifeblood of two worlds merging to form a third country — a border culture" (3). In *Cactus Blood*,

Carlota has learned to live on this ever changing border — hunted, or temporarily protected by a fake green card or friends, her voice limited, but speaking out for the rights of all Chicanos or recoiling in the shadows to recover — she has continued to move across the abyss that continually opens and closes at her feet.

Anzaldúa's poem "El otro México" that precedes the quotation above expresses very clearly the loss and desire for an affirmation of Mexican origin, and the desire to effect a change in the United States:

> This land was Mexican once,
> was Indian always
> and is.
> And will be again [3].

The borderland described by Anzaldúa is the "land" that is to be Mexican Indian again. Its geographical location is the Southwest and Mexico. Even though Anzaldúa does not use "Aztlán" to describe this area, but uses instead "borderland," her poem expresses the desire for continuity expressed by "El Plan Espiritual de Aztlán" ("The Spiritual Plan of Aztlán") of 1969.

However, Anzaldúa's desire is not for a political unification, rather a spiritual one. The *New Mestiza*, Carlota and Gloria Damasco work within the sociopolitical structure of the United States. They are cognizant of its restrictions as well as the opportunities it presents for change. Carlota maintains ties to Mexico's indigenous heritage that Gloria Damasco has lost, but recovers at the novel's conclusion. However, Carlota, not Gloria, is the activist on the "border." Her experience bridges indigenous heritage and U.S. political activism.

The foundational fictions of Latin America, according to Doris Sommer, attempt to project a nation where the romantic pair will be able to live and work in peace. Josie's abusive childhood and her rejection of her Mexican heritage and Carlota's continual, but frustrated, battle against an abusive socioeconomic system underscore the need for a more fecund environment for Chicanas and Chicanos alike.

With the murder mystery solved Gloria, her family and Justin have gathered for dinner and to watch the third game of the "Battle of the Bay" on television when the catastrophic earthquake of 1989 strikes. Symbolically, the earthquake can represent the open bleeding wound of Anzaldúa's borderland.

When the earth rents itself, the game stops. Baseball is the "national pastime" of the United States. Akin to a U.S. concept of progress that defines worthwhile human endeavor in terms of a lineal progression towards an ever greater goal, the expectations of the fans of baseball are best satisfied by players and teams who are in a constant battle to improve their records of previous seasons. The earthquake stops the baseball game and symbolically turns to rubble this concept of western progress.

The earth sustains an actual open wound. However, in the poetical perspective suggested by the novel we can assume that the earthquake is also a symbolic wound to the dominant sociopolitical structure whose opening and eventual closure will have made an incremental difference in the environment of the Chicana feminist. Both geologically and metaphorically speaking, this wound will be opened again along the lines of the San Andreas Fault and along the lines of the U.S. sociocultural border. Gloria's final comment and the last lines of the novel are: "'Tomorrow, or when this is over, I will plant the tiny nopal at the foot of Luisa's grave,' I promised aloud, looking up at the morning star punctuating the canvas of the night" (249). From her teacher Carlota, a Chicana "Scarlett O'Hara" has absorbed the lessons of hardship, and also of renewal and hope.

The earthquake has stopped momentarily or permanently. The movement of the earth has destroyed material representations of the dominant culture and again wounded minorities. The earth has hemorrhaged like the border in Anzaldúa's description, but a scab will form, and the earth will have changed. With the knowledge that the "borderland" is always shifting, Gloria Damasco recognizes the challenges that she will have to face as she works for positive change for the Chicana and her community.

# 5

# Breaking the *Macho* Mold
## *Manuel Ramos*

What is "*macho*"? This ubiquitous word has an identity crisis. Its original meaning is "male" in contrast to *embra* ("female") and is used to distinguish the gender of animals and plants, and in a secondary meaning refers to one half of a mechanical pairing. However the most common usage, as an adjective or noun, describes the human "male." Women can be very "*macho*" when acting like a man and this is where the difficulty begins because the qualities of being "*macho*" in gender in a patriarchal society are more valued than those described as feminine. In the United States "*macho*" becomes even more problematic because it has been used historically as a derogative adjective to describe Hispanic males.

In an attempt to clarify this I am enlisting the detectives of Manuel Ramos and Michael Nava. Lawyers by profession, Ramos and Nava are the most prolific writers of Chicano detective novels, having published between them 13 novels. Their lawyer detectives, Luis Montez and Henry Rios respectively, present first-person narratives reminiscent of 1930s and 1940s hard-boiled fiction. Like their predecessors, they are unmarried city dwellers, have lived hard, are familiar with urban low life and are keenly aware of local government corruption. My analysis, in this chapter and the following one, will concentrate on their representations of Chicano masculinity as narrated through the male gaze of their detectives. Their constructions of maleness depart from those of the "founding 'fathers' of Chicano Renaissance," a term used by many Chicano critics to describe the prominent authors of the 1960s and 1970s (Pérez-Torres 27).

Anglo American writers of fiction, history and the social sciences have abused the Chicano male for almost two centuries. As if this were not enough, just when Chicano critics were working to construct a uniquely Mexican American literary canon they were blind-sided by a definition of "Mexican" proffered by an eminent figure of Mexican letters. Their *paisano*, Octavio Paz, who in 1990 would receive the Nobel Prize for literature, portrayed his countrymen as the insecure sons of a woman who has been raped (Paz 72). His definition in conjunction with his criticism of the *pachucos*[1] he observed in Los Angeles in the 1950s denigrated the culture Chicano literature and criticism were in the process of defining. Chicanos vociferously contested Paz's *Labyrinth of Solitude.* In 1967 Américo Paredes took up the gauntlet and distanced himself from Paz, from the "they" he writes about here: "*Machismo*— so they tell us— has its origins in the Conquest, when Hernán Cortés and his conquistadors arrived in Mexico and raped the women of the Aztecs. From this act of violence is born the *mestizo*, who hates and envies his Spanish father and despises his Indian mother — in both cases as a result of his Oedipal complexes" ("The United States" 17). Paredes was part of a group of Chicano critics who took offense to the Paz definition of the *mestizo*[2] because the rebirth of this literature celebrated Mexican Americans' indigenous origins.

For the Chicano patriarchy the rape of their Indian mother was seen as the rape of a culture.[3] Her inheritance was celebrated because it was through her that Indian and European combined. The *mestizo* bloodline stood in sharp contrast to the historical contempt for and ignorance of racial mixing in the United States. For the next 20 years a majority of Chicano critics followed the example set by Paredes. However, their defense of *mestizo* was equally patriarchal and ambivalent toward the anguish of their Indian mother as the writings of Paz.

In *Movements in Chicano Poetry* published in 1995, Rafael Pérez-Torres agrees with this previous generation of critics that "literary criticism serves to found cultural identity," but differs with those who would limit this identity (27). In reference to criticism from the perspective of Chicano Renaissance "founding fathers," Torres writes: "While advocating and celebrating a sense of self, Chicano literary criticism effects a disenfranchisement felt strongly among gay and lesbian Chicanas/os, among monolingual speakers of English, among the many Chicana writers who were not included among the founding 'fathers' of the Chicano Renaissance" (27). In 2004 the body of this literature and its criticism includes a diversity of experience. Chicanas, heterosexual and lesbian, are recognized despite the fact that some male critics include them only grudgingly. However, the voice of male homosexuality continues to be radically marginalized and the nuclear patriarchal family is still emphasized as a cultural marker.

Américo Paredes is one of the most respected and frequently cited of

Chicano authors. Of those included in my bibliography the following have referred to his writings: Héctor Calderón, María Herrera-Sobek, Rolando Hinojosa, Luis Leal, José Limón, Francisco A. Lomelí, Genaro M. Padilla, Rafael Pérez-Torres, Tomás Rivera, José David Saldívar, Ramón Saldívar and Charles Tatum. There is no doubt that Paredes' contributions to the formation of the Chicano canon are important and will be long lasting. It is, however, necessary to view his writings with a critical eye in order to underline some of the more abusive restraints imposed on Chicano identity by his definition of Mexican American masculinity.

Paredes has written short stories, novels, and studies of ethnography and folklore. In *With a Pistol in His Hand* (1958), he almost single handedly shattered the foundations of Anglo Texan "Alamo" mythology. There is no doubt that this is a well-researched tome, but its perspective with regard to the community as a whole is limited by its subject matter: men fighting men. In his article "The United States, Mexico and *Machismo*," first published in 1967 in Spanish, Paredes describes the masculine culture he knows so well. His essay is both a defense and an affirmation of the Chicano male. Comparing fictional (popular and elite) renditions of masculinity in Mexican and Anglo American literature, he uses the terms "*macho*" and "*machismo*" (Paredes' translation: "manliness") in reference to Anglo American and Mexican American males and their actions.

Paredes states: "The characteristic traits of *machismo* are quite well known: the outrageous boast, a distinct phallic symbolism, the identification of the man with the male animal, and the ambivalence toward women — varying from an abject and tearful posture to brutal disdain" (17–18). Paredes states that he does not support this limited view. He does not, however, recognize that *both* "authentic" and "false" *machismo* are "ambivalent" at best toward women and outright exclusionary of the homosexual male.

His definition of *machismo* follows that of his fellow scholar of the *corrido* tradition, Mexican folklorist Vicente Mendoza who derives his view of the *macho* from this popular traditional ballad. Quoting Mendoza, Paredes states: "'there are two kinds of *machismo*: one that we could call authentic, characterized by true courage, presence of mind, generosity, stoicism, heroism, bravery' ... and 'the other, nothing but a front, false at bottom, hiding cowardice and fear covered up by exclamations, shouts, presumptuous boasts, bravado, double talk, bombast'" ("The United" 18). Paredes goes on to declare that "the fundamental attitudes on which *machismo* is based ... are almost universal" (35). I question the use of "universal"; it would be more descriptive to call these attitudes "dominant" in any patriarchal society.

For Paredes the configurations of authentic *machismo* are bound to a "growing sense of nationalism" ("The United" 26, 36) for the North American during the initial years of westward expansion between 1820 and 1839 and for the Mexican during the Mexican Revolution of 1910 and until 1930. During these years "the sense of manliness [authentic *machismo*] is exaggerated" (36), but it is authentic because "despite all its faults, [it] has been part of a whole complex of impulses leading toward a more perfect realization of the potentialities of man" (37).

I assume that Paredes uses "man" to designate "humankind" and, because he is addressing the question of masculinity, that the actors in this "realization of the potentialities of man" are all males. However, when he defines the authentic *macho* he excludes the homosexual male: "We all know that courage and virility have always been identified as the ideal traits of the male, and that both primitive and modern man often have equated the coward with the homosexual" (Paredes "The United" 25). That, of course, is true and Parades has no intention of questioning this dominant perspective. From his viewpoint, it is unfortunate that the authentic male has become less evident in the United States: "After World War I, a decided shift from *machismo* to feminism occurs in the United States, but it is not immediately apparent in literature" (28). His use of "feminism" does not refer to any feminist movement, but to a feminization of male behavior — the adaptation of feminine characteristics by a gendered male. The characteristics of the "authentic" *macho* cannot be those of women because his are the delineators that separate him from women.

It must remembered that the views expressed by Paredes in 1967 could be understood by any male in the United States and were expressed in defense of the assault on Mexican American masculinity from more than one front. However, because his stature in Chicano letters is so great some contemporary critics do not question his underlying patriarchal and homophobic perspective, or his dismissal of women, and inadvertently or intentionally allow this perspective to limit the Chicano canon.

His article goes on to cite two examples of North American fiction that highlight the differences between "authentic" and "false" masculinity after World War I. The fiction of Ernest Hemingway "shows us the attraction the *macho* still had for the North American" population (28), but since the example of manliness was lacking among the North American Anglo-Saxon population — "in real life the man of the United States made less and less of a show over his masculinity" (28) — Hemingway chooses to "develop the theme of *machismo* in Spain, Mexico or Cuba" (29). For Paredes, a bravado display of masculinity is distinguishable from Hemingway's portrayal of masculine show.

Hemingway is not as widely read today as he was in the period between the two World Wars. According to Paredes this is because the critically "acclaimed" contemporary protagonist "no longer is the *macho* but the homosexual — the other extreme, or perhaps the same thing seen from another point of view" (29). Paredes finds the "same thing" or "the other extreme" in the hard-boiled genre in works "of the type begun by Mickey Spillane." This whodunit genre began in the 1930s and was contemporary with Hemingway's writing. The hard-boiled "*macho* heroes are fierce, sexual, and brutally sadistic with the female" (29). Thus, from Paredes' perspective "brutally sadistic with the female," "homosexual" and "feminine" are extremes that are in direct contrast to his definition of authentic masculinity.

Paredes equates Spillane's pulp fictional Anglo American hard-boiled *machismo* with the "false" *machismo* that is demonstrated by "[a]rtistic boasting ... found among Mexican males" (20). Paredes notes that among the Mexican American population, it is "the buffoon of the group who cultivates this genre ["false" *machismo*]. Usually he is the drunkest and least courageous member of the group, whose lack of valor and manliness give him a certain minstrel-like license" (20). His "show" is different than the "show" of the "authentic" *macho* because it is "artistic" and not serious in nature.

For working class Mexican Americans the term "*macho*" is more complex than distinctions between "authentic" and "false." Among native ethnographer José Limón's subjects *macho* is associated with *chingar* ("to fuck") and as the opposite of *joto* ("fag") ("Dancing" 224). As a Mexican American male in a working class environment Limón's choices for sexual identification are limited; he must be either a *macho* or a fag: "O es muy chingón, o es joto" ("Dancing" 224). In English this translates as "you are a big fucker or you're a fag." There isn't much room in this definition of *macho* for the nuances described by Paredes. These *machos* are artists of the one-liner and vigorously defend their turf from Anglo American intrusion.

In northern Mexico, that is assumed to influence the perspectives of Chicanos in the United States by virtue of its proximity and emigrant population, anthropologists Ana Alonso and Maria Koreck conclude that the term "*macho*" does not exclude the homosexual male. "*Macho*" connotes a male whose sexual identity is based on the erotic act of penetration, regardless of whether a female or a male body is penetrated. The northern Mexican usage follows Octavio Paz and his definition of *chingar* as an "act of taking anything by force" (116).

Force, for Limón, Alonso, Koreck and Paredes, appears to be the underlying common denominator in the definition of *macho*. The liberties that Paredes' authentic *macho* took before World War I, what he euphemistically describes as "faults," did not detract from the character of these men because their cause was just. "Force" does not dominate the definition of the authentic *macho* for Paredes, but from the popular perspective, as researched by Alonso, Koreck and Limón, it is the single characteristic that separates maleness from femaleness and cannot be properly distinguished as a justifiable gesture.

I use "*macho*" to describe a masculinity that is characterized by the use of force and as a term that describes a gendered male, who aggressively promotes his own prerogatives and who lacks respect for domestic occupations and those physically weaker than him, whether or not his cause is justified. This is the *macho* mold inadvertently promoted by some Chicano literature and the mold that Chicano detective protagonists Luis Montez and Henry Rios break.

Montez, the Denver based lawyer detective of Ramos' first four and sixth detective novels, is a wannabe *macho*. Luis wants to be characterized as an ardent Chicano activist, but he just can't quite put aside his respect for women's labor, his reluctance to use violence in the defense of justice and his fondness for a self-deprecating one-liner. His self-criticizing jokes connect him to the Anglo American private eye of the 1930s and 1940s and separate him from *macho* self-aggrandizing bravado.

Looking back on the Chicano movement of his youth, he recognizes the contributions of women as positive and undervalued at the time and the confrontational male-centered rhetoric that initially dominated his memories as having actually worked against the movement's sociopolitical goals. Decades later, Luis Montez associates with Chicanas whose influence has measurably expanded beyond the limitations of the caregiver role relegated to them during the movement. These are women who work in leadership roles inside and outside their homes. Luis is not domestic, regrets that he does not possess any talent in this area and admires its labors whether performed by women or men.

In *The Ballad of Rocky Ruiz* (1993), *The Ballad of Gato Guerrero* (1994), *The Last Client of Luis Montez* (1996) and *Blues for the Buffalo* (1997), Montez battles his conscience as he takes a nostalgic trip back to his youth and the Chicano movement. The prevalent *macho* attitude of the male activists is sometimes seen as having hurt the movement and is always viewed as out of place in the context of the last decade of the twentieth century.

As the series begins Montez, a twice-divorced father of two sons, is 41 years old and "determined to have" a "midlife crisis" (*Rocky* 14). He meets a young Chicana who fits the bill. She is "[t]he most beautiful, the most sensual" woman he has encountered for a long time, and in his words, "ten years of crust fell off my skin" (5–6). Teresa Fuentes is in his favorite bar, the Dark Knight Lounge, with his buddy Tino, who Luis describes as a "*macho*" from the Movement. Teresa and Luis manage to dump Tino and share a late night or early morning conversation over hot *menudo*. Montez wants to tell Teresa his "old movement stories, brag about our days as Chicano radicals fighting cops and university deans," but he resists the temptation because she must be "scarcely old enough" to even remember the "big names like Cesar Chavez and Corky Gonzales" (8).

During a midlife crisis men of a "certain age" are reportedly consumed by nostalgia for lost youth and attempt to recover their vigor in the company of much younger females. For Luis his youth and the Chicano movement are interconnected. He tries to avoid Tino and other aging reminders of times past, but the opportunity to relive his youthful enthusiasm for the cause of a marginalized population encourages him to share the history of these times, and in the fourth novel of the series, *Blues for the Buffalo*, he finds in Rad Valdez another youthful ear.

A few years after the case of Rocky Ruiz, Luis, a bit worse for wear from his knight errant pursuits, is still seeking youthful affirmation of his Chicano movement nostalgia, but he isn't chasing skirts or dreaming of sexual gratification in *Blues for the Buffalo*. In this whodunit Luis uses his knowledge of the protest decade to flavor his middle age masculinity with the *machismo* of activism in contrast to the physical virility of a young Chicano detective. Rad Valdez is searching for his girlfriend and asks Luis to help. Luis is required to reevaluate his nostalgic view of masculinity and qualify as negative the *macho* attitude of an actual Chicano movement icon — Oscar Zeta Acosta, the "Buffalo" of the title — while viewing Acosta's social activism as positive (65).

In *The Ballad of Rocky Ruiz* and *Blues for the Buffalo*, a Chicana is the pivotal mysterious figure, and women and their actions become central to the detective's reevaluation of the Movement or the "Chicano mystery" as his character Charlotte calls this era (*Blues* 28).

When Luis meets Teresa, a top law school student, in *The Ballad of Rocky Ruiz*, she has completed her bar exam and has been hired by one of the most prestigious law firms in Denver. As the novel's pivotal mysterious figure, we do not learn that she is Rocky Ruiz's daughter until late in the story when she becomes a suspect in the murder of Tino Pacheco and the disappearances of Judge Hector Garcia and Orlando, "Orlie" Martinez. These three along with Rocky Ruiz formed a secret Chicano revolutionary group led by Ruiz.

Contrary to Luis' initial evaluation of her ignorance of the movement, Teresa proves to be more knowledgeable than himself. She has read all her father's writings from that era. Teresa wants to learn more about her father's death because she suspects his killer may have been one of his activist buddies, all of whom live in Denver. She has come to Denver to get in touch with Luis, Tino, Orlie and Judge Garcia. The novel explores what motivated each of these men to participate in the movement and in the secret revolutionary group.

With the exception of Rocky, whose leadership style will be explored shortly, each member of this group, Tino, Orlie and Garcia, aspired to positions of power. Luis, unable to recognize his lack of talent for *macho* heroism, learned early on that he was missing something the other men possessed. The reader finds that Luis' capacity for violence is minimal and his respect for women is genuine.

In *The Ballad of Rocky Ruiz*, the Ramos protagonist describes this secret revolutionary group of men with words reminiscent of Paredes' description of the "authentic" *macho*: "They molded a world where they were the protectors of the people, the vanguard of the revolution" (29). They were *corrido* heroes. The novel ends with the "El Corrido de Rocky Ruiz" (200–201). However, Rocky is the sole *corrido* hero and the novel demystifies the other members of the group.

The youthful Luis Montez "sat in on some" of the meetings of the secret society, but he never became a member, "I never passed the test, whatever it was" (30). Montez lacks Rocky's ability to "mold" others. In his failing law practice he defends the losers of society and infrequently wins his cases. In *The Last Client of Luis Montez* he is disbarred, and when *Blues for the Buffalo* begins he no longer has a secretary or even an office.

As Luis looks back on the Chicano movement in *The Ballad of Rocky Ruiz* he remembers a better time when a "wave of Chicano pride and enthusiasm ... swept the Southwest" (29). It is this social embrace that he misses most. He recalls that shortly after Rocky's death, "Everybody gave a speech. Hours of rhetoric. Political babble I didn't care about anymore" (50). Previously the student protest groups had erupted in "factional fighting, turf disputes, and maneuvering for leadership of a movement that had lost its direction" (31) as it took up other causes, "the Black Panthers," "the truth about Viet Nam" (30), the need to create a "new Communist party" and "Chicano capitalism versus Third World unity" (32). He sees these divisive tendencies promoted by each organization, led almost exclusively by males, not as manifestations of courage but as male posturing for dominance.

Rocky Ruiz, however, was different. When Luis remembers Rocky, he recalls his role as a mediator between these factions: "[H]e had a way of understanding, of picking out what was important. He could see things clearly" (51). According to Montez his "death ended the movement for most of us" (32). Luis admires Rocky's skill as a mediator more than his skill as a revolutionary activist. However, Rocky's dedication to the move-ment takes him away from his wife and daughter, and for Luis this "fault" of his hero is not easily forgotten. In all his mysteries mediation, rather than confrontation, and confirmation of female perspectives, rather than their dismissal, seem to be what Ramos emphasizes as his novels move between different groups of Chicanos in the Southwest. His protagonist's nostalgia is for unity, not a single configuration of Chicano, but rather for a mediated Chicano identity.

First person narrator Montez describes his contribution to the secret revolutionary group as that of "an anchor, a sounding wall to help keep them somewhere near reality" (*Rocky* 30). His role was similar to that of Rocky's wife Margarita. She did not "fall for ... *macho* city jive" (107), was able to let the young men know that she had no time for "their youthful endeavors" (107), and yet was the person who looked after all of them by providing a place to sleep and meals (108). Neither Margarita or Luis is directly involved in the political power plays, but both support the move-ment as caretakers to the active males who surround them. Almost thirty years later, Luis is again the caretaker for the surviving members of the secret revolutionary group: Tino, Orlie and even the powerful Judge Gar-cia.

Over the years since the Movement, Luis has pulled Tino out of more bar fights than he would like to recall, but he was "an old friend" (4). After Tino is killed, Orlie and Judge Garcia both call Luis; they have been receiv-ing threatening phone calls and ask him for support.

The participation of Tino, Orlie and Garcia in the secret organiza-tion, the *Guerillerros* ("Warriors"), was motivated by selfish interest. Tino wanted to use his muscle and a worthy cause gave him this opportunity. Two decades later he is still using *macho* force. Garcia, a straight-A stu-dent who graduated *summa cum laude*, joined the organization to estab-lish his Chicano leadership name. He has bribed Tino over the years in order to silence him. It seems that Tino's recollections of the movement would have jeopardized Judge Garcia's Chicano credentials. Orlie's moti-vation was power and money. He was paid by the government to sabo-tage the revolution by promoting violence, but this is not revealed until late in the novel. Orlie's good work in guiding disadvantaged youths would also have been tarnished by any revelation from Tino, so he cooperates with the judge and acts as his go-between by delivering hush money to Tino. Rocky, in his papers written during these years, dubbed the organization he led the "Gorillas" which reflects the fact that he was having a hard time keeping them focused on the goals of the movement (29).

When the reader meets the three of them two decades after Rocky's death, Tino is trying to impress Teresa with his "belligerent and hostile" attitude (*Rocky* 6–7). His come-on "line" is blatantly confrontational because he is looking for the opportunity to display his physical dominance over other males. He works to win Teresa by brawling with the other customers in the bar. In contrast, Luis tries to avoid physical confrontation, but in the heady company of *machos* he is rarely successful. Garcia, now Judge Garcia, has always used his movement credentials to political advantage, but they were tarnished by the death of Ruiz. Because he witnessed Rocky's death and never testified against the killer, he has paid for Tino's silence for decades. Of the three Orlie, who works with minority youth, appears to have been the most faithful to goals of community service, but he has used his connections with these young people to make money as a drug dealer.

On Paredes' *machismo* scale these three characters represent corruptions of genuine masculinity. Tino is a buffoon who uses violence for violence's sake; Garcia is a coward and untrue to the law he represents, and Orlie is a hypocrite who uses morality to hide his lust for power and money. However, during the movement they would have been outwardly recognized as true *machos* whose characters showed "courage, presence of mind, generosity, stoicism, heroism [and] bravery" ("The United" 18).

The wannabe *macho*, Luis Montez, only managed to demonstrate generosity. He participated in the Chicano movement by marching in demonstrations and finding locales and supplies for those who debated and lectured on the university campus, and in addition to these chores he found time to tutor minority high school students, preparing them for college. He probably enjoyed the marijuana and beer more than the discussions because Rocky noted in his diary that Luis "parties too much," and he must have been interested in females because the *corrido* hero called him a "Chicano playboy" (125).

Montez was fond of women, but not in a narrow "playboy" sense. He asked for Rocky's wife's help in tutoring young females from "strict, traditional families who lived in the San Luis Valley [Colorado]" because, as he confesses, "I had no idea how to reassure them, how to convince them that they really did need to attend this college, where they would be totally out of place, surrounded by strange, alien people who spent more on clothes than their parents would have for food all year" (109). He is obviously interested that these young women succeed.

Though "not involved" in the movement, Rocky's wife, Margarita, makes a more lasting contribution than the radical activists portrayed in the novel. During the movement, she was instrumental in helping others form productive lives by tutoring the Valley Chicanas. When Luis sees Margarita again after 30 years, he learns that she graduated from college after Rocky's death and became a teacher and an artist. She is also the mother of Teresa, the Chicana lawyer. Teresa took the law firm job primarily to learn more about her father's mysterious death. As the novel concludes, she is working for a firm "representing refugees and immigrants, demanding asylum and decent housing," and following her mother's example of selfless community service (197).

The characterization of Margarita and Teresa as strong, caring, intelligent and independent women is typical of the Chicana characters in the *Luis Montez* series and the detective's preference for this type of woman. Luis was in love with Margarita 30 years ago and, unaware of the mother-daughter relationship, falls in love with Teresa as soon as he meets her. Pursuing her affection, Montez tells her what he wants in a woman: "A strong person who doesn't really need me, I guess. A contradiction. Someone independent enough to say she wants me the way I am" (*Rocky* 86). Luis admires Teresa for her intelligence and independence in addition to her beauty. "She had a feel for the law that I envied, and I assumed she would continue as a lawyer, somewhere in Texas. There was no mention of her returning with me" to Denver (135). Even before Teresa has taken the job with the nonprofit organization, Montez seems to recognize that the help he gives to his clients is insignificant in comparison with Teresa's potential for social service.

In *Blues for the Buffalo*, Chicana poet Charlotte Garcia dies in an arson caused fire. Her death is mysterious because she is the only one who does not escape the flames in this bookstore frequented by Luis and his old guard generation of Chicano movement activists. Charlotte's lover, an Anglo woman, asks Luis to investigate. Typical of the hard-boiled genre, seemingly disconnected crimes turn out to have a connection: plagiarism, arson and a missing person. We learn that Charlotte wrote the "song" that identified the movement, not the fictional iconic Chicano male poet Bobby Baca who has taken credit for it, and that the fire was started by the half-brother of Rachel, a young Chicana who is missing.

The title Ramos gives to Charlotte's Chicano poem, "Pachuco, Low Rider, Xicano," is a slightly disguised reference to the poem "Yo soy Joaquín" by Rodolfo "Corky" Gonzales of Denver that defines the Chicano male by referring to Indian, Spanish and *mestizo* heroes of Mexico and the United States and contemporary Chicanos who have died in war and urban violence. The title of Charlotte's poem incorporates various linguistic registers of Mexican Americans evident in Gonzales's poem that refer to the vocabulary of a triple cultural heritage — Mexican (pachuco), U.S. (low rider) and indigenous (xicano)— and all of which refer to emblems of the Chicano population.

Mexican critic Octavio Ignacio Romano-V., writing in 1967 shortly after the dissemination of Gonzales's poem, lauds it as an example of the complexity of the Chicano heritage: "Joaquín is many men. Joaquín is every man" (37). Luis describes "Pachuco, Low Rider, Xicano" as having "captured the minds, hearts, and sentiment of young militants" and as "the anthem of the Aztlán nation" (27).

For the hymn of the "authentic" Chicano *macho* to have been written by a woman who furthermore is lesbian suggests that there might be something wrong with limiting Paredes' adjectives "courage, presence of mind, generosity, stoicism, heroism, bravery" to males. Charlotte unselfishly let the poem be mistakenly attributed to Bobby Baca. Only Bobby and Charlotte's lover knew that she was the author. Baca's only claim to fame is "Pachuco, Low Rider, Xicano" and his failing career as a poet along with some mysterious and violent behavior seems to indicate that he may have been the arsonist. For the reader his movement credentials, his *macho* heroism, is tainted by a lack of courage. He is the coward. Charlotte turns Paredes' definition of the "authentic" *macho* into that of an "authentic" *embra*.

Ramos expands the definition of "Chicano" to include Chicanas and lesbians as "every man" and "young militants." It took two decades for the authorship of the fictional epic poem to be acknowledged and this belated acceptance reminds us that it also took more than twenty years for Chicanas to be accepted as equals in the ranks of Mexican American politics and letters.

In *Blues for the Buffalo*, when Charlotte first meets the young Chicano detective, she suggests that he "deserves his own novel … a movement mystery" (28). *Blues for the Buffalo* and *The Ballad of Rocky Ruiz* are movement mysteries. They question the unwillingness of militant radicals to support broader, more encompassing and realistic goals for the Chicano population.

A successful former boxer, Rudolfo "Corky" Gonzales, author of "Yo soy Joaquín," put his time and money into helping urban youth in Denver. The actions and programs of his organizations kept many young people out of the drug culture and improved the education of Chicanos. He originally supported the Democratic Party, but later established the Colorado La Raza Unida Party (LRUP), that called for ethnic autonomy in the Southwest. Gonzales was adamantly anti-drug, but he was an egotistical leader. His attitude and actions estranged many moderate Mexican Americans, and along with other heady leaders of the LRUP he managed to effectively split this community politically. The infighting among student activists, the characterization of Orlie as a youth-group leader in *The Ballad of Rocky Ruiz* and the veiled reference to Gonzales' poem, "Yo soy Joaquín," may not be meant as criticisms of Gonzales personally, but do criticize excesses of the Chicano movement. These along with Charlotte's comments about Oscar Zeta Acosta demystify the *macho* mystique of 1960s and 1970s Mexican American activism.

As Charlotte notes in *Blues for the Buffalo*, in a comment on lawyer-writer and activist Acosta, in-fighting among those who would definitively define "Chicano" continues to be a problem: "The first, and some would say, the only real Chicano lawyer.... A pig of course — he had no respect for women. And some think he was a provocateur, and a drug dealer. Of course he was called a sellout too, but then who among us is ever really Chicano enough?" (29). This is the mystery the *Luis Montez* novels explore.

Manuel Ramos's Luis Montez and Raymond Chandler's Philip Marlowe, both protagonist narrators, share these traits: they distrust local government, they "need" a drink when stressed, often drink too much and suffer the consequences, constantly remind the reader that they are in pain, pass out frequently, lie to and annoy the police, give colorful physical descriptions of other characters, of poverty and wealth, and emphasize female sexuality in their descriptions of women. Each is at times painfully aware of his shortcomings, but tries to live up to an ideal of masculinity that is supposed to be, in Chandler's words, that of the "common man" (qtd. in Abbott 17). However, the "common man" admired by each detective graphically points out the difference in each author's configuration of an ideal masculinity.

Detective Marlowe's "man's man" is always a loner like himself, and Marlowe will rarely accept his collaboration, even if offered. Luis's "man's man" is his father Jesús, who continually bails him out of personal, financial and investigative problems.

In the first four *Luis Montez* novels the detective's almost 80-year-old father represents an ideal of Chicano masculinity that the protagonist despairs of ever emulating. Meet Luis Montez's dad: "Jesús Genaro Montez, migrant worker, coal miner, construction laborer, father of four sons and three daughters, admired and respected by his friends and neighbors, feared by his children. He outlived my mother and I knew he would stand laughing over my coffin when I cashed in" (*Rocky* 24). Luis's offhand tone cannot disguise his admiration for his father. Jesús is the keeper of his cultural inheritance. The twice-divorced detective, with rusty Spanish, obviously ignored the lessons his father attempted to teach him, but won't let his sons be so negligent. Jesús will teach them Spanish. The movement ideology that Luis spouted as a youth was easily recognized by Jesús as incongruent. It struck him as "funny" that his son was learning about his culture from "books" (57). As an adult Luis realizes that the movement would have benefited from the lessons of people like his father (57).

Jesús will not be ignored. He cantankerously demands that Luis recognize how a real *macho* lives. The novels contrast Jesús's stability with Luis's bungled attempts to put some order in his life. Jesús is characterized by his role as a father and a good neighbor, his frugality, his ability to manage for himself and his courage in the face of poverty and prejudice. Jesús, old, independent and cranky, is the center of a family of males: Luis and his two sons. Luis ignored too many lessons as a young man, but Jesús will not give up trying to teach them.

In *Blues for the Buffalo*, Jesús takes over the education of a rich and tormented young Chicana, and also resolves the mystery. In the novel a mysterious young Chicana, Rachel, is looking for her supposed father, Oscar Zeta Acosta, who disappeared in 1974.[4] Rachel is the daughter of a poor single Mexican immigrant woman who died in childbirth. After several years with foster families, she was "adopted" by her natural father who is a promiscuous married man and the head of a wealthy old Mexican American family from California. Rachel comes to live in a luxurious mansion with her half-brother and sister. Since her earliest days in this wealthy household Rachel's half-brother has violated her. Her life has been defined by the *macho* sexuality of her father and half-brother. Jesus's pupil, Rachel's half-sister, tells him her sister's story.

The dysfunctional wealthy family is a staple in Chandler's detective fiction. However, he, unlike Ramos, does not offer any insight or future hope for the degenerate rich. In *Blues for the Buffalo*, Rachel's half-sister communicates Rachel's true story and all the sordid family history to Jesús because he makes her feel comfortable and at home for the first time in her life. With this information, her brother is exposed as the arsonist and Charlotte's murderer, and the reader is given an explanation for Rachel's disappearance. Like Acosta, Rachel is running from her past, searching for herself and is never found.

Luis Montez's bungled life and career manage to obscure false distinctions between male and female. His interaction with secondary characters, with his ex-wives, sons and father, are not typical of the heroic *macho* of the past. Ramos's characters are multifaceted: his heroes have weaknesses and his villains have redeeming traits. He breaks the *macho* molded hero and amplifies and integrates Chicano definitions of masculinity and femininity. This wise perspective allows the reader to recognize the pitfalls inherent in the idealistic zealousness of the '60s and '70s. It also affirms the difficulties these Chicano activists faced and affirms their lasting accomplishments evident in the strengths of the women Ramos describes in his novels and the continuing interest in civil rights, socioeconomic justice of this community.

# 6

# Marginalization in Aztlán
## *Michael Nava's Gay Detective*

Michael Nava's detective fiction has won several awards, been well received by critics from the *Los Angeles Times*, the *New York Times*, other major newspapers and magazines and has been translated into German and Japanese, but the author doubts that many "Latinos" are interested in his Mexican American gay protagonist. "'I write about my experience as a Mexican American man. It's not an experience that many Latinos want to hear about, but that's not my problem; that's theirs'" (Nava qtd. in Gambone 139).

It is their problem, and it exists for various reasons explored in the previous chapter and others that will be explored in this chapter. There is, however, one reason that is easy to correct. Chicano literary criticism, history, sociology and ethnography must recognize the fiction of gay Mexican Americans and not shy away from studying their social and historical presence.

Ramón Saldívar's critical work, *Chicano Narrative*, published in 1990, referred to by many researchers as a defining analysis of this literature, includes female authors, heterosexual and lesbian, but does not analyze any narrative of male homosexuality. Saldívar mentions that he has not included either Arturo Islas or John Rechy for lack of space, but does not mention that these authors' works refer to Chicano male homosexuality. Even though he analyzes Richard Rodriguez's autobiography, *Hunger of Memory*, he does not address what role Rodriguez's sexual orientation may have had in defining his relationship with the Mexican American community and his political views. Even if Saldívar did not read between the lines in *Hunger of Memory*, he had to have been aware of Rodriguez's homosexuality since Rodriguez had come out of the closet before his autobiography was first published in 1982. Saldívar's criticism of *Hunger of Memory* is important to consider when analyzing the configuration of masculinity presented by Michael Nava and Manuel Ramos, because his perimeters for "Chicano" contrast to the more inclusive ones of the detective novelists.

In *Hunger of Memory: The Education of Richard Rodriguez*, the author does not specifically address his homosexuality. However, he does include painful passages of homoerotic longing, which he remembers from the perspective of an adolescent who knows, from his reading, from socialization at school and from his family, that a woman should be the object of his sexual desire (127). He is confused because his romantic imagination does not leave room for his fascination with male bodies (113, 126, 131, 132). Looking at Mexican laborers, Rodriguez describes what he sees: "They were the men with brown-muscled arms I stared at in awe on Saturday mornings ... frightening and fascinating men ... powerful, powerless men. Their fascinating darkness— like mine — to be feared" (113–114).

As a child, the women of his family warned him to stay out of the sun or he would be taken for a *pobre* ("poor"). The *braceros*[1] are "to be feared" because their dark skin is associated with the poverty of hard labor that his parents fled. Richard's parents fear them so much that they are willing to sacrifice money and the use of Spanish in their home in order to further his education and save him from the horror of poverty.

As an adult, Rodriguez is incapable of bridging the distance that has grown between him and his parents. Even though he blames this on his "education," it is not in school per se where this begins, but rather with his voracious reading as a child. He hides himself in his books: "My father opened a closet one day and was startled to find me inside, reading a novel" (45). He suspects that there is something "effeminate" about his reading (127). He even suggests this by telling the reader that he spent many hours in the closet. Rodriguez is different from his whole family. His siblings are also good students and become professionals, but Richard hid himself in his education, in his books. "'What do you see in your books?' It became the family's joke" (45).

In his analysis of *Hunger of Memory*, Saldívar does not acknowledge the similarities between the experiences of Rodriguez and those of Chicana lesbian author Cherríe Moraga whose work is also analyzed in *Chicano Narratives*. In *Hunger of Memory*, Rodriguez, like Moraga, felt the need to put aside the Spanish language of his home and embrace English as his only language. English was for Rodriguez a "'public language'" that initiated his separation from his "'private'" self and from his family according to Saldívar (qtd. in Saldívar 158). Saldívar prefers to use "private" to indicate the self that Rodriguez describes more frequently with the word "intimate." Rodriguez's intention was not to separate himself from his family, but this did, however, occur. Furthermore, in my opinion, his "public" English language allowed him, as sociologist Tomás Almaguer points out in the case of Moraga, to assume an "'anglicized'" identity in order to begin to understand his sexual otherness apart from the "intimacy" of his heterosexual and Spanish speaking family identification (Almaguer 266).

Saldívar praises Moraga and condemns Rodriguez for the same act: "[k]nowing at ten years old that 'she is queer' ... does not produce ... the kind of alienation that Rodriguez blames on his education.... Rather it produces the political poem of her life as she embraces and celebrates her multitudinous difference" (*Chicano Narrative* 190). Unlike Moraga, Rodriguez was unable to recognize his homosexuality as a child, but he does perceive that in his family his reading is not considered *macho*: "I knew that I had violated the ideal of the *macho* by becoming such a dedicated student of language and literature" (128). Saldívar fails to recognize what Almaguer points out: Moraga is only able to create her "political poem" after having rejected her ethnicity and after a long process of reconstructing a Chicano ethnicity compatible with her sexual identity (266). Gloria Anzaldúa did the same. Saldívar approves of Moraga's "political poem," which speaks out for the Chicana lesbian and disapproves of Rodriguez's stance against bilingual education and affirmative action. He fails to acknowledge that what he calls Rodriguez's "overpowering order of the *private* world" could actually be representative of the adolescent's as yet unformed perception of his homosexuality and that, like Moraga's sexuality, Rodriguez's homosexuality may have effected his political views.

Men, Anglos and Mexican, are expected to be achievers, whereas in both cultures women are not expected to carry this burden. When women are achievers, because of economic or personal needs, their willingness to participate in the U.S. economy is not seen as "assimilationist" but as an expression of need which is not competitive in the same sense as male achievement when bracketed by the norms of a patriarchal society.

Because Saldívar recognizes that the traditional configuration of Chicano families has limited women's identity and quieted their sexual and political voices, it is difficult to understand why he avoids recognizing "family" as problematical for the homosexual male (21–23). Furthermore, by condemning Rodriguez as "assimilated" (158) and "the voice of 'Hispanic America'" (155) Saldívar is effectively questioning Rodriguez about his Chicano credentials. Charlotte, in the Ramos novel *Blues for the Buffalo*, as mentioned in the previous chapter, points out the pervasiveness of this attitude by asking, "who among us is ever really Chicano enough?" (29). Rodriguez defines himself as middle-class. He avoids using any ethnic identity because to do so would limit the credibility of his jealously guarded independent political voice.

Because of the lack of literature on Chicano homosexuality and to construct a frame of reference for Nava's series, it is pertinent to review Rodriguez's three autobiographical works: *Hunger of Memory* (1982), *Days of Obligation: An Argument with My Mexican Father* (1992) and *Brown: The Last Discovery of America* (2002). Rodriguez is a Mexican American gay man of a similar age and background as fictional Henry Rios. Like Nava, Rodriguez describes his experience as his alone. He claims that life is unique and representative of an individual's particular path. In *Brown*, Rodriguez stresses that his life will always be a paradox to himself and to others. His autobiographical journey can help us understand the characterization of Henry Rios. However, before any comparisons are made between these two it is proper to note that author Rodriguez, unlike the detective-protagonist Henry Rios, who actively supports gay rights in America, refuses to take on the roll of a spokesperson for any label that could be attached to him other than middle-class American.

Rodriguez and the fictional Henry Rios are Mexican American males from the northern interior of California, the well-educated sons of working-class immigrant parents. Rodriguez was an undergraduate at Stanford and has a Ph.D. in English literature and Rios is a graduate of an unnamed prestigious private northern California university who as an undergraduate studied English literature.

It is obvious that the focus of my book is "ethnic" literature. What is not so obvious is that as much as this category is my point of departure, the ethnicity "Chicano" is not fixed. Chicano literary criticism was initiated during the activist years of the 1960s and 1970s and has influenced education in the United States. This does not mean that there is an equal amount of influence from Chicanos as from the mainstream "Anglo-Protestant"[2] perspective. There is now, as compared to before, a limited representation of the Chicano historical experience and literature included in the U.S. public school curriculum from grades one through twelve.

For those who were educated before the 1980s, there was no representation of the political Chicano, the Mexican American immigrant or the historical viewpoint of Mexican Americans, citizens of the United States since 1850 and colonizers of the Southwest who preceded the east coast Mayflower pilgrims. As José Limón points out representations of Mexican Americans in literature of the social sciences have been dominated by a "colonial" perspective where the cultural outsider, an ethnographer or sociologist, observes the cultural *other* (Limón *Dancing with the*

*Devil* 7). This viewpoint dominated representations of both popular and elite configurations of the Mexican American until the last decade.

Authors Richard Rodriguez and Michael Nava grew up in this educational system. Chicano critics have taken Rodriguez to task for not challenging this curriculum, for actually embracing English for its universalism and for calling what he learned, English literature, his own (see Alfredo Villanueva-Collado, Tomás Rivero, Gary Soto in addition to Ramón Saldívar). I feel that it is very important to recognize, as Chicano critics have recognized, that part of self-identity is to have role models with whom to identify. This has been, and still is, a project of Chicano criticism.

However, in our Anglo and Chicano cultures there has been a concerted effort to deny readers access to literature that describes nonheterosexual relationships. Between the years of 1990 and 2000, 515 books were either challenged or banned in libraries and public schools across the United States for "promoting homosexuality" (American Library Association web site).

Chicano history and literature offers young Mexican Americans historical and literary examples of Mexican American identities, just as the traditional curriculum presented outstanding figures from the majority Anglo-Protestant population. However, there is an inherent paradox when Chicano critics base their criticism of Rodriguez on his refusal to identify himself as Chicano or Mexican American and then loudly denounce him for a viewpoint that does not reflect that of this community.[3]

Rodriguez's autobiographies refer to a search for self that is outlined by perimeters set by specific literary genres. In *Hunger of Memory*, Rodriguez tells the reader that he found a portrait of himself in *The Uses of Literacy* by Richard Hoggart: "I found, in his description of the scholarship boy, myself" (*Hunger* 46). He relates to the scholarship boy because they share a similar history: a working-class background, an educational journey, and finally — as result of education — a middle-class identity and the loss of family and community ties. He introduces this autobiography by calling it a "kind of pastoral.... I write in the tradition of that high courtly grace" but not from an aristocratic perspective, rather from a middle-class perspective (*Hunger* 6). In *Days of Obligation*, he begins to trace his family roots and refers to the Mexican authors Octavio Paz and José Vasconcelos, who both explored traits of Mexican identity.

Rodriguez addresses the paradoxes of his identification in *Brown*, and his conclusions are not unlike those of the character Charlotte in *Blues for the Buffalo*; Chicano mysteries exist and perhaps each Chicano has his own. For his mystery Rodriguez cannot find a conclusive solution. *Brown* is the "volume [that] completes a trilogy on American public life and [his] private life" (xiv) and it accepts that there will be no resolution to Rodriguez's personal paradox. Nava explores this same "mystery" through the characterization of his detective. Henry Rios, like Rodriguez, searches for self-identification through the study of English literature; each novel contains references to its prose or poetry. Neither author refers to Mexican American literature, or the "corrido paradigm" that has been so influential in Chicano literature (Saldívar, R. *Chicano* 160). Rodriguez and Nava initially choose literary models that might appear incongruous to ethnic labelers. In *Hunger of Memory*, Rodriguez chooses that of the "pastoral" into which he inserts the "scholarship boy," and Nava chooses the genre of hermetic white male detective. However, as these authors' narratives evolve, they move away from their original models.

Rodriguez's *Days of Obligation* speaks with the conversational tone of an editorial. He continues to present paradoxes, but these are less personal and more historic. Attempting to define the immigrant experience in the United States, he frames this narrative with the genre of "comedy and tragedy" (xviii) in *Brown* where he returns to the more intimate perspective of *Hunger of Memory*. With *Brown*, however, the autobiographer now tells his paradoxical tale with confidence. The voice in *Hunger of Memory* was painful to hear; his loneliness is palpable.

After having searched "class, ethnicity and race" respectively in his three autobiographies, he concludes in *Brown* that the world is brown, "not skin, but brown as an impurity" (194). "Sodomy," he states, "is among the brownest of thoughts" (207). However, he does not say this sadly; the pain is no longer unbearable. He prefaces this statement with "Where there's a will, there is a way" (207). Rodriguez will most likely be criticized for identifying "brown" with race, love and sodomy. The equation is presented as a paradox because for Rodriguez, and for the fictional Rios, "Mexican American homosexual" is an uneasy identity. It has few literary and public models and stands in sharp contrast to familiar representations of the Mexican American male.

*Hunger of Memory* is a threat to the prevailing ideological construction of family. According to literary critic Sonia Saldívar-Hull, this family is seen as the stable center where resistance to the dominant hegemony is constructed or is the refuge where the political activist finds solace in tradition. "Family" becomes problematic for the homosexual because, as sociologist Almaguer notes, "[t]he openly effeminate Chicano gay man's rejection of heterosexuality is typically seen as a fundamental betrayal of Chicano patriarchal cultural norms. He is viewed as having turned his back on the male role that privileges Chicano men and entitles them to sexual access to women, minors, and even other men" (266). Furthermore,

"Chicano family life remains rigidly structured along patriarchal lines that privilege men over women and children. Any violation of these norms is undertaken at great personal risk because Chicanos draw upon the family to resist racism and the ravages of class inequality" (266). Rodriguez's education is not the only aspect of his life that separates him from his family. When he becomes aware of his sexuality he feels an even greater estrangement from the traditional values he was taught at home.

Almaguer analyzes Cherríe Moraga's very open expression of her sexuality, *Loving in the War Years*, not because his topic is the lesbian Mexican American or Chicana literature, but because of the lack of literature, fictional and autobiographical, anthropological, ethnographical and sociological, that describes Mexican American male homosexuality (256). He makes his point on familial relationships by quoting Moraga: "'[L]esbianism, in any form, and male homosexuality which openly avows both the sexual and the emotional elements of the bond, challenge the very foundation of la familia'" (qtd. in Almaguer 266).

Late capitalism, in a process begun more than two hundred years ago in the United States, has completed the destruction of an environment conducive to the nuclear patriarchal family. In his article "Capitalism and Gay Identity," John D'Emilio argues that there have always been human beings who engage in homosexual eroticism, but that in New England of the seventeenth through early eighteenth century an agriculturally based capitalist economy did not allow for any sexual identification other than that of biological male or female as defined by the heterosexual family. "Although there was a division of labor between men and women, the family was truly an interdependent unit of production: the survival of each member depended on the cooperation of all" and birth rates were high because of the need for children's labor, therefore "sex was harnessed to procreation" (469).

It was not until the beginning of the twentieth century that the gradual shift from a family-centered agricultural economy created a sufficient number of individuals living in urban areas and supporting themselves outside of this economy, that an active homosexual identity became possible. Currently, as in the past, the nuclear family as an institution is supported economically by populations of recent immigrants who rely on family and co-nationals for financial and moral support. This group can include recent Mexican immigrants, but does not include the great majority of the urban-dwelling Chicano population. It could be assumed that upward mobility and the generational distance from subsistence farming would change Mexican American attitudes towards homosexuality, and that a change in attitude would not signify assimilation, but would be reflective of a change in economic circumstances and environment.

There is a "contradictory relationship of capitalism to family" (D'Emilio 473). Having "undermined the material basis of the nuclear family by taking away the economic functions that cemented the ties between family members," the capitalist government continues to have a political interest in maintaining the nuclear family as the site where future citizens are nurtured, educated and socialized (473). Capitalism "maintains that reproduction and childrearing are private tasks, that children 'belong' to parents, who exercise the rights of ownership" (473). By refusing to support in a significant manner programs that nurture, educate and socialize children outside of the traditional nuclear family, capitalism "scapegoats" those who, because of capitalism's material foundation, have been able to sexually identify themselves as "lesbians, gay men or heterosexual feminists" (473).

The Mexican American homosexual is accused by his community of being "assimilationist," of simulating alien values and rejecting his culture for that of the Anglo majority, that in turn accuses him of being antifamily and therefore against the capitalistic values of the United States. What a fix! Furthermore, the characterization of the hard-boiled detective has been subject to similar paradoxical criticism.

Américo Paredes was not alone in accusing the hard-boiled detective of being "homosexual" ("The United" 29). In 1949, just before McCarthyism, a pamphlet published by Gershon Legman undoubtedly influenced and supported congressional claims that hard-boiled "pulp" fiction posed a "national threat against the era's dominant conception of the American way of life" (Abbott 76). "For Legman, homosexuality, rather circuitously, threatens normative Oedipal development, the family romance, and by extension a bourgeois nuclear family structure" (78).

How do the novels of Ramos and Nava demonstrate that they are not "sell-outs" to assimilation? The fact is these texts transform the hard-boiled genre. Chandler's white male detective, mired as he was in "depression era gender anxiety," attempted to bury any conflicts between his "feminine" and "masculine" self. In contrast, the detectives created by Ramos and Nava manage to confront their anxieties precisely because their introspections combine masculine and feminine perspectives. They overcome the *macho*'s and the "hermetic" white male's fear of self-love, of displaying, in Moraga's words, the "emotional elements of the bond" between males (qtd. in Almaguer 266). From my perspective the detectives' vision is more radically confrontational of U.S. hegemonic ideology than the emphasis on the patriarchal nuclear family espoused by the founding fathers of the Chicano Renaissance. The depiction of *la familia* in their mystery novels demonstrates that strong emotional bonds between males in the absence of females can be incorporated into a Chicano identity. Detectives Montez and Rios posit and affirm strong bonds between males, straight and gay, and describe these bonds as nurturing of other males, women and children.

The hard-boiled detective persona provides a critical perspective that allows the Chicano sleuth to criticize government corruption, urban decay and focus on marginalized populations. Moreover, the hard-boiled male stance taken initially by Ramos and Nava is a vehicle well suited to criticizing from within the contradictions inherent in Anglo American and Chicano generalizations of Mexican American masculinity.

The paradoxes inherent in the characterization of the hard-boiled detective serve as a point of departure for Ramos and Nava. The following is a review of three analyses of Raymond Chandler's seminal works of hard-boiled detective fiction: Fredric Jameson's Marxist analysis, Megan E. Abbott's analysis of white masculinity and Jeffrey Langham's Freudian analysis.

Surprisingly, Jameson focuses on the stylistic and not the materialistic content of Chandler's fiction: "[t]he detective story, as a form without ideological content, without any overt political or social or philosophical point, permits such pure stylistic experimentation" ("On Raymond" 124). However, he does find in Chandler's style — his use of slang, his carefully detailed portraits of anonymous figures, his descriptions of the urban environment of 1930s and 1940s Los Angeles—covert references to the urban failures of late capitalism:

> For Los Angeles is already a kind of microcosm and forecast of the country as a whole: a new centerless city, in which the various classes have lost touch with each other because each is isolated in his own geographical compartment.... Los Angeles is ... a spreading out horizontally, a flowing apart of the elements of the social structure [127].

In this milieu, the detective provides a means by which the reader can "know the society as a whole" (127).

In Chandler's "microcosm" the detective visits the sites of local "injustice, racism, corruption, educational incompetence" (130). The same can be said for both Ramos's detective in Denver and Nava's in the Bay Area and later in Los Angeles, with the qualification that they attempt to construct a social whole out of the conflicting pieces of the society they observe. Curiously, Jameson does not elaborate on the economic circumstances that surround Chandler's literary production and the characterization of his detective. He notes briefly that "[a]s an executive of the oil industry, he [Chandler] lived in Los Angeles for some fifteen years before the Depression put him out of business, enough time to sense what was unique about the city's atmosphere, in a position to see what power was and what forms it took" (123). Both the Chicano detectives, like Chandler's alter ego Philip Marlowe, struggle economically and show an intimate familiarity with the locales where their investigations take place. But they go farther than Marlowe, because they want to resolve the conflict between the powerful and the powerless. Marlowe's view is basically pessimistic, whereas Montez and Rios begin to develop a more optimistic outlook.

Critic Abbott makes a direct connection between the hard-boiled detective persona and "depression era gender anxiety" (21). The white male's masculinity is under assault. He is no longer able to function as the provider for his family. This is a situation that displaces him from his role as a patriarchal leader. He has become "dependent in many ways that women had been thought to be" because in addition to being unable to provide for his family he is he unable to provide for himself (24). He is forced into a situation where his only stable employment opportunity is with the federal government "as a 'selfless public servant' devoted to the needs of community" (25). The New Deal's "masculine ideal" posits the male as a caregiver, a role traditionally delegated to women. Not only does the white male's role change, but the white woman's role also changes; she is now part of the work force and this further threatens traditional patriarchal masculinity. Finally, the white male's loss of economic privilege puts him in direct competition with ethnic and racial minorities; this contact threatens his "whiteness" and all the privileges American society grants to "white." Depression era Los Angeles demonstrates "a particularly volatile xenophobic atmosphere in which the hero's whiteness is very much up for grabs" (9).

Abbott concurs with Jameson that Marlowe does not "experience"[4] the various social strata he narrates (Jameson "On Raymond" 127); in her analysis he is a "hermetic" figure who does not, as Jameson suggests, provide "knowledge" of "society as a whole" (Jameson "On Raymond" 127), but instead seals himself off from the various "others": female, non-white, non-heterosexual. However, this construction of hermetic masculinity actually embodies that which it fears most, the contagion of the *other*.

> Masculinity is situated as weak, changeable, even hysterical, with the feminine characterized as potentially lethal in strength and amoral will. But this unsettling binary is thrown into question, as it is through weakness that these protagonists often find pleasure and eventually solidify power. Such episodic male pleasure in infirmity or temporary loss of agency, however, unsettles certain basic hegemonic structures— most notably the patriarchal family, a

structure that rests on potent masculine control offsetting any exog-
amous threat [Abbott 27].

This is the detective that Paredes classifies as a false *macho*.

Paradoxically, Chicano detective Henry Rios initially adopts a "hermetic" posture, to escape that which he fears most, the "authentic" *macho*.
Luis Montez tries to act *macho*, and talk *macho*, but never quite pulls it
off: *machismo* is what he criticizes most about Chicano identity. Masculinity and femininity are unstable in Chandler's fiction and in the detective fiction of Ramos and Nava. However, in Chandler's fiction Marlowe
is completely unaware of this fact. Montez and Rios are forced to first
acknowledge the unstable characterization of masculinity and then accept
as positive a degree of feminization of the gendered male and visa versa.

Langham's Freudian analysis of Chandler's *The Long Goodbye* concurs
with Abbott's observations outlined above. His analysis refers to the work
of Judith Butler that "revisits Freud in order to make a persuasive claim
that gender can be understood as an effect of melancholy, recalling that
Freud ... argues that melancholy is the structure through which egos are
formed" (Langham 148). A "consistent, continuous gender" is seen as "a
fantasy constructed" by privileging, "libidinizing," those parts of the body
"that give it gender while disavowing" this very "zoning" by positing that
this gender "had always been that way, even before the subject's story
began" (150–151). In other words, the construction of a "consistent, continuous gender" perforce denies an erotic or traditionally male or female
part of the subject, and as a result the subject feels a loss, Freudian melancholy. Therefore gender must not be consistent or continuous because any
limited construction will result in a feeling of loss for that part left out of
the equation and undermine the subject's ego.

Langham goes on to show that the purported hermetic white male persona contradicts himself; that his "apparent lack of desire to be attached
to anybody, especially another man" is undermined by the relationship
between the "detached" first person narrative and the melancholy voices
of others incorporated by the narrative, in particular those of "emasculated" white males.

So Paredes was right: the Depression era male was an "emasculated"
male. In Chandler's *The Long Goodbye* characters Marlowe and Lennox
seem to need each other; there is a "homoerotic dimension of their friendship" (Langham 147). In her analysis of the relationship between Red and
Marlowe in *Farewell, My Lovely*, Abbott concurs that "the primary lure is
the entanglement of masculine and feminine signifiers" (Abbott 87). The
pessimism and melancholy of these male characters is certainly reflective

of the historical circumstances, but it is moreover psychological because it is the result of their isolation, a circumstance framed by a radically limited concept of masculinity. They are homophobic to the nth degree. Any closeness between themselves and another male is seen as deviant.

Langham's discussion of *The Long Goodbye* shows how Nava transforms Marlowe's hermetic narrative into Rios's heterogeneous narrative in his novel *The Little Death*. Following Butler, Langham states: "[i]n the mouth of the other ... the citation [of the detective genre] dislocates both authority and origin" (154). Nava's style has easily recognizable hard-boiled roots and in *The Little Death* the story of the detective's relationship with the victim parallels that of Marlowe and Lennox. The "mimicry" of a heterosexual narrative "carries with it a subversive potential to displace heterosexual authority" (Langham 155) which Nava accomplishes by undermining the "stability of heterosexual subjectivity through his grief for another man," a grief that Marlowe denies himself (162). Marlowe is melancholic; he does not morn the loss of Lennox, but more significantly cannot morn his own loss of a heterogeneous masculinity. He, like Paredes, is completely unaware that an "authentic *macho*" need not adhere to a "consistent, continuous gender."

Nostalgia can bring on melancholy. Film *noir* and Chandler's fiction, according to Jameson, have a nostalgic appeal because their definition of social types is indicated by socially specific lexicons that have, "except in certain very specialized situations," disappeared (135). Along with these lexicons of yesteryear, Jameson notes the references to stable "brand names" of "simpler" forms of "market capitalism" (136). When written Chandler's fiction was not overtly nostalgic, but for current readers the chaos he portrays and the absence of the nuclear family and a stable economy inspire longing for a past when these situations were still seen as temporary aberrations.

The nostalgia that Jameson doesn't mention, in my opinion the most obvious "nostalgia," is for brand name, visible, "white" masculinity. The original hard-boiled genre did not question "white" identification, but through its portrayal of the detective's interaction with others showed that the white male was feeling threatened. In the 1940s, and even now in 2005, the "universal" of "whiteness" is either defensively denied or openly threatened. As Abbott points out, "these texts [Chandler's] seek to perpetuate and maintain the illusion of whiteness as a universal, as an invisible, raceless man" (95). Ramos and Nava confront and deny the "universality" of the white male by making this perspective visible. By locating their hard-boiled detectives outside of the perspective of a white male hegemony they destroy the covert and overt nostalgia typical of the hard-boiled genre.

Nava's detective Rios begins his career as a hard drinking, hard working loner detective. After the murder of his client and lover, Hugh Paris, in the first of seven *Henry Rios* novels, *The Little Death*, the lawyer-detective begins to take stock of his life. He recognizes that his drinking is a problem and joins Alcoholics Anonymous. As he ages and gains experience in personal and public spheres, his life begins to change, his law practice improves, he makes connections with powerful and responsible people, he becomes a sought after speaker for gay rights and he conquers his alcoholism. At this point, it is not difficult to see him as an assimilated Mexican American, a man who simulates the lives of those around him. But, he is unhappy, his love life is unsatisfactory and he is estranged from his only family, his sister Elena. He is weighed down by personal grief, but is unable to identify its cause.

In the last novel of the series, *Rag and Bone*,[5] Henry finds happiness in a stable relationship with another Mexican American male and has reunited with his sister, her daughter and his young nephew. The loner detective of the hard-boiled tradition completely disappears, and the middle-class gay man is able to live comfortably with his dual identities, Mexican American and gay.

Nava's series openly portrays a multitude of problems that gay men face and the loving relationships that many of these men form. In the majority of his novels, with the exception of *The Hidden Law* and *Rag and Bone*, the Mexican American community is absent. Rios is characterized as a gay activist; he is part of the homosexual community. That he is essentially the only Chicano character in most of the novels is not surprising because his life intersects with the lives of other men who share his interest in gay activism and who are also professionals. These "white" men, like those defined by Almaguer, have forged their sexual identity, live in or frequent a "'gilded' gay ghetto," have learned to be unafraid of being visibly homosexual, and are able to do so because of the "unique class and racial advantages" their whiteness affords them (263). By openly living their sexual identity, the autobiographer, Rodriguez, and the fictional lawyer-detective, Rios, are "assimilated" *by* the "white" community.

From personal observation, Almaguer notes that the middle-class Latino gay male is "more likely to be assimilated into the dominant European-American culture," than the homosexual working-class Latino (265). These men are less likely than middle-class Latinos to identify themselves as homosexual, or *internacionales* in Spanish. It is also more likely that the working-class Latino will remain in his community. If he remains there he must meet certain conditions as anthropologists Alonso and Koreck and autobiographer Moraga point out. In this space his homosexuality is tolerated as long as he does not try to establish an emotional bond with another man. As long as he maintains close ties to family and community he is essentially prohibited from pursuing what many Euro-American gay men seek. Economics or family can easily immobilize him. In other words, for lawyer Henry Rios, the possibility of meeting another openly gay Chicano who is interested in a long term relationship is significantly less than that of meeting a "white" gay male with these same interests.

Race or ethnicity as an identifier of the homosexual characters in Nava's series is not stressed because this identification loses its significance when a man comes out of the closet. Even though he is not specifically addressing the topic of sexual identity or "white" in relationship to the gay community, Rodriguez likens the process of becoming American in white America to that of an "acid bath" (*Brown* 140). A lesbian or gay identification, as D'Emilio points out, usually requires that the homosexual individual be financially independent of his family and be willing to sacrifice an ethnic identity or, in other words, his or her family ties (472). This is when he or she takes the "acid bath" Rodriguez once took. The fictional protagonist Rios has also taken the "acid bath" and, until the conclusion of the series, he is estranged from his only living sibling and has no knowledge of the fact that he has a niece and a great-nephew.

The relative safety of the gilded ghettos of San Francisco and Los Angeles do not have much appeal for lawyer Rios. He lives his life as part of the greater heterosexual and homosexual communities. Many of the accused or victims in his series are homosexuals who do not live openly; they have not passed through the painful process of coming out of the closet (*The Little Death, Golden Boy, How Town, The Burning Plain, The Death of Friends,* and *Rag and Bone.*) In *Golden Boy* and *The Hidden Law,* Rios explores the coming out process and the obstacles white males, even with all their "unique class and racial advantages," must face and as a consequence reveals a personal struggle between his ethnicity and sexuality.

In *Golden Boy,* Henry is enlisted by a powerful consortium of wealthy Angelinos to defend a young homosexual man, a waiter, who is accused of having killed a co-worker. Jim has continued to proclaim his innocence in the face of overwhelming circumstantial evidence. Henry is confused as to why his good friend Larry from Los Angeles has come all the way to San Francisco to ask him to defend this young man. He does not understand why Jim's Public Defender has withdrawn from the case and what interest his friend, a powerful lawyer, has in the defendant. Surprised, Larry retorts, "'Isn't the reason for my interest obvious?'" Henry relays that he is still confused and Larry answers:

"Everyone's abandoned him, Henry. His parents and now his lawyer. Someone has to step in —"

"I agree it's a sad situation. But why me, Larry? I can name half a dozen excellent criminal defense lawyers down there."

"Any of them gay?"

"Aren't we beyond that?"

"You can't expect a straight lawyer to understand the pressures of being in the closet that would drive someone to kill," he said.

I put my pen down. "What makes you think *I* understand?" I replied. "We've all been in the closet at one time or another. Not many of us commit murders on our way out" [9].

It turns out that Jim did not commit murder on his way out of the closet. He is still hiding there. Though accused of having committed murder to hide his homosexual relationships, he refuses to acknowledge his sexual orientation. When Henry meets with him for the first time, Jim asks if he is "gay" which Henry confirms, and Jim shoots back "'Do you wear a dress in court?'" (47).

Jim's parents are Catholic, but Catholicism itself is not what is specifically criticized. Throughout the series all religious condemnation of homosexuality is criticized for foisting an unfair choice on young people who have only begun to construct their philosophical and sexual identities.

In *Golden Boy*, Henry meets a young middle-class Jewish man, Josh Mandel, who becomes his lover. The relationship continues in *How Town* until, in *The Hidden Law*, under the strain of AIDS, the pair separates. Josh is at least 12 years younger than the 36-year-old lawyer. With Henry he had discussed coming out, and in an emotional scene after hearing Henry speak on the campus of his university about gay rights, he sits his parents down in Henry's company and tells them that he is HIV-positive, that he is gay and that Henry is his lover.

Nava describes a scene that lasts from the late afternoon into early hours of the morning, resumes at breakfast, and then, after Henry leaves, resumes again. Josh's parents bring the Bible, AIDS as "divine retribution," the "unborn grandchildren" and corruption by an older man into the discussion, but ultimately and reluctantly accept his homosexuality (*Golden Boy* 149). The hurdles did not seem that difficult, because after Josh's point blank revelations the emotionally charged group, Josh's parents, himself and Henry, was able to continue to talk to each other in a civil manner. This, however, will not continue.

Religion does not disappear from the equation. After Josh's death, in the *The Burning Plain* Rios recounts the court battle mounted against him by Josh's grieving parents. The Mandels have accused Rios of asserting undue influence over their son, of having infected him with AIDS (completely false) and most importantly of having estranged him in death from his cultural inheritance. The Jewish faith prohibits Josh's own last wish to be cremated and have his ashes divided between Henry and his family. As the executor of Josh's estate, Henry must face the Mandels.

The reader learns in *The Hidden Law* that Henry, who seems so comfortable with his gay identity, has wrestled for many years and continues to struggle with this identification. His conflicted self is brought to the forefront when his relationship with Josh is strained because of Josh's personal confrontation with AIDS. Henry wants to protect and insulate him; Josh wants to gain more courage by living independently. He leaves Henry and becomes the lover of a man who, unlike himself, is now having to face the debilitative stages of AIDS. Josh says to Henry:

> "I'm not in love with Steve's diagnosis, but I am in love with his courage, the same way I was in love with your courage when I first met you. Do you remember how I was? I was a closet case who knew that being HIV-positive was the judgment of God for letting myself get fucked in the ass." He grimaced. "You taught me I could be gay and still live with dignity. You taught me to be brave" [31].

Josh gives up trying to gain his independence in his relationship with Henry, recommends that Henry consult a therapist and storms out.

Through the sessions with his psychiatrist, Henry begins to realize that he is more like his abusive *macho* Mexican father than he had ever suspected. "I still bore a residue of homicidal rage toward him [his father]" (169–170). He makes a similar observation about his father's anger that ethnographer Limón has made of some of his working-class subjects (Limón *Dancing* 140). Henry recalls that "[o]utside, in the larger world where they labored under the contemptuous eye of Anglo bosses, the fathers were social and political ciphers. No wonder, then, that in the families they tolerated no dissent from their wives and children. And they drank" (*Hidden Law* 169). However, at this point in the lawyer protagonist's life narrative, Henry does not recognize that his behavior toward Josh, though not violent, shows a lack of respect and acknowledgement similar to his father's in relationship with wife and children. Henry confesses to his therapist that "[g]rowing up, I was sensitive and strong-willed. It was a combination that didn't make sense to his [his father's] notions of being male. He thought I was simply weak and disobedient" (73).

Henry's father's view of him parallels his own stance towards Josh. As an active member of ACT UP,[6] Josh attends meetings and participates in confrontational demonstrations where he could be injured. Henry is sympathetic to the cause—help for AIDS victims and a cure for the disease—but he wants to protect Josh from injury, and moreover be assured that Josh will be home when he arrives from work. In one scene between the former lovers Josh tries to explain his need to participate in ACT UP and his need of a lover, who like himself will not live to reach "seventy-five" (*Hidden Law* 52). Henry is so upset with Josh and himself that he is about to "explode" (52). Josh is reduced to tears. He is unable to break through Henry's possessiveness and "I know more than you" stony stance. Henry does not admit to himself, but the case is that he thinks that Josh is weak and disobedient, and unappreciative of the protection and stability he, the dominant male, has provided.

Josh's make-up favors femininity more than masculinity. He is more sensitive, smaller in stature, less ambitious, more conscious of his appearance and more interested in cooking than Henry. However, he will not allow himself to be abused mentally or dismissed by Henry. This is his accusation: "'You think this is some cheap faggot farce, don't you' he said thickly. 'This is my goddamned life'" (*Hidden Law* 52).

Henry's mom suffered physical and verbal abuse when her husband was not categorically dismissing or ignoring her. In therapy, Henry is forced to revisit the abusive patriarchal marriage of his parents and his youthful self-defense. After hearing from his psychologist that "'perhaps ... you live out his [your father's] judgments of you,'" he is forced to reconsider his identity. "When I was a child I had worked hard at making myself invisible and I emerged from it without an identity. Over the years, I had crafted one for myself, and now Raymond Reynolds [his therapist] was telling me it was all wrong" (*Hidden Law* 75). After his session with Reynolds, Henry decides to call Timothy, a friend from AA, to talk to him about his relationship with his father.

In his conversation with Timothy, Henry again shows he is incapable of resolving his conflictive masculinity and femininity. After hearing his story Timothy comments, "it sounds like your dad went to the same school of child rearing that mine did" (*Hidden Law* 77). Henry defensively answers that his father in contrast to Timothy's did not know he was gay, Henry himself did not know he was gay, and that his father had only recognized him as "different" from himself. There is a shade of Rodriguez's experience in this passage: the youth and his family recognize, but are unable to identify, "difference." Timothy wisely comments, "You know, Henry, we're the only people who get born into the enemy camp ... we get born into straight families" (77). Besides stating the obvious—your parents were heterosexuals and you are not—he is trying to tell Henry that the sharp divisions he witnessed as a child between male and female should not be part of a healthy identity, or relationship. Timothy tries to cheer Henry:

> "You're smart, sensitive, successful —"
> "Trustworthy, loyal and obedient." [retorts Henry sarcastically]
> "OK, then don't take a compliment, as long as you understand what I'm saying. There's nothing wrong with the kind of man you are."
> I laughed. "That means a lot from someone who dressed up last Halloween as Barbara Bush."
> "Bitch," he replied. ... "Now can I finish?"
> "Please."
> "...Let go of what your father wanted you to be and maybe you'll stop hating him so much" [Hidden Law 77].

Eventually, in Rag and Bone, Henry learns to stop hating him so much.

Henry continues to be influenced by his perception of what his father wanted him to be: a controlling and abusive macho who belittles sensitivity as feminine. Raised by a brutal father and a cowering mother, Henry has not learned to respect sensitivity in others, male or female. He has constructed a stark and uncompromising binary: man is brutal and woman is weak.

In The Hidden Law, a prominent Chicano politician, Gus Peña, is murdered. Peña, like Rios, grew up with an abusive working class father. Rios recalls

> his [Peña's] spectacular success had not been enough to break the circuits of resentment, any more than my fine academic degrees had, and we had both ended up like our fathers, seething alcoholics. There was a crucial difference though — I had not had a son to visit this fury on. He had [170].

Peña's son, in complicity with his mother and sister, murders his father. In Rag and Bone, Rios becomes a father figure to his nephew Angel. The relationship has to weather religious and ethnic negative perspectives toward homosexuality and femininity. Henry finally grows out of his machismo. His barricaded door opens, rigid heterosexual binaries disappear and he becomes the benevolent director of an extended Mexican American gay/lesbian family.

The choice of the name Angel is significant. It is a popular first name for a Mexican male that lacks, unlike the also common name of Jesús, an exclusive reference to Christianity. Furthermore, in U.S. popular culture angels have become talismans. Sold at the local Hallmark Store, or attached to the logos of charitable organizations, angels are workers of secular miracles. Nava chooses for his unbelieving detective a savior who is not the exclusive property of organized beliefs, but can bridge the detective's discarded religious education that continues to weigh on his imagination and his faith in secular solutions.

Angel is the ten-year-old son of Henry's niece Vicky, the daughter of his long estranged sister Elena. She left Vicky with an adoption agency days after her birth, while a student at UC Berkeley. Vicky was never adopted because "[t]hirty years ago, brown-skinned girl babies were not very placeable" according to Elena (22). She grew up in an abusive and intellectually sterile environment in a series of foster homes and finally in the house of a Catholic charity group where she was sexually molested. As a teenager she was impregnated and then married.

Vicky only initiates contact with Elena because she and her son Angel have no where else to turn. Her husband Pete has been released from jail with a new identity to protect him from the gang he was a part of and informed on to the police. Vicky had been "hiding" from the gang in a home for battered women, but this became impossible. She could not go to Pete's mother, who loves her like a daughter, because she would be recognized in the gang's neighborhood, so she arrives on her mother's doorstep. Pete misses her and she joins him in rural California where he is living out his new identity. But he gets bored with the farmer life, and the little family returns to southern California and, with the financial help of Pete's mother, is hiding out in a series of different motels. Pete has again picked up his drug habit, when he is murdered. Angel turns to his uncle Henry because he believes that he has witnessed his mother kill his father.

We later learn that Pete was homosexual and heavily influenced by his aggressive *macho* cousin. He married to hide his sexuality from the community, not an uncommon act of defense. He was neither aggressive nor effeminate, but was very weak-willed. Angel's birth father was actually Butch, Pete's cousin and a Mexican American gang leader, drug dealer and super*macho* type. Vicky had her own run-ins with the law that seem to coincide with Pete's vacations from jail. When they met in rural California, as an evangelical Christian, she was adamant about saving Pete from drugs and jail and keeping a Christian home. Because of her religion, but also through her experience of having lived with a man whose denial of his sexuality is perceived as having made him weak and susceptible to victimization, she condemns uncle Henry's homosexuality and is fearful that he will sexually abuse Angel. She is in a difficult situation; accused of murder, she has no one else to turn to but Henry Rios.

Nava is clearly a talented author. The *Henry Rios* series improves in plot development and description with each novel. In *Rag and Bone*, the "murder" does not occur until the middle of the novel, but by then Nava has so well constructed his characters that a relatively common story of poverty, sexual abuse and gang violence becomes a gripping mystery. The "mystery" is couched in family characteristics and history that Henry, Elena, Vicky and Angel share unbeknownst to them. Several other characters, John DeLeon in particular, help the Rios family resolve the "mystery" of themselves.

As the novel begins, *macho* Henry has suffered a myocardial infarction, been very near death and while in this state called for his estranged sister, Elena. He still sees the "terror" of their childhood in her eyes, but now he also sees "love" (6). When he awakens in the hospital he is surprised to see her and wants to know why she is at his bedside. Elena, his senior, an independent woman, a lesbian and a professor of English, explains that she always felt responsible for him as a child, and that now, unlike when they were children, she can help him. When Vicky comes on the scene, first described as a battered wife, Elena immediately connects her situation with that of their mother. Henry does not understand why Vicky has not left her husband, and feels that she is not worthy of his sister's sympathy. He is still resentful that his mother did not leave their father and take him and his sister away from his abuse. Elena points out that their mother did not have this option: "She had a grade-school education, no job skills and her family was far away" (108). Henry still is not convinced, but later when he learns the history of his niece and her mother-in-law and recalling the efforts his mother made to show him her love, he understands that poverty, lack of education and societal pressures can force even strong women into situations where they become powerless to act in their own behalf.

Angel, despite having been warned about his uncle's homosexuality, shows early on that he is drawn to Henry, but tries, as children do, to manipulate Henry by taunting him. With a conscious effort on his part, Henry refuses to take the bait. He learns that the "control" on which he has always prided himself is not part of a *macho* need to prove himself, but is first and foremost a learned self-control, that incidentally has given him a successful career as a lawyer. He is able to reject both physical and mental coercion in his relationship with his "son," Angel.

In one scene, Angel asks him if he can have Henry's grandfather's pocket watch when Henry dies:

> I laughed. "Yeah, but I'm not dying anytime soon."
> "My mom said—" he exclaimed, then caught himself.
> "What did your mom say? You can tell me, I won't be upset."

He weighed my credibility as carefully as a judge. "My mom says you're a *joto* and probably have AIDS."

*Joto* was Spanish for the letter "J," but in the vernacular, *joto* meant, essentially faggot. To hear the word from him was like being stabbed, but I knew better than to be angry with him, so I calmly explained, "*Joto* is not a nice word, Angel. Please don't use it again. I don't have AIDS and I'm not dying" [85].

This is not the only negative stereotypical labeling that Henry must face in his relationship with Angel. He is much less patient with Vicky, who has taught her son this and other abusive labels, until later in the novel when he has absorbed the totality of her life history.

Economics and education — poverty and affluence, the drop out and the college grad — are stereotyped on both sides of the family equation. Angel says to Henry, "She [Vicky] said you think you're better than us" (147). Elena, facing a hysterectomy at forty, went in search of her daughter. When she found her, she did not identify herself: "My maternal instincts weren't even as strong as my snobbery" (23). She saw a "chola," a girl of fourteen in tight pants and make-up that looked like the girls she and Henry "grew up with ... the bad girls, the gang girls" (23). Having been given up for adoption as a baby is not as hard on Vicky as her mother's confession of having searched for her, found her and again abandoned her as a teenager.

Henry and Elena's "snobbery" extends to educated and middle-class Mexican Americans. Elena tells Henry in a "rueful but affectionate" tone about Vicky's father: "He was the first Chicano I ever met. He couldn't speak ten words of Spanish and his dad was an accountant in L.A., but he lectured me about *la causa* [the goals of the Chicano movement] and told me that studying American literature was assimilationist" (19). Even though she does not identify herself as a working-class Chicana, she will not accept that "Chicano" can be anything other than herself: a Spanish speaker from a humble background. Conversely Vicky's dad perceives that reading any literature which is not Chicano is a traitorous act. In *The Hidden Law* Henry reveals that he is skeptical of Chicano movement rhetoric. He describes college Professor Ochoa, who has a "yellowing poster calling for revolution" (86), as "a believer, and though I thought his beliefs were foolish, I had to envy his tenacity" (85). Ochoa is supportive of Chicano gangs because, in his opinion, they show Chicano solidarity, a stance that Henry finds abhorrent. In the same novel, he faults the affluent parents of a troubled Chicano youth for not having shown any interest in their son, who then seeks his identity within Chicano gang culture. Henry and Elena are at a loss when asked to affirm their ethnicity: they reject the poverty and abuse of their home, but at the same time will not accept that anyone who has not had this experience can truly be aware of what it is to be Mexican American. Furthermore, Henry's dismissal of violent gangs as a cultural markers contradicts his claim that the abuse he suffered in a traditional home defines his ethnicity.

Henry and Elena were raised Catholic. Their "snobbery" includes Vicky's faith: a "storefront," "Holy Roller" Christianity (34). When they first meet Vicky's pastor, Reverend Ortega of "La Iglesia de Cristo Triunfante," Henry perceives that Elena wants to "get rid of him" (191). Elena justifies her loyalty to Catholicism because this was her only entry to education; she became a nun because otherwise their father would have forbidden further education after high school. However, both Henry, the nonbeliever, and Elena consider the Catholic Church as a defining trait of their culture; other Christian denominations are viewed as upstarts and not sufficiently Mexican.

Henry, by committing himself to care for Angel and respect his niece's wishes, is forced to take Angel to his mother's church. Angel sees that his uncle does not feel comfortable and asks him why. Henry answers that "Most churches don't like gay people very much" and Angel reassures him that "Reverend Ortega is really nice" (242). Henry meets the minister at his place of work: the local mall. Ortega is a janitor and narrator Henry points out the contrast between the humble and hard-working pastor and his place of employment where "such essentials as German nose-hair clippers and two-thousand-dollar Italian suits" abound (273). His congregation cannot support him and his family, and Henry recognizes that Ortega's dedication to his people is not so different than his own dedication to the law: "There were vast divides of education and experience between Ortega and me, but we were at least of the same genus" (273).

In *Rag and Bone*, Henry and Elena are forced to face the fact that Mexican American gangs are stepping into an "identity" vacuum in poverty stricken Mexican American neighborhoods. Parental guidance is lax or the traditional stabilizing influences cannot compete with the twenty-first century's youth culture, poor education and lack of employment opportunities. From their positions of privilege (a lawyer and a university professor) they could have made an effort to step into this community and project a positive identity. But they were rejected by the Mexican Americans because of their sexual orientation and they in turn rejected the political Chicano community because of its emphasis on traditional values and culture, and are only now awakening to a sense of communal responsibility through a family experience.

In *The Hidden Law* and in *Rag and Bone*, Nava explores gang influence in Mexican American neighborhoods through Henry Rios' perspective. Two pivotal characters in these novels are both young men who are drug addicts, have become involved in gangs and whose social identification is confused, but whose ethnic identity is secure. In *The Hidden Law*, a young man, the son of wealthy and prominent Mexican Americans who have completely abandoned community ties and have left the care of their son to his *barrio* grandmother, searches for a powerful Mexican American identity by trying, unsuccessfully, to join a gang. He rejects his parents as imitators of Anglo culture and his grandmother's traditional humility as un–Chicano. Pete in *Rag and Bone* attempts to find a family, his father is dead, and to hide his homosexuality, his "weakness," by becoming a member of a gang.

In *Rag and Bone*, Henry gets a better understanding of the pressures these neighborhoods live with because he must visit Pete's mother, Angel's other "grandmother," Jesusita Trujillo in Garden Grove, south of Los Angeles. Jesusita, not unlike the *barrio* grandmother of *The Hidden Law*, is a widow who has worked all her life and owns her own home. But she must live behind a tall chain-link fence, barred windows and locked doors, as do all her neighbors (124). She would like to be as trusting of the young people in her neighborhood as the grandmother in *The Hidden Law*, but her neighborhood has become a battle ground. She is later beaten by gang members, young men who are actually related to her and are searching for her son.

Henry and Elena recognize how much Vicky looks like their mother but beneath her *chola* and Christian veneer she, unlike their mother, is capable against all odds of extricating herself from a no win situation. In Angel they see a survivor, intelligent and curious, like themselves. They step back from their middle-class identities and return to their childhood by taking a closer look at Vicky's Mexican American *barrio* to eventually realize that they are hers and Angel's *familia*.

In *Rag and Bone*, Henry meets a middle-class blue collar Mexican American for the first time in the series. John DeLeon, Mexican American, working-class, Catholic, a divorced father of two college students, an imperfectly reformed alcoholic, a fit former baseball player, a construction worker becomes Henry's first Mexican American lover. Through their relationship, Henry's identity conflicts— professional and working-class, English speaker and Spanish speaker, lower-class and middle-class, American and Mexican American, non-believer and Catholic, gay and straight, male and female — begin to be resolved.

John is not invincible, but he rolls with the punches. Henry finds him dirtied by his own vomit after a drinking binge. Bisexual John's girlfriend had called him a "faggot" and accused him of trying to give her AIDS (130). John's view of Mexican American homosexual relationships is rarely heard: "Most gay Latinos I meet are still pretty much into role-playing. One guy's the man, one guy's the woman" (71). He is equally critical of gay Anglos, "man, they treat each other like shit, like they're taking out on each other all the hate they have to deal with for being gay in the first place" (71). He refuses to follow the Mexican American norm: keep his love for another man hidden or, like his cousin, dress-up like a woman and live with mom. He also does not subscribe to the model of self-hate he has observed among Anglos.

In contrast to Henry, John has a close relationship with his family, has had a long-term relationship, marriage, and finds solace in Catholicism. Unlike Henry, his bouts of self-criticism are few and far between; he does not intellectualize or stereotype his identity. He accepts that he is "attracted to men and women" and does not allow himself to dwell on negative criticism thrown his way (70). His grown daughter has rejected him because of his homosexuality, but he is confident that she eventually will be able to accept him. He recognizes that it would be disrespectful of his Mexican workers' "different place" and "time" to kiss Henry in front of them, but he also requires that his workers respect the gay men who employ them to work on their homes (95). Henry recognizes that both he and John "come from the same world," and John concurs, but with a qualification: "we ended up in different ones" (203). Henry has lost his Mexican American identity and continues to struggle with his sexual identity, but through his relationship with John and his family is able to face both and begin to resolve the battle they have fought inside him for so many years.

John has never left the world he came from; Henry is still trying to understand the Mexican American male identity that they share does not necessarily need to be homophobic or misogynist. John's father comes to talk with Henry and gets straight to the point, "John says he's in love with you" (236). Immediately Henry becomes "tongue-twistingly lawyerly even to [himself]" (236). Henry comments that when the senior Mr. DeLeon speaks Spanish he *does*, as John has told him, sound like a "formidable patriarch" (237). However, Henry is surprised because Mr. DeLeon's message is not the condemnation that Henry's own father would have expressed. Henry hears from John's father that "God gives us children to love, not to hate" and for that reason his message is: "In my house, you will always be treated with respect" (237). The senior Mr. DeLeon's brother committed suicide because their father rejected his homosexuality.

Both the autobiographer Rodriguez and the novelist Nava have, through different genres, made peace with their conflictive identities. Rodriguez asks in *Brown*, "The way we are constructed constructs love? Limits love? (We die.) The making of love? No. That is a heresy. God so loved the world that the Word became incarnate, condescended to mortal clay. God became brown. True God and true man. Where there's a will there's a way" (207). Nava concludes *Rag and Bone*, his last detective novel with a similar but secular expression of acceptance.

As Henry Rios sits down with his nephew Angel to watch a baseball game on television and remembers that "[w]here once I would have spent hours wondering about the meaning of life and my place in it, now I am more apt to wonder what to give Angel for dinner. A much smaller question, to be sure, but one to which there is at least a concrete answer" (*Rag and Bone* 289). Rodriguez, like Elena, resolves the conflict between his Catholicism and his homosexuality and by accepting a paradox. Henry resolves the conflict between his domineering controlling self and his homosexuality by recognizing the positive qualities of his "masculine" control and his "feminine" sensitivity. Henry has questioned the usefulness of an ethnic identity, but concludes that an ethnic identity, like his gay identity, is ultimately like family. For him family is something that you accept with love and respect.

Neither Rodriguez's autobiographies nor Nava's detective novels present a clear dialectic. For both of them, Rodriguez and the fictional Henry Rios, "white" does not offer as clear a dialectical contrast as it does for many writers of ethnic literatures. This is not because they have not felt marginalized by their skin color or ethnicity, but because, as Rodriguez states to become an "American" in "white" America requires "an acid bath" that results in the absence of color. The hermetic "white" detective does not openly recognize that his absence of color is what he fears most. Without color, Philip Marlowe may be colored by the many others of Los Angeles (Abbott 27). Nava and Rodriguez show that Marlowe's fear was indeed well founded. Marlowe, the hard-boiled *white* detective, is no longer distinguished by his "whiteness." His "whiteness," his invisibility, was appropriated by Nava's detective and the young autobiographer of *Hunger of Memory*, only to be rejected later by both as valueless. For the mature Rodriguez, brown colors life, and presents a vibrant contrast to white invisibility. What Henry Rios has feared most is himself — the Mexican American male — was invisible. When brought again to his conscious, Henry is able to complete his identity, Mexican and gay American, and abandon the hermetic white male detective persona that *literarily* obscured his ethnicity.

In the "Acknowledgements" that follow *Rag and Bone,* Nava states: "This book brings to an end this series of mysteries." *Rag and Bone* breaks with Nava's six previous detective novels, and most definitely with the hard-boiled genre itself. In all the previous novels the crime has been inflicted upon or committed by someone outside of the detective's family. Now the crime has come home and the work-alcoholic lawyer's "client" is his own family, and he must get to know them in order to defend them. The hard-boiled detective who had previously personified the series disappears and Nava ends his "career as a mystery writer" after investigating the mystery of his own family (*Rag and Bone* "Acknowledgements").

# 7

## More *Salsa*

### *Latino Detective Fiction in the United States; and Interviews with the Chicano Chefs Anaya, Corpi, Hinojosa, Nava and Ramos*

In 1944 Joseph Wood Krutch wrote "Only a Detective Story," an essay that is included in Haycraft's collection of literature on the genre. Krutch, a critic and biographer, was an editor for the *Nation* and a professor of English at Columbia University. Before writing his essay he read about 150 volumes of mystery tales in one year. "Even this, I realize, leaves me still a novice," he wrote (179). As for me, I don't even know my prayers in comparison. In the body of this book I've explored in detail only one novel each of the 21 written by five Chicano authors. Below are introductions to other Latino authors, including six Chicanos, writing in the United States and its territories. These are 19 authors who have written more than 30 novels.

Something new is happening in detective fiction. It began in the United States with authors who wrote about themselves; their detectives were women or African Americans. Now there are Latino and Native American detectives (and perhaps Asian American and Pacific Islanders). Mainstream authors are also taking a different perspective toward the minority detectives they create by writing from an informed and intelligent stance that was unheard of in Krutch's time. Two examples are Tony Hillerman in the United States and Alexander McCall Smith from Scotland.

Americans Dashiell Hammett and Raymond Chandler transformed the British classic. For Haycraft's critical volume of 1946, Chandler wrote:

> How original a writer Hammett really was, it isn't easy to decide
> now, even if it mattered. He was one of a group, the only one who
> achieved critical recognition, but not the only one who wrote or
> tried to write realistic mystery fiction. All literary movements are
> like this; some one individual is picked out to represent the whole
> movement; he is usually the culmination of the movement ["The
> Simple Art of Murder" 233].

At some point in time there may be one "minority" writer recognized, as
Chandler is now in for the hard-boiled genre, as the primary example of
a new interpretation of detective fiction, but at this time the field is open.

In my research I have identified twenty-four Latino authors. Why
are there so few? In speaking with Manuel Ramos, he suggested one explanation: "We're a full dimensional community of people, and characters in
books have to portray all dimensions or the book is not very realistic."
Expanding on his point, it is necessary to note that crime committed by
members of marginalized communities has been the fodder of the mainstream genre, therefore it is not surprising that writers whose cultures
have been treated with disrespect are reluctant to present "a full dimensional community" to the reading public.

Chandler wrote: "Murder, which is a frustration of the individual
and hence a frustration of the race, may, and in fact has, a good deal of
sociological implication" (223). The classic novel of England divorced the
sociological implications from the crime itself. Murder became a parlor
game where an outsider could always arouse suspicion. Chandler and the
Latino writers in the United States do not shy away from realistic connections. Chandler had a good ear for the life in the alleys and dives of Los
Angeles, even though he did not live there. Historically the alleys and ten-
ements of urbanity have been the residence of minorities in the United
States. Chandler portrayed them realistically from a 1940s segregated distance, and unfortunately his minority characters served the same function
as those in the English classic novel.

In Latino fiction, murder stories from an insiders' point of view have
been few, but times are changing. Latinos are no longer relegated to urban
ghettos, but have become upwardly mobile. This is a diverse community
now looking at all its members. Their detective fiction crisscrosses all segments of the U.S. population because this is Latino contemporary reality.

A span of almost thirty years separates Rudy Apodaca's two detective
novels. His *Waxen Image*, published in 1977, was the first Chicano whodunit. To the best of my knowledge this was the first mystery written by
a Latino in the United States. When published, however, the novel's focus
on an African idol, an Anglo protagonist and the use of a popular mid-

dle-class genre — the problem-to-be solved detective novel — limited its critical Chicano audience, and it was generally ignored by the mainstream audience.

It may have received wider interest if it were published today. It is no longer a convention that Latino authors must limit their creations to the confines an Hispanic milieu. The three detective novels of Martín Limón take place in Korea. Sergio Troncoso's recent psychological crime thriller, *The Nature of Truth*, explores New Haven, Connecticut. While the majority of Chicano detective fiction is set in the Southwest and focuses on the lives of Mexican Americans, the genre, with the possible exception of Rudolfo Anaya's *Sonny Baca* series, has grown away from the "nostalgic panegyrics to the movement" common among "old guard Chicano activists" (Novoa 116). Below I introduce seven new novels, three old hands, four new authors, an exciting array of settings, protagonists and characters for further reading of Chicano detective fiction.

## Rudy Apodaca: Pursuit (2003)

Rudy Apodaca, now retired after more than thirty-five years as a lawyer and judge in his native New Mexico, has a new novel, *Pursuit*. For this mystery, Apodaca calls on his experience as a jurist and as a family man. He has justifiably dedicated this second work to his four children, and his wife who has accompanied him throughout his career.

*Pursuit* moves back and forth from New Mexico to Washington, D.C. Apodaca describes these locales with the confidence of someone who knows them well, easing the task of the reader and enhancing the pleasure of exploring these settings. Unlike many detective novelists, Apodaca takes the time to explain the inner workings of the justice system, surveillance, police procedure and the coordination of special police forces when confronted with hostage situations. *Pursuit* uses the Vietnam War to question government oversight of military spending. It is a timely topic during the continuing conflict in Iraq. Apodaca's presentation of graft and mismanagement during the Vietnam War shows careful research.

This is not a short novel. Three plots intersect and each one works to create tension in the protagonist's life. John Garcia, a successful lawyer who has not practiced criminal law for eight years, agrees to defend the son of a former client — a Mexican American laborer whom he defended in a civil case — against the charge of attempted murder. Garcia soon observes that he is being followed and finds out that his wife has noticed a strange car parked in their neighborhood. The surveillance is related to his experience as a soldier in Vietnam, and a second mystery, in contrast with the murder case, evolves.

The murder case and the story of wartime intrigue underscore and aggravate the tension in Garcia's marriage and this presents a third and personal mystery. Will John and Deli Garcia's marriage survive these additional pressures? This anatomy of a marriage sets the novel apart from the majority of detective fiction and is rewarding reading. Written in the third person and told from the perspective of Garcia, the novel provides an intelligent and sympathetic view of the pressures that assault any couple when the vocation of one assumes more importance than their life partnership.

## Martín Limón: Buddha's Money (1998)

A retired U.S. Army officer, well educated in the Chinese language and culture who spent ten years of service in Korea, Limón has written a series of three mystery novels. These take place in Korea and feature George Sueño and Ernie Bascom, a contrasting pair of M.P.s. In addition to his novels, Limón has published short stories in the *Alfred Hitchcock Mystery Magazine*.

*Buddha's Money* starts with an assault on a Buddhist nun, moves on to the abduction of a young Korean girl working for all practical purposes as a slave, then connects the two crimes with a dark and terrible Mongol Buddhist sect from mainland China. As in the earlier novels, *Jade Lady Burning* (1992) and *Slicky Boys* (1997), the action is fast paced, rough and sometimes unsavory. Bascom, Sueño's Anglo buddy from Vietnam, is the push and grab arm of the pair, whereas Sueño, who speaks Korean, is the communicator. Both take their share of hard knocks. Giving a local flavor to the story, Limón spares no detail in presenting the sights, sounds, smells and language of Korea.

In an interview published in 1998, Limón said that he was at work on a novel that would bring George Sueño home to East L.A. to find his "long-lost father" (*Troutworks* "Interview"). Limón, a L.A. County native whose family roots go back to the state of Sonora, Mexico, was born in Compton and grew up in Gardena. Perhaps we can anticipate that Sueño's search for his father will reflect some of Limón's own background: his father fought in the Pacific during World War II and his grandparents immigrated to Los Angeles during the Mexican Revolution.

## *Max Martínez:* Layover *(1997)*

"Redneck noir" is what Ramos calls the genre written by Martínez. *White Leg* (1996) and *Layover* are set in Martínez's native south Texas and dissect the poverty the late Martínez knew and observed (Ramos "Chicano detectives"). These crime novels explore the rural life of Anglo and Mexican Texans. Racism and intermarriage fuel the mix.

In the first novel, Deputy Sheriff Joe Blue, a Mexican Anglo who leans toward his Mexican side, has to investigate his Anglo cousin. Poverty, sustained by a lack of opportunity, fuels the frustrations of the protagonist. In both *White Leg* and *Layover*, the primary focus is on the criminal. *White Leg* offers a Chicano vision of despair that recalls the Spanish classic *La Familia de Pascual Duarte* (1942) by Camilo José Cela. Blue's cousin is pushed by poverty and a lack of education into a maelstrom of violence.

*Layover* is not as dark perhaps because it more closely follows the suspense genre and the protagonist does not live in poverty. There is a beautiful and intelligent San Antonio Chicana who has lost her way, an enterprising Mexican American Vietnam vet and the dead body of the son and heir to the local white trash petty crime family. Martínez skillfully leads the reader down false trails without resorting to exotic improbabilities. The novel is about promiscuity, female assertiveness, marijuana farming, rural crime and money. As in *White Leg*, Blue is the investigator and his role requires perseverance and intelligence, but no extraordinary qualifications when honesty and dedication are attributes of police officers. This character is unassuming, but not unassertive.

Mr. Martínez also wrote *Schoolland* (1988), a *bildungsroman* set in 1950 rural Texas, and *A Red Bikini Dream* (1989), a collection of five stories that describe Chicanos in contemporary settings from New York City to rural Texas. Martínez is one of the few Chicanos to have been included on the Best Texas Writer list of the "Texas Monthy" ("Max Martínez, interview").

## *Ricardo Means Ybarra:* Brotherhood of Dolphins *(1997)*

A poet and novelist, Ybarra's venture into crime reflects both of his talents as writer. Ybarra, a sixth generation *Californio*, knows his people and his home well. His descriptions of urban Los Angeles County and southern beach towns resonate with atmospheric sounds, sights and smells.

The beauty of the Sea of Cortez as seen from the Baja California coastline encourages the reader to swim with the dolphins despite the violence portrayed in this setting.

The protagonist, Pete Escobedo, is a Los Angeles Police Department detective, but the novel does not focus on his limited investigative skills. Rather crime — the scenes of crimes, the action of pursuit and confrontation of the criminal — pushes the detective to explore memories of childhood and youth that he had been reluctant to confront. The investigation forces his return to his Echo Park and Chavez Ravine neighborhood where he confronts the contradictions of his life. Pete is a very complex character in conflict with himself, his past and the females close to him.

There are three novels masquerading as one in *Brotherhood of Dolphins*. One is a love story that involves Pete and a much younger Carmen, a childhood friend and currently a student at Stanford. Another, not fully developed, is the story of a Sylvia, a Chicana fire fighter. This character, like Pete, records a conflict between traditional male and female roles and the changing expectations and opportunities of Mexican American women. Sylvia's relationship with her African American co-worker causes distress among the men of Echo Park. This relationship and Sylvia's professionalism as a firefighter along with the crime of arson could make another novel.

The third storyline is that of the deranged villain. This character is intriguing, but his background and motivation, well told from his perspective, leave many questions unanswered. All three histories converge around the 1986 arson-caused fire that resulted in the destruction of Los Angeles's sixty-year-old central library built by Mexican brick layers, a group that included Sylvia's father. Ybarra brings complex *Californio* history to his story and treats the genre with innovation and insight.

## Sheila Ortiz Taylor: Coachella (1998)

Ortiz Taylor's *Coachella* takes another real life "mystery," the spread of AIDS in the Coachella Valley of California in 1983, and creates a detective novel distinguished by its multiple perspectives. Generally when whodunit authors return to the scene of an actual crime it is one committed by a single person with the intent to harm. The spread of AIDS in the Coachella Valley was not intentional, unless the attitude of the residents toward its gay population can be viewed as premeditated. Prejudices toward homosexuals and minority ethnicities are shown as the result of fear and lack of knowledge. Ortiz Taylor's novel asks the reader to join the lone detective-phlebotomist Yolanda Ramírez, and together form a community that will not allow public negligence to be committed in its name.

Yolanda not only investigates the blood supply at the local hospital where she works, but also delves into her Indian and Mexican ancestry that have challenged her lesbian identity. In the hospital and in the community she confronts prejudices and hypocrisy that support the dominant Anglo heterosexual medical industry in their refusal to consider that blood, not sex practices per se, is the primary carrier of AIDS.

Yolanda's nickname "Yo," the Spanish word for "I," functions in this third person novel to form a bond between the reader and the protagonist. This is perhaps the most subtle of the literary devices used by Ortiz Taylor in this innovative narrative. The perspective is constantly changing between more than four characters, principals like Yolanda and secondary figures like the hapless wife of the hospital director who is infected by the blood supply.

Ethnic vanity and heterosexual arrogance contribute to the deaths of several Anglo women and confirm Yolanda's hypothesis. The "mystery" in 2004, is not the transmission of AIDS, but continues to be, as in 1983, the lack of concern for the spread of AIDS within minority populations. This problem outlined in Ortiz Taylor's novel and the current one avoid solutions because of uninformed allegiance to traditional values in the majority and minority communities.

Ortiz Taylor, a California native and a professor of English at Florida State University, is an award winning scholar and a renowned Chicana author of novels, poetry, essays and literary criticism.

## *Sergio Troncoso:* The Nature of Truth *(2003)*

Son of Mexican immigrants and a native of El Paso, Troncoso is not afraid of taking an off center view of his heritage. He mixes Mexican and German, the Southwest and European haunts of World War II Nazis. A graduate of Harvard and Yale, Troncoso, in the tradition of Dostoevsky, brings philosophy to the crime novel.

Akin to Martínez in *White Leg* and Ybarra in *Brotherhood of Dolphins*, he explores the inner workings of the mind of his criminal protagonist. However, in *The Nature of Truth* the role of investigator and criminal are not easily distinguished.

Sexual abuse, the Holocaust, scholarly investigation, academic power plays and the politics of a prestigious university in conjunction with the poverty, racism and crime of New Haven all combine for a heady mix of

violence and reflection. The protagonist, son of a German soldier and a
Mexican American mother and a graduate student at Yale, explores his
European roots through the personality and professional life of his men-
tor, a German national, Professor Werner Hopfgartner.

Suspense is maintained by the characterization of protagonist Helmut Sanchez. The narrator suggests a conflict between his German ancestry and his Mexican American heritage. His commitment to Ariane — his
love interest — first presented as the object of his sexual desire, is continually suspect. The reader is in doubt until practically the last page as to
whether Helmut is truthful with Ariane. The same can be said for his relationship with Hopfgartner. It is difficult to predict whether his admiration for, or aberration of his mentor will dominate, and whether Helmut's
rational logical self or emotional self will control his behavior. The plot
perhaps suffers from the enormity of its topics, but the youthful angst of
the protagonist rings true.

Troncoso teaches at Yale and recently won the Premio Aztlán for his
first published work: *The Last Tortilla and Other Stories.*

## *Alicia Gaspar de Alba:* Desert Blood/ The Juarez Murders *(2005)*

More than 250 young women have been brutally murdered in Juárez,
Mexico, since the early '90s. Despite outrage on both sides of the border
the Mexican government has been unconscionably lax in its investigation.
Gaspar de Alba is a native of El Paso, Texas, the U.S. city that looks at its
neighbor, Ciudad Juárez, from across the Rio Grande.

These killings and the lack of interest shown by the Mexican government have led to rumors, investigative journalism articles and literary
treatments of the topic. In Gaspar de Alba's novel the protagonist, Ivon
Villa, has arranged to adopt the unborn child of a young Mexican national
and resident of Juárez. The mother-to-be, Cecilia, falls victim to the crime
wave. Then Ivon's younger sister disappears.

Gaspar de Alba interweaves the cultural bias against Ivon, her lesbian
protagonist, and the lack of interest on the part of the authorities in the
exploitation of women sex workers. Ivon begins to investigate and with
the help of four others, including a rookie detective, is able to contribute
some insight into the motivation for the crime wave and the lack of interest on the part of the authorities.

The novel explores "the use of Internet tourist sites, forced contra-
ception, illegal medical testing, and the inhumane working conditions in

the maquiladoras [factories, held by foreign corporations that manufacture export products]" of Juárez in addition to the corruption of government agencies on both sides of the border, according to the author's synopsis provided by Arte Público Press (Gaspar de Alba).

Gaspar de Alba has also written another novel, *Sor Juana's Dream* (1999), short stories, poetry and critical studies.

Mexican Americans comprise the largest group of Hispanics in the United States: 58.5 percent of this population in the year 2000 according to U.S. census figures. The second and third largest single groups are Puerto Ricans (9.6 percent) and Cuban Americans (3.5 percent). Hispanic is not a racial descriptor; Hispanics come in every color, including "white." The overwhelming majority of U.S. residents of Hispanic origin are from the Americas; only one-twentieth of 1 percent is from Spain.

Puerto Ricans, residing on mainland United States or on the island, are U.S. citizens and in approximately equal numbers reside in Puerto Rico as on the mainland. Both Spanish and English are spoken and taught in Puerto Rico. The majority of Puerto Ricans residing on the mainland live in the Northeast and the majority of Hispanics living in New York continue to be of Puerto Rican descent.[1]

## *Soledad Santiago:* Room 9, a Novel of Suspense *(1992)*

Santiago, born Sabire Vural of Swiss-Turkish parentage, came to the United States when she was ten years old. She has lived in Anglo and Puerto Rican communities and, judging from her name, identifies positively with her Hispanic neighbors.

*Room 9* is one of three novels she has written and is, in my opinion, her best mystery genre work. *Nightside* (1996) is more akin to a police procedural and *Streets of Fire* (1996) is episodic, which is logical as much as it was originally written as a serial for *New York Newsday*. All three of Santiago's novels reflect her activist background and her experience as a single mother who divorced a drug-addicted husband.

In *Room 9*, Santiago expertly weaves trust and love with corruption and betrayal. This is a book that makes one glad to be just reading the detective genre and not living in this milieu; the story will end and hopefully the situation described will improve. The portraits of rich and powerful New Yorkers contrast sharply with those of the homeless, drug dealers, addicts and juvenile prostitutes. However, the truly bad guys are corrupt politicians who betray the city's trust.

The Latino flavor of Miami and New York City figure prominently in the narrative. The protagonist, Maria Terranova, is the 38-year-old widow of a police officer shot mysteriously in the line of duty. She has a 12-year-old son who is trying to rebel and a grumpy old-country Italian mom. As the mayor's administrative assistant, Maria is put in contact with a Cuban American newspaper reporter. "Room 9" is the pressroom at New York's City Hall.

The protagonists of her other two novels are female police officers of Puerto Rican descent. They are tough ladies, in contrast to the rather timid Terranova. However, this protagonist learns the ropes with the help of her Cuban American friend and lover. Not only does she actively investigate government corruption, but she also stakes out her independence as a woman and learns to make accommodations in relationship to her son's developing maturity and responsibility.

## Ana Lydia Vega: Pasión de historia y otras historias de pasión (1987)

A professor at the University of Puerto Rico, Vega, born on and a resident of the island, has been interested in crime and passion from the age of eighteen when she wrote stories in English that are unpublished and jealously guarded to this date (Colón 1). *Pasión de historias y otras historias de pasión*, a collection of short stories, won the prestigious Juan Rulfo International Prize. Two of the stories, "Pasión de historia" and "Caso Omiso," cleverly rework formulaic genres of hard-boiled detective fiction and contemporary horror. The influence of Daphne du Maurier, Agatha Christie, Alfred Hitchcock, Stephen King and Raymond Chandler's adaptations of the genre, both written and cinematographic, all contribute to these narratives.

The language in Vega's stories reflects contemporary usage in Puerto Rico, with its infusions of English and regional Spanish vocabulary and construction. Reading the dialog and descriptions in her stories is similar to reading the best of Chandler. Though written in a tongue in cheek style with humorous laugh out loud moments, these narratives are deadly serious.

Vega's perspective is decidedly feminist. When the question is "passion," men pull together to support brutal men, but women condemn women whose passion is nonviolent. These stories require that the reader reconsider how men view women, how women see themselves and why many women see themselves from a male perspective. "Pasión de historia" underscores a lack of solidarity among women.

Suspense is Vega's strong point, but the interaction between the characters and the settings, from San Juan to provincial France, are well presented. The movement and vibrancy of the Puerto Rican settings and people contrast with the static and tension-laden French.

Three Cuban Americans— Alex Abella, Carolina Garcia-Aguilera and John Lantigua — have put together a volume of work initiated in 1987 with Lantigua's *Heat Lightning*. Between them, there are now fourteen published detective novels. Back on Castro's island in 1971, a genre never before explored by native authors was initiated. Translations of detective fiction had been popular since the 1920s, but Cuban authors were few and those that wrote followed the British formula. However since the triumph of revolution of 1958, Fidel Castro's strict guidelines—"'Our art and our literature should be valuable means of educating youth within revolutionary morality'"— have attempted to dictate an ideological agenda for the genre (Simpson 98–99). Rolando Hinojosa recommends two Cuban nationals who write in Spanish, live in Cuba and have been critically acclaimed: Amir Valle and Leonardo Padura. They manage to bend the island guidelines and write great mysteries. Cubans and Cuban Americans are resourceful and in the United States have had their say using what East German critic Ernst Kaemmel called a "Capitalist" genre (56). Lantigua, Abella and Garcia-Aguilera are talented writers who present distinct viewpoints and adaptations of the detective genre.

## *John Lantigua:* Player's Vendetta, a Little Havana Mystery *(1999)*

Lantigua, of Caribbean heritage — a Cuban father and a Puerto Rican mother — is a novelist and a journalist who won the Pulitzer Prize as an investigative reporter for the *Miami Herald*. He has published five detective novels.

The *player* in the *vendetta* was a "Peter Pan" kid. In 1962 many Cubans, hoping for the best, but frightened for their children or having no way out for themselves, put boys and girls on airplanes and sent them to the United States. These children were divided among participating families all over the United States, or arrived on the doorsteps of family friends or relatives. *Player's Vendetta* is a political novel about U.S. involvement in Cuba.

But it is for the reader to decide if mistakes were made and if there might be something to be learned from this history.

The protagonist, detective Willie Cuesta, is a divorced single man. His former wife, a Cuban, was a "boat" person, and his widowed mom owns a *botanica* (hers is a combination herbal and religious "drug store"). Dad was a musician and both parents were Cuban refugees. Willie came to the United States as a baby with his parents and has no memory of his native land. He was formerly an intelligence police officer in Miami, but is now a private detective.

Gambling is the focus of the novel; the Spanish translation of the title takes its name from the poker chip that Player brought with him as a child: *La ficha roja*, "the red chip." In pre–Revolutionary Cuba, the Mafia controlled gaming and pocketed the majority of the money. The involvement of the Mafia in these gambling casinos represented a convergence of interest between the United States and the Mafia in regard to communism on the island. The confusion of the last days and weeks before the United States broke relations with Cuba forms the background for this novel, which explores loyalties that have endured decades. The crimes are not committed by nostalgic Cubans, but their nostalgia is portrayed as mind altering, self-debilitating and a danger to themselves and others.

## *Alex Abella:* Final Acts *(2000)*

Abella with his parents came to the United States from Cuba as a child in 1961. He is a journalist and creative writer who has worked for the *San Francisco Chronicle* and in television where, as a reporter for KTVU, he won an Emmy for the Best Breaking News Story in 1982. He has written drama, a nongenre novel and three detective stories. His first mystery was *The Killing of the Saints* (1991).

In *Final Acts*, the story unfolds in two first person narratives. Abella shows his skill as a dramatist with these highly contrasting voices. Rita Carr — Chicana Irish lawyer, with little skills in Spanish, young, hip and just starting her own private legal practice — tells her story. Charlie Morrell, a prominent attorney, fortyish, graying-at-the-temples handsome, a classy dresser and fluent in the language of his Cuban birthplace, writes his history. Abella gives a plausible *chola*[2] edge to Carr's narrative and makes Morrell's long autobiographical letter — broken into parts in the novel — sound like the English a native speaker of Spanish would write.

The premise of the novel revolves around a series of ritual killings that Morrell is accused of have having orchestrated and that carry the signs of an African Cuban religious cult identified as "Abakuá." The beleaguered lawyer chooses novice attorney Rita as his legal council because he has apparently burned all his bridges in the legal communities of northern and southern California.

This novel also takes a political stance. Any positive social changes that might have come from Castro's revolution have been severely compromised by his opening of the country to commercial tourism. As in Batista's 1950s capitalist regime, foreign tourists and investors in destination sites are subjecting the majority of the population to the power of a moneyed class. While in Cuba investigating the cult in attempt to exonerate himself, Morrell talks to Lee (named for Robert E. Lee) Gutiérrez, deputy head of security for Havana and an officer of the Interior Ministry. In reference to a ritual killing by members of the Abakuá cult, Gutiérrez comments, "This, this horror you just saw, is the product of capitalism. We never had it before this..." (156). The accusation is that Castro has encouraged native cultural traditions not because of their intrinsic value, but rather to bring international tourism to the island.

Abella's language provides a poignant description of a beckoning tourist destination: "At the far end of the bay that opens like a crooked smile at the docile Caribbean I can see the rhomboids, spheres, and cylinders of the other Cuba, the one where tourists flock, the country of domesticated communism, syrupy ballads, and spicy guarachas, fabricated for foreign consumption out of the hopes of a starving revolution" (297).

## *Carolina Garcia-Aguilera:* Bloody Secrets *(1998)*

Garcia-Aguilera knows her trade; her seven *Lupe Solano* mysteries show a wonderful conversational familiarity with the genre that make them extremely readable additions to the North American canon of detective fiction. Garcia-Aguilera was born in Cuba, came in her parents' arms to the United States in 1960, studied history and political science as an undergraduate and language and linguistics for her Master's degree.

Her novels are political and romantic, with more emphasis on the latter. Lupe Solano, her protagonist comes from an elite Miami Cuban American family. In *Bloody Secrets*, Solano's conflicts with her family stem from differences of opinion as to the proper role of women. Garcia-Aguilera is adept at employing many conventions of the genre. References to name brand products act as cultural markers of the well educated and affluent first wave of Cuban immigrants, and suspicion falls on the subsequent waves of the less-than-white labor-class former islanders.

This fast-paced and entertaining novel's themes are the Cuban homeland, the reestablishment of privilege and the abandonment by the U.S. government of the Bay of Pigs invaders. Private detective Solano's client was betrayed by a powerful married couple of the Miami exile community. Their betrayal is mitigated by the fact that this couple have used their money to establish a fund for a post–Castro government in Cuba. The reader is adroitly led to erroneous summations of the action, but is rewarded by a conclusion that follows the logic of the text and subscribes to the classical whodunit tradition.

Garcia-Aguilera is no slouch. In addition to her education mentioned above, she has a degree in finance, has studied Latin American literature at the Ph.D. level, interned at an investigative agency in Miami and has worked as a private investigator ("Carolina Garcia-Aguilera").

A documented 66,520 Central Americans immigrated to the United States in 2002, half of whom were from El Salvador. Ninety percent of all Hispanic immigrants who have originated their journey in South America and south of the Mexican border are Central Americans. Even with the tremendous problems in Colombia, El Salvador with only a fifteenth of Colombia's population sends almost twice the number of immigrants to the United States. Central Americans live all over the United States. In the southern United States, Hispanics who do not belong to the larger immigrant groups, Mexican Americans, Puerto Ricans and Cuban Americans, outnumber the combined population of these groups.

## *Marcos McPeek Villatoro:* Home Killings, a Romilia Charcón Mystery *(2001)*

McPeek Villatoro attended the Iowa Writers' Workshop and currently is a professor of creative writing and Latin American fiction at Mount St. Mary's College in Los Angeles. He has written a volume of poetry, a memoir and an autobiographical novel. In *Home Killings* he uses his knowledge of his mother's native country, El Salvador, his experiences in Guatemala and his knowledge of his father's native Tennessee. *Home Killings* was his first mystery novel. The sympathetic Ms. Charcón appears again in *Minos* (2005) and *A Venom Beneath the Skin* (2005).

Romilia has just moved to Nashville with her mother and young son from Atlanta where they have lived for several years. She is hired as a homicide detective, a new job for this policewoman. Because Nashville has a growing Latino population and no Spanish-speaking detectives Romilia is able to take a step up on the career ladder. Her mom, who only speaks Spanish, is unhappy about the move because she misses their Hispanic neighborhood in Atlanta. Grandmother, mother and little boy have to make an adjustment to a new city and a life outside the *barrio*.

David Sáenz, the bilingual reporter for the local paper, is murdered. Romilia's careful treatment of evidence, her ability to speak Spanish and English and her familiarity with her mother's history — a refugee from the civil wars of El Salvador — help her solve a difficult case. The author weaves drug trafficking, police corruption, illicit love and the historic death squads of Guatemala into a convincing and exciting mystery.

Customs of the various Hispanic populations of Nashville and the mysteries of the hot Cold War in Central America provide interesting reading. Character development, including that of the multifaceted protagonist Romilia, is solid. She has always had a problem controlling her temper, which makes her job more difficult, but at the same time is a loving mom and daughter. Her volatile and domestic personality, uncommon in the genre, adds to the interest and suspense of the novel.

According to the novels of Eric Garcia, another minority group, some of whose members have Spanish surnames, compose a significant percentage of the current U.S. population. To date, I have not found any demographic information about this population. However, Garcia who has documented their experience in his *Victor Rubio* novels assures his readers that dinosaurs make up about 10 percent of the total U.S. population.

## *Eric Garcia:* Anonymous Rex *(2000)*

Victor Rubio is a dinosaur, with an Hispanic last name, a pervasive odor of Cuban cigars, no family connections, conversational in L.A.-Spanish and English, distrustful of any species of minor intelligence, suspicious of teleological narratives and transformative states of mind. With humor and without referring to specific ethnicities, the *Victor Rubio* series confirms that minority persecution is pervasive and the benefits of claiming an exclusive ancestral identity are dubious.

In *Anonymous Rex*, the first novel of three in the series, Rubio describes the parameters of the dinosaur's life in human society. Imagine that you have a large anatomical appendage that is necessary for balance and defense and that it is held against your body by a cumbersome and at times painful array of clips and elastics and that, along with the rest of your anatomy, it is contorted underneath a tight fitting suit. This is what Rubio suffers with his tail everyday. The dinosaur-detective comments, "All it takes is one slipup from any of us ... and the last hundred and thirty million years of a persecution-free environment could all be over" (162). Presumably shot, or at best locked up in zoos, all the dinosaurs would be systematically rounded up and their properties confiscated. Garcia may be writing about dinosaurs, but their story sounds familiar. Haven't some human populations disguised their differences in order to meld with a majority population intent on their destruction? The Dinosaur Council polices conformity to the disguise. Of course, as humans we are familiar with various types of group-imposed acts of conformity to the majority population.

The Dinosaur Council firmly maintains that scientific evidence has proven that different species of these ancient reptiles cannot mate. A bi-species dinosaur would initiate the loss of identity. Each ancient reptilian species has distinctive physical features and personality characteristics. Rubio comments to himself while at the meeting of the L.A. chapter of the Dinosaur Council: "Most of all, they are worried that they will lose their identity. But it is pointless to fret in this manner, we lost it a long time ago" (208). The council members do not see the perversity of their stance: they live their lives from birth to death disguised and acting as humans, yet insist on the preservation of an unseen identity. Whereas humans of different ethnicities are successful at cross-ethnic reproduction, many races, ethnicities and religions forbid mixed matches. Some of us, akin to the dinosaurs, allow ourselves to be divided by allegiances to exclusive group identities that do not serve any practical purpose.

Rubio is proud to be a "Velociraptor," but among humans he cannot express this pride. When "Compys," the dinosaur dunces, participate in an exclusive dino event, the detective compares the repugnance he feels toward them to what he feels toward many humans. It's a toss up, because ultimately he values an intelligent intelligence. The detective respects the multifaceted. Therefore even an extremely competent human who is unwilling to inspect other forms of intelligence is as lacking as the Compy who doggedly follows the path he knows.

When labels are employed paradoxical problems arise. In an interview, Garcia states that the *Victor Rubio* series is comedy, but booksellers insist on shelving the novels with mysteries. He would prefer that all fiction were shelved together, *but* then "any damn lit major [would be] reading my pulp novel" (qtd. by Soyka).

Garcia was born in Miami, Florida, studied at Cornell and the University of Southern California where he pursued creative writing and filmmaking. In his short career he has written three *Victor Rubio* novels and the screenplay for the movie *Matchstick Men* based on his novel of the same title.

For Latinos the detective genre provides a functional armature for the discussion of contemporary socioeconomic, political and cultural conflicts. When presented with the opportunity to publish my dissertation on Chicano detective fiction, I suggested that I would like to interview the authors. I knew the fictional detectives— Sonny Baca, Gloria Damasco, Rafe Buenrostro, Henry Rios and Luis Montez — after having spent two years reading and evaluating novels, but I was curious to meet their creators— Rudolfo Anaya, Lucha Corpi, Rolando Hinojosa, Michael Nava and Manuel Ramos— and learn how they felt about their mysteries.

I formulated my questions based on assumptions I drew from reading their novels, my experience as a reader-student of mysteries and as a teacher. Chicano detective fiction is written by active members of a socially conscious group and reflects contemporary regional Mexican American populations. I did not feel that the social issues of the novels were presented for a didactic purpose or directed to a particular audience. I relax reading detective fiction, but I also value it as an educational tool. Because it is more accessible than a "highbrow" variety of literature, it can introduce the basic components of the novel to anyone able to read who has the patience to spend time in this pursuit. It has been my job to read between the lines and discover those subliminal associations with literatures that cannot be purged from any writing. But, I wanted to know from the authors, which were their favorite mystery stories.

As a wannabe writer of fiction, I have a vested interest in the writing process, so I asked them what advice they might offer to students interested in writing detective genre fiction. All five authors received the same questions.[3]

I have organized these "interviews" by presenting the written responses first. These were received by mail and email from Rudolfo Anaya and Rolando Hinojosa. I was unable to interview Michael Nava, but have included information from his conversations with Philip Gambone that answer some of the questions I posed to the other four authors. My phone conversations with Lucha Corpi and Manuel Ramos are presented last. I have decided on this organizational scheme because the written word is the center for the authors and myself. The spoken word breaks the eggs, heats the tortillas and selects the chiles for the salsa. In other words, I assume that a written answer has been edited, by the author or the interviewer, whereas an oral response is less structured. I have therefore used the written interviews as an outline, a recipe, to aid in editing my conversations with Corpi and Ramos.[4]

## Rudolfo Anaya

Born in the small town of Pastura on the eastern plains of New Mexico, Anaya has lived and worked close to his New Mexican roots. He has published nine novels, seen seven of his nine plays produced, edited numerous collections of fiction and nonfiction, and has written four children's books. This abbreviated list also includes a journal of his travels in China, *A Chicano in China* (1986). His productive career began with *Bless Me, Última* in 1972. His writings have been published in translation in Mexico, Russia, France, Germany, Italy and Japan. He has lectured in Mexico, Central and South America, Europe, Israel and China. Anaya began his teaching career in the Albuquerque Public Schools in 1963 and after almost twenty years as a professor of English at the University of New Mexico, he retired in 1993. Among his many awards, Anaya has received the National Medal of Art (2002), the Wallace Stegner Award (2001), a three year W.K. Kellogg Foundation Fellowship in 1983, and a Rockefeller Foundation Residency in 1991. His novels *Bless Me, Úlitma, Tortuga* and *Alburquerque* have each won awards.

With a Dr. Seuss stamp and 23 cents postage due, a signed letter from Rudolfo Anaya answering all my questions appeared like a miracle in my mailbox. Anaya is proud to state that he *was a founding writer in the Chicano literary movement* in answer to my first question about social activism. He has not only been active through his writing but through his teaching and his promotion of educational opportunities. *In the 90s my wife and I founded (and funded) Premio Aztlán for Chicano/a writers; Critica Nueva, a lecture series; and La Casita, a writers residency for Chicano/a writers.*

About his audience, Anaya says, *My audience has always been my community, which is diverse.* He describes it thus: *I write for the world but my sense of place and community (New Mexico) is the ambience.* In other words, he does not direct his narrative to a particular readership. However, Anaya is very clear about his communal commitment: *Our literature is based on giving back to the community what is theirs, the soul.*

Anaya acknowledges having read *a few* authors of detective fiction that he does not name. However, he is fully aware of what he is doing with the detective genre: *I hope there is a lot in my detective fiction which is not genre. We're really using the genre to illustrate our world view. It's a subversive play. The themes of my "serious" fiction appear in my detective novels. Of course the genre demands some of its established formulas, but the genre can also be used to advance the concerns of the author's mythopoetic world, his ideology, environmental concerns, the nature of reality, history, culture, et cetera.*

When asked to compare his "serious" writing with his detective series, Mr. Anaya's answer illuminates his creative process: *I fell into writing detective fiction because a character, Sonny Baca, sprung full-blown from my unconscious, my dreams, the fountain of my creative inspiration. I had to honor him. So he fits in the genre but the world that conspires against him is the same world all my other characters live in. Sonny's adventures are deadly "serious." I had no intention or plan to write detective fiction until Sonny Baca appeared. Since I don't read the genre I had a lot of fun experimenting with my first novel,* Zia Summer. *It was a pleasant change in my writing. And good for me as a learning experience. I continued in the genre because the force of Sonny Baca's character demanded I continue. His character had to evolve and complete itself.*

I asked about the accessibility of detective fiction with a poorly phrased question, and Anaya answered by commenting on the availability of Chicano literature: *Look at the bookstore shelves or best seller lists. Detective fiction seems to do well for a few writers. The world is not ready for Chicano/a detectives. But one or two writers will eventually break through.* The solution will come when *Readers have ... got[ten] use to and interested in the cultural reality of our characters.*

Anaya was at that time working on a fourth *Sonny Baca* novel, *Jemez Spring*, which was published in 2005.

## *Rolando Hinojosa-Smith*

Hinojosa was born in Mercedes, Texas, not far from Brownsville on the southern tip of the state just across the Rio Grande from Mexico. He grew up in a bilingual home. His father's family came to this area, Nuevo Santander, in the eighteenth century from southern Mexico. His mother's family, with the surname of Smith, settled there in the late nineteenth century. Hinojosa has had a long and varied career: a soldier in Korea, radio announcer and editor for the Caribbean Army Defense Command, a high school teacher, a laborer, a graduate student and finally a college professor. He has written since his youth and began publishing fiction in 1970. His work has received noted recognition: Quinto Sol prize in 1970, Premio Casa de las Américas in 1976, Southwestern Conference on Latin American Studies prize in 1982. In 1983 he was inducted into the Texas Institute of Letters and in 2003 was invited to be a juror on the committee for the selection of the Pulitzer Prize novel of 2004. Currently Hinojosa is a professor of English at the University of Texas in Austin.

Hinojosa responded to my questions by email. He has been an active promoter of social, educational and political opportunities for the Chicano population *[n]ot only as a writer of detective fiction but also as a writer and a professor.* Perhaps, his longest lasting contribution is his work with NCCHE.

*Back in the '70s, when there was a dearth of raza[5] Ph.Ds., I served on NCCHE (National Chicano Council on Higher Education) whose mission was to secure money for the purpose of encouraging graduate study with an emphasis on college teaching. We did not look for graduates planning to study law, medicine, or dentistry, in brief, the free professions. We concentrated on young men and women who wanted to be college and university professors. We were highly successful in our searches because of Ford Foundation funding. One of the products achieved with that level of education is the creation of socioeconomic opportunities for the graduates. The formation of NCCHE, then, had a defined political agenda: the creation of a concentrated mass of future university professors.*

Role models are important for all students and in academia the growing number of minority faculty can only serve the interests of all by encouraging the education of a larger group of Americans.

Akin to Anaya, Hinojosa has not sought out a particular audience. His readership is *composed primarily of future book buyers, the educated class* [because] *in the main* [this group] *is composed of university men and women and their instructors.* His books have been *translated into Dutch, French, German and Italian,* which serves to show that he has *no core audience in mind.* Furthermore, he says, *I also think it is dangerous for one writer to tailor one's work for a particular audience; it defeats the purpose of universality.*

Hinojosa read *much detective fiction as a youngster.* The authors he names *may not be known or remembered by current readers* of the genre, but they are among some of most popular authors of the late 40s and 50s: *Ellery Queen, Mary Roberts Rinehart, Mignon Everhardt, Erle Stanly Gardner, Manny Coles, Agatha Christie, S.S. Van Dyke, Rex Stout and so on.* As a professor of English he returned to the genre *in 1977, when a friend recommended Nicolas Freeling and the husband/wife team of Maj Sjowall and Per Wahloo,* [whose works], *if pushed,* [he would name as his] *favorites.*

The work of Freeling, an English author who began publishing detective fiction in the 1960s, is characterized by an abundance of day to day details and the Dutch detective, Van Der Valk, who is uncommonly cynical. Sjowall and Wahloo are Swedish and their *Martin Beck* series criticize 1960s social disintegration and the invasive policing of society.

Asked about a seminar for writers of detective fiction, he responded: *I would tell the students what I tell all of my students: read. Without reading, no writer gets anywhere. Imagination is helpful but it will flag without reading.... At present, I go to bed with Cervantes, whom I've read a great number of times, and with Montaigne. If one plans to write, one must be like a shark, which, by the way is what defines a writer: you read everything, and like a shark, you have no natural enemies. When Mexican American students tell me they do not relate to Shakespeare, I tell them they're in trouble, and that their language will be deficient as will be their thinking. Someone may think I'm being hard nosed, but that's what writing is ... tough. It's not for people whose feelings are hurt easily.*

Furthermore, *Living, observing, listening, undergoing a varied number of experiences, knowing the language, and the language used by the different social classes of this country and any other where one's characters appear and so on is not only important, it is also essential.* But a seminar is not necessary: *one does not need to take classes in creative writing to be a writer,* [but one does need models and] *Graham Greene would be someone who would be a model for any writer of any type of fiction.*

*The Texas-Mexican border, close to where the Rio Grande/Rio Bravo empties into the Gulf of Mexico* is the setting for *Partners in Crime* and *Ask a Policeman,* and, with the exceptions of *Korean Love Songs* and *The Useless Servants,* for all the works of the *Klail City Death Trip Series: the communities, on both sides of the river reflect contemporary reality. Since* Partners in Crime *and* Ask a Policeman *form part of the series, it is inescapable that Mexican Americans form a large part of the characters.*

Contemporary *demographic and economic changes in the Valley* along with Hinojosa's need to experiment with different genres influenced his selection of the detective genre. *Given the violence produced by the drug smuggling, it is proper that crime fiction made its entry in the series.* Hinojosa chose to use the detective genre in 1985 for two reasons: *to show young writers not to restrict themselves to one form of the novel—I knew of no Mexican American writer who had published a crime novel prior to 1985—*[and] *it fit the Series given the changes in the Valley.*

When asked if he distinguished between his "serious" literature and his detective novels, Hinojosa further explained the project of the *Klail City Death Trip Series* (1972–1998). *There is no difference for me; the two detec-*

*tive stories fall within the Series. I'll explain. In the late seventies, I noticed that the Lower Rio Grande Valley, one of the poorest sections in the United States ... was undergoing a transformation. I was born there, and the Series focuses on the place and its people.... I wanted to use as many forms of the novel as possible to tell my story and ... I did so. The detective fiction, then, because of its linearity and because it fit with the influx of a false economy due to illegal activities, was a perfect fit for the Series. As a consequence, the two novels form part of the Series and thus, are not separate from it.*

Hinojosa agrees that detective fiction *is more accessible to the general reading public; it isn't merely entertaining although many readers find it so and buy the books because of that.* However, he finds *non genre work more exciting.* Here's his current reading list: *Over the Edge of the World: Magellan's Terrifying Circumnavigation of the Globe* by Laurence Bergreen; *The Peloponnesian War* by Donald Kagan; *Chasing the Sun: Dictionary-Makers and the Dictionaries They Made* by Jonathan Green. For Hinojosa reading never stops, and I look forward to reading his recommendations.

As a juror on the Pulitzer Prize committee, Hinojosa was very busy reading *a great number of novels* between 2003 and 2004, but he found time to write four short crime stories. Two have been published electronically by *Prótesis*, a literary magazine based in Madrid and a third, "El puñal de Borges," was published in the pages of the same journal in April 2004.

## Michael Nava

Nava, the son of a Mexican American working-class family, was born in Stockton, California, and grew up in Sacramento. In 1975 he collaborated with James Byers and David Owen to publish a volume of poetry. He graduated Phi Beta Kappa with honors from Colorado College in 1975 and then, with a Watson Fellowship, studied the poetry of Ruben Dario in Buenos Aires, Argentina, for a year. He received his law degree from Stanford in 1981 and served as a deputy city attorney for the City of Los Angeles between the years of 1981 and 1984. That year he began a private law practice and from 1986 to 1995 he acted as a research attorney for the California Court of Appeals. In 1995 he left Los Angeles for San Francisco. His first *Henry Rios* novel was published in 1986 and the last in 2001. He has written autobiographical essays that appear in the three volumes edited by John Preston about the lives of gay men in the United States. Nava's *Henry Rios* novels have been widely translated and have won numerous prizes.

Philip Gambone interviewed Nava in the fall of 1992 and in August of 1993, when Nava was working on a fifth novel that would be titled *The Death of Friends* (1996). These interviews are published in Gambone's *Something Inside: Conversations with Gay Fiction Writers*. I have selected information from these that give insight into Nava's process as a mystery writer and his community perspective.[6]

Gambone puts this statement to Nava: "There seems to be a growing trend among writers ... to adhere to certain politically correct ways to portray characters in fiction" (135).

> What I've decided is that I'll write what I need to write.... In *The Hidden Law* I was nervous about some of the AIDS stuff I was writing because Rios ... is not of the generation or persuasion of ACT UP or Queer Nation.... We're going through a hard time because all of us gay and lesbian writers are aware of the vicious stereotypes which have been perpetrated against us in literature since the novel was created. And with this in mind, it's very hard not to be sensitive about what you are writing [135]. It does seem to me that any gay writer cannot avoid the issue of AIDS, because it's such an overwhelming fact in out world. So I needed to write about it [137].

Nava's community is "gay and lesbian," and he is sensitive to its need to present a positive image, but refuses to compromise his literature by creating new stereotypes. With Robert Dawidoff, Nava wrote about civil rights in the gay community in *Created Equal: Why Gay Rights Matter to America*. There is no doubt that this was a forward-looking volume that has influenced thinking and action in this area since it was published in 1994. In *Created Equal*, Nava has done the public a great service. He wrote the book with the hope that the members of the homosexual community would give a copy to each of their heterosexual friends (140).

In his conversations with Gambone, Nava talks in detail about his childhood and the fact that he has no relations with his family (125). However, when Gambone asks if he considers himself a "Latino writer" he answers positively. Nava characterizes the Chicano and Mexican American culture as *socially conservative, family-oriented* and *pretty homophobic* (138–139). He rejected this community because of these attitudes, but he has taken a new perspective:

> I had a revelation, which is that simply because I am Latino and I write about those things [the cultural attitudes of Latinos], that qualifies me to be a Latino writer. I thought I had to be someone else, and now I see, Well, no. Maybe just by being myself I'm lengthening the spectrum. So I accept that identity (139).

Nava read and wrote poetry as a child and young man. He had little interest in detective fiction until an English professor gave him some Rex Stout books and then he became a fan of the genre (130). He has read with pleasure Katherine Forrest, Raymond Chandler, whom he calls a *bigot*, Ross MacDonald, *a great poetic writer*, Sarah Karetsky and Reginald Hill, but Joseph Hansen's mysteries gave him the confidence to create his *openly gay* protagonist, Henry Rios (129).

Nava's stance is that a writer must write about what he knows which in his case is the lives of homosexual males and the law. However, his detective novels have not been directed at this particular audience. He has a large crossover audience including heterosexual women. He has written mysteries, and his books have respected the genre's formula: *If you write a book that satisfies the expectations* [of mystery readers], *then they're willing to accept a lot of the commentary that goes with it* (132).

Before he wrote his first mystery, Nava had only written poetry. He wanted to try his hand at prose fiction, but he wanted to avoid a *self-indulgent, first, autobiographical novel* (130). With a friend he began discussing the details of a plot they planned to develop together. He and the friend separated and Nava started writing the novel that took him three years to complete: *The Little Death* (129). Writing a mystery imposed a discipline that he felt would have been lacking if he had chosen a more the typical *bildungsroman* as his first work of fiction.

Gambone concluded his interview by asking if Nava had any advise for "aspiring gay writers" or "Latino writers" (141). Nava said his advice would be the same for each: work hard, because even though it may be painful it is *deeply satisfying work* (128). There are no miraculous shortcuts and the aspiring writer should not put off his writing while waiting for the impossible (141). In the body of the interview Nava describes what this work entails. His first word of advice is to write about what you know (128). Learning how to plan a plot is of paramount importance. When he began writing whodunits he made extensive and detailed outlines of the plots to be developed (128). After having gained experience, these preparations became less important. Any writing experience is important for the aspiring novelist. For Nava the economy of poetry and the clarity that is a paramount necessity in legal writing have made him aware of the importance of choosing the *precise word* to convey meaning (131).

In his interview with Gambone, Nava spoke of a possible future project, a memoir of his childhood:

> Because of the response I get from the Rios books, it's clear that I'm a teacher of another kind — just sort of a moral example for people

who struggle through some of the same things I've struggled through. And I want to set it down without the veneer of fiction [133].

Ten years and three novels after the interviews of 1992–93, Nava retired as a mystery writer ("Acknowledgements" *Rag and Bone*). There are considerable autobiographical elements in the *Rios* series, and in particular in this last novel. Nava is reported at this time to be working on his memoir ("Nava [Michael] Papers").

## Lucha Corpi

Corpi was born in Jáltipan in the state of Veracruz, Mexico. According to tradition, Malintzín, the interpreter and mistress Spanish Conquistador Hernán Cortés, was born in Jáltipan.[7] From this colorful past Corpi arrived in Berkeley, California, at age nineteen and has remained a resident of the Bay Area since. She graduated from the University of California–Berkeley and has a Master's degree from San Francisco State. She has taught English to adults in the Oakland Public Schools Neighborhood Centers Program since 1977. Among the awards bestowed on her are a National Endowment for the Arts Fellowship, a Pen award, the Oakland Josephine Miles Literary Prize in fiction and the Multicultural Publishers Exchange Book Award for Excellence in Adult Fiction. She has written several volumes of poetry including *Palabras de Mediodía* (1980), recently republished in a bilingual edition, has edited a collection of Chicana autobiography, *Máscaras*, and has authored one bilingual children's book, a story that reflects her childhood experiences: *Where Fireflies Dance-Ahí donde bailan las luciérnigas*.

During our phone conversation I was impressed by her story-telling skills and the insight she provided on the writing process. I was particularly interested in the relationship between Corpi's poetry and narrative.

*What happened was that I was writing stories in Spanish and writing poetry in Spanish and there was a lot of — well — my first stories were really weird, surreal kind of, and I realized that I was looking at things and the narrative was coming out as if I were a poet, and I couldn't get a handle on it. Then I decided forget that — poetry, that's your natural voice. Go with it. For ten years I wrote exclusively poetry. Then I had a poetic silence for two years. I have no idea how those things happen — of course it drove me almost to madness and to a stomach ulcer. Just to keep myself occupied—there was still that demon in me — I started writing narrative. My first was a short* story, *"Shadows on Ebbing Water."* With Delia's Song [her first novel] *it was interesting how I could begin to blend, have the poet serve the narrative, the writer. Poetry's just that connection between that part where all of that— subconscious streams— is going on, and then connecting it to the hand that writes it— that part of the brain where you make selections. Narrative comes from an entirely different place. I don't know how to explain it.*

I asked, "How do poetry and narrative work so well together in *Cactus Blood?" The poet is now subject to the writer and is not interfering, but is aiding the narrative process and for that reason, in some ways, I have stopped writing poetry.*

For Corpi producing poetry and detective novels are experiences whose differences go beyond the requirements of the genres. Corpi's poetry is written in Spanish and her novels in English. She did not explain her decision to write her novels in English, but she said she could have just as well have used Spanish. English is her second language and she feels compelled to check her work in a way that she does not with her Spanish language poetry. She rewrites both, but with the poetry she knows when a poem is finished. Writing a novel she says *is a lot of work and a laborious process. I like doing it, of course, or otherwise I wouldn't be doing it. Poetry comes in a more natural organic way.* In my opinion, Corpi loves a challenge, and writing mystery novels confronted her with the problem of learning a new genre and expressing herself in English. Her husband has challenged her to give her male detective, Justin Escobar, the opportunity to star in a "thriller" and she confesses that the proposition is intriguing.

A precocious reader at the age of seven, Corpi read the newspaper to her father while he was recovering from a cornea transplant. The local paper carried a crime page, "La página roja," that her father would not allow her to read. Her curiosity aroused, she looked for this page, and could always find it where he assumed it had been safely discarded and out of her reach. There were of course many stories of crimes of passion that a seven year old could not comprehend. However, she began to follow the stories, some lasting years, that pointed to *an intelligence behind the crime.* The crime pages were the beginning of her interest in the genre, but later, she recalls, *mystery became an obsession.*

In 2000, at a seminar on Chicano detective fiction at the University of New Mexico she presented her personal essay, "Las páginas rojas." Our conversation was an example of what this audience heard: Corpi is a natural story-teller who mesmerizes her audience with ease.

When she wrote the novel *Delia's Song,* she had for many years been interested in writing a mystery. Shortly afterwards, her good friend, the poet Francisco Alarcón, suggested that because she was so good at "setting mood" she should try the mystery genre. Three years later she did just that.

She described her preparations for writing her first detective novel as a reading process: *I didn't know how write a mystery. I mean I have read mysteries, and I knew mostly what I knew subconsciously in just getting tidbits of how people put together a mystery novel by reading them. I also read essays on the conventions of mystery writing and I have broken I don't know how many of those.* Corpi is justifiably proud of having crossed some of these lines.

Corpi views her five published novels, *Delia's Song* (1989), *Eulogy for a Brown Angel* (1992), *Cactus Blood* (1995), *Black Widow's Wardrobe* (1999) and *Crimson Moon* (2004) as representative of her learning process as a novelist: *The monologue* [in *Delia's Song*] ... *was something very interesting for me because I became very aware of the different levels from total consciousness to subconscious streams. In writing the monologues I became a lot more aware of my process as a poet and a writer, and so I realized that poetry comes from inside of me some place. I realized with* Eulogy *that I could develop character and setting — that seems to my strength in writing mystery novels, but mystery novels tend to be plot driven.* Cactus Blood *was actually my apprenticeship — it was my first plot treatment novel. I felt I did a fairly good job there, although I still needed to study as an apprentice a little more. So here comes* Black Widow's Wardrobe, *where I felt I had learned so much with the other novels that this one had to be better for that reason. And in some ways it is. I learned to develop character well, setting, creating mood, the mystery, tension — you know that plot. My challenge in* Black Widow's Wardrobe *was to make minor characters more interesting. With* Crimson Moon *I thought I'd challenge myself by writing a mystery novel in narrative voice, rather than first person with my three detectives in it* [Gloria Damasco, Justin Escobar and Dora Saldaño].

An integral element of Corpi's process is the part her protagonist Gloria Damasco has in the creation of her mysteries. Akin to Anaya's Sonny Baca, Corpi's Damasco has had a prominent role in directing the novels. *Gloria wakes me up — tells me she is ready and when she tells me she is ready then I have to do my research for whatever she's going to get involved in. She usually lets me know what I have to research without telling me exactly what is going to go on. She's been speaking to me a little lately, but not coming and offering me something yet that she's interested in telling me.*

Abandoned by Damasco and her first person insight, Corpi decided to challenge herself with a third person narrative and began to write *Crimson Moon. I think I was over-ambitious with the first draft and Gloria kept telling me, 'I don't belong in this story,' and I kept saying 'yes you do, yes you do.' But I finally listened to her and revised the draft. Sure enough she didn't belong in there ... so I had to take her out thread by thread of the whole story and what was left was* Crimson Moon, *with Gloria just making a cameo appearance.*

One of the conventions Corpi recognizes that she breaks is the classical genre's exclusion of history and day to day culture. *I was interested in writing history and mystery and culture and everything that my world is. I've been criticized because there is too much history and too little mystery in my novels. I think the mystery story lends itself to dealing with things that people would just deal with in passing in other kinds of novels. Even Carlos Fuentes has a mystery. The mystery is very attractive to a lot of writers; Vargas Llosa has a mystery. There are quite a few writers who write mysteries because it is actually very disciplined and kind of a humbling experience in some ways. To write a mystery, where you have plot, and if you are able to bring in anything else into the mystery story — that's a challenge for the writer — to make it more than just a mystery.*

I asked all the authors about the use of pen names by writers of genre fiction. None of them had even considered using one, but Corpi was made to feel that perhaps writing mysteries might jeopardize her prestige as a poet. *My editor called me one time. She was very, very concerned that I wasn't going to get another grant, another fellowship or another literary award writing genre literature. Well, it doesn't matter that much; a grant helps me, and an award does wonders for my ego, but in the end they don't help me write better, you know. Most Latino authors will write under their own names, and not use pen names, just simply because we're there. We are who we are and you know it doesn't matter to us — we haven't learned shame yet.* She laughs.

When I asked her about her uncommon name, "Lucha Corpi," she told me that a friend translates it as "*Struggle of the Body.*" "Corpi" is the surname of her grandfather, *an Italian wet-back in Mexico.* "Lucha," which in Spanish means "struggle," is the nickname her grandmother gave her as a child and is the name she has always been known by. I suggested that her name "Struggle of the Body" sounded like the title of a mystery novel and she answered with a laugh, "*It's my destiny.*"

Corpi confirmed that my question about accessibility was indeed poorly worded. As was the case with Anaya she pointed out that a small circle of readers in the United States, principally Chicanos, read Chicano detective fiction. However she sees the lack of readership in the United States differently than Anaya. Latin American writers in general are not translated as widely as they could be. She puts it this way: *There is a reticence on the part of the mainstream to acknowledge all of these writers* [Latin American and Chicano]. Like Hinojosa, her reading public is larger in Europe.

Her advice for beginning writers of the genre: *Read as many novels as possible — discover different voices.*

Corpi does not back away from any writing challenge. She's looking forward to retiring from teaching and, now that she has honed her narrative skills, to rewriting *Delia's Song*. She assures me that there will be other cases for the Brown Angel investigators, another children's book is waiting to be written and perhaps soon there will be a thriller featuring Justin.


## Manuel Ramos

Ramos was born in Florence, Colorado, a small community about thirty-five miles from Pueblo. In 1970 he graduated with honors from Colorado State University and in 1973 received his law degree from the University of Colorado. He has used his skills as an attorney to provide legal aid to the indigent and is currently the Director of Advocacy for Colorado Legal Services. His duties include "staff training, backup and support, overall direction for the agency's litigation, and resolution of issues involving professional ethics" ("Manuel Ramos"). Very active in his community, he has participated voluntarily on "numerous boards, task forces, and court committees" ("Manuel Ramos"). In addition to his legal career, he teaches in the Chicano Studies Department of the Metropolitan State College of Denver. *The Ballad of Rocky Ruiz* won the Irvine Prize for Literature in 1992 and was nominated for an Edgar, the E.A. Poe Award for Best First Novel. He has also received recognition for his legal work. Northwestern University Press has republished his two early *Luis Montez* novels, *The Ballad of Rocky Ruiz* and *The Ballad of Gato Guerrero*, with introductions by noted critic of Latin American literature, Ilan Stavans.

When I spoke with Ramos my interview skills were nonexistent and I am glad for his patience and sense of humor. I promised not to print anything embarrassing, but I can't resist. Near the beginning of our conversation I expressed surprise when I learned that he was a teacher. *I've teached. I've taught. Right.* His answer, given with a laugh made me feel quite at ease, since I am an expert at confusing verbs for my university students of Spanish.

Ramos has been actively promoting Chicano detective fiction for ten years. But his interest in community does not end there. As noted above, his commitment to community encompasses the practice of law and teaching. When we spoke about community involvement he responded with humility and with insight. *We do what we can. It's just the way things are.*

*I've found out in my experience at my work* [Colorado Legal Services], *teaching and from other writers, that if I want something done and I want help, I ask the people who are the busiest people that I know.* In other words, he knows how to organize motivated people in the interest of the community.

As a teacher he is well informed and approaches his subject with insight and wit. *I've taught a survey of Chicano literature. And a course I developed on the Chicano Novel. Everything published after 1990. Less of the early masters, the early golden age, more of Yxta Maya Murray and Alfredo Vea. My original title was "Post-Chicano-Chicano Lit." I like to say that teaching Chicano lit is a little difficult because every time a Chicano or Chicana publishes something new the definition* [of this literature] *has changed. It's just that dynamic — it's just like us.*

I asked about an online comment he made regarding Max Martínez' *White Leg*: "Too many labels and not enough readers willing to take a chance on something different" ("Max Martinez"). *We're a country of labels. We love to put labels on people, on our art, on our politics and we like the shorthand method. We're, you know — a people. In North America we live in an age when everything has to move at the speed of light. Whether you're on the internet, whether you're trying to get a book in a book store — you need to rush in over lunch hour and get it. As a people we've developed this cult of fascination with speed and so that's why labels are so welcome. If somebody knows that there's a quick label on something then they know what to expect and they won't be disappointed — they think. So what that means is that they are just missing out on so much that is going on because of the labels. I understand it as a marketing tool — it's certainly something that publishers use.*

Related to marketing, and because he has been published by the academic as well as the commercial press, I asked him if he could discern any differences between these publishers' promotion of his mystery novels. *I think that there's a difference, but maybe it's just because so much time has passed. She* [his editor at the commercial press] *didn't really know what to do with a book like mine, wasn't sure where it fit and what to do with it to attract the widest audience as possible. Now, I find the same thing but at a different level. A university press is used to thinking of their audience in one way, so that's what they're going to do, which is fine, but there is a whole mystery audience that needs to be brought in, but I think that's getting better.*

If academia is taking mystery more seriously, perhaps critics of the genre will be more widely read. Relative to readership, I asked: "Do you have a core audience in mind when you are writing?" *Frankly no. It would really hinder me as a writer if I were trying to create with a specific reader in mind. I write for myself. It's got to be something I enjoy, something I read, that I like and that's what I'm doing. And then when its finished, then of course I want everybody to read it. Not just one particular audience, one kind of reader. I know that's impossible, not very realistic, but that's the attitude I have.*

I asked if he felt "serious" versus "pop" Chicano literature had different audiences. We discussed these labels and I suggested that a novel like *House on Mango Street* could be an example of "serious" literature. Ramos pointed out that it is still in print and is very popular. I suggested that part of its popularity, and the popularity of *Bless Me, Última,* was that both novels are part of "minority canon" reading lists in high schools and colleges. We both agreed that this was a *great* thing. When talking about his fiction and he agreed that it might be more "intellectually accessible" than some Chicano fiction, but not necessarily. *From my own point of view one of the things that I do try to accomplish is to tell a good story and to me that means that a reader, any kind of a reader, can pick it up and enjoy it at that level and anything else they get out of it is going to be extra.*

Our conversation moved to the topic of reading habits in the United States. "If," I said, "each person in the U.S. reads on an average one book a year — one per person — this could mean that some may read 50 and others none." *Reading is something that has to be encouraged and cultivated. It is an issue within the Chicano Community about what emphasis families place on reading and how it fits into a life style. And it's something I try to impress on folks. It's something that starts in the family. I've always been reader. Since I was a young child, I was reading what I could get my hands on and some of the stuff was clearly detective stories, and crime fiction. At an early age I read Raymond Chandler, James M. Kane, Dashiell Hammett. The* Dain Curse *by Dashiell Hammett must have made an impression on me 'cause — you know — I love that kind of stuff. I continue to read crime fiction, mysteries and detectives and there's excellent writing going on. I also think that it's a type of literature that allows the author to speak about social issues, political issues, in a very broad canvas and not hitting anybody over the head with those kinds of issues — part of the context of crime fiction is to put those kind of issues into the story.*

Relative to sociopolitical issues, I asked Ramos about the Chicano movement and its current importance in the community he portrays. *Certainly it is historically important to the community, and the type of story line, in* Rocky Ruiz *for example, had to deal with a man who was middle age or so, who was trying to confront issues in his present life, but in order to do that had to go back into his past and resolve certain things that occurred in his youth to understand where he was in middle age. So that whole back drop was historically in his life and the community that called itself "Chi-*

cano" at the time. It was a very politically motivated term; the whole term is not just an ethnic term. So that was crucial for the character, Montez, and the story that he was involved in.

And today the same kind of political issues continue, it's just a different motif, a different struggle, a different venue, different attitudes. It's much more mainstream politicized. What used to be almost a counter-cultural movement in the 60s and 70s is now, I think, part and parcel of mainstream politics going on in the Southwest: bilingual ed., immigration, higher ed., voting rights. Those are issues that now the Mayor of Denver, a white businessman, will have opinions about. He has to. In the 60s and 70s those were things that a white politician would just as soon ignore — they didn't think that they had to deal with 'em. There were only the crazy Chicanos raising those kinds of issues. It's a different thing today.

The past and present are part of Ramos's fiction and he is very aware of their push and pull. I wonder if there is another novel in the works.

At this point there is not one. But I haven't decided to end it [the Luis Montez series].

Have you ever thought of using a pen name?

Never even occurred to me. Lawyers in town who write, all the lawyers who do it, we all use our actual names.

I've read that you've been criticized by the Chicano community for your portrayals of violence in the community.

Well, I wouldn't go that far. We're a full dimensional community of people and characters in books have to portray all dimensions or the book is not very realistic. And if you dwell on stereotypes, then you're in trouble and you've done some bad writing. Do we need to show the negative side of our community? No we don't need to, but in this kind of a book, for some verisimilitude — reality — you're going to have good and bad.

How do you get the time to write?

It's an act of will. I take time out, carve out time. I'm systematic about it, when I make the commitment.

Why do you write?

It is something I want to do; I enjoy it, like it. The whole creative process is a mystery. When I finish with a session with the computer, I'm often surprised and amazed, because I had no idea that was lurking in my head.

Do your legal writing skills contribute in any way to your mystery writing?

There's some connection and I don't know what it is yet. I think it has to do with a couple of things: one is the kind of work lawyers do on a daily basis — often personal crises of other folks — and that's good fodder for stories. And the technical aspect of the kind of writing that lawyers do makes a *lot of them want to be more creative. This one friend of mine who teaches has this theory that too often lawyers deal with the basic core of the story and then throw on it all kinds of legal theory as analysis. You can see this in opinions that come out from appeals courts. You get a real short summary of the facts to the case and then they're all kinds of legal analyses to the case. So her theory is that lawyers who write want to fill in the gaps, expand on the story to tell the human side of things.*

We finished our conversation by discussing *Brown on Brown*, the latest *Luis Montez* novel that I had not read at the time. Ramos suggested that I needed to see what had changed in Luis's life. After reading the current chapter of my detective friend's saga, I was a little put out; Luis seems to have grown up, and didn't need as much of my sympathy as he did before. Now, I want to reread this novel because maybe I was jealous of his almost successful relationship with another woman.

Chicano authors seem to have approached the genre from a perspective similar to that of Raymond Chandler. They have not shied away from "loosen[ing]" the formulas they have worked with, but contend that writing within the constraints of the genre has been a means to expand their abilities ("The Simple Art of Murder" 235). They agree that reading is of vital importance to anyone who would write because writers learn from their predecessors, and perhaps especially from those who do not write detective fiction (233). Unanimously they do not recognize any difference between genre writing and "serious fiction." I did not specifically ask them but I would surmise that they would agree with this statement of Chandler's: "I do not know what the loftiest level of literary achievement is…. It is always a matter of who writes the stuff, and what he has in him to write it with" (231–232). Anaya, Corpi and Hinojosa make no distinction between the quality of their nongenre work and that of their detective novels. Nava and Ramos show equal respect for the masters of the genre and "serious" writers.

As easy, entertaining and relaxing as a detective story may be, all the authors agree that it is hard work to write one. It requires discipline to write in English and get up at five in the morning for Lucha Corpi, to explore a new genre for Anaya and Hinojosa, to be faithful to the craft for Nava and to just find the time away from work, from family and social obligations for Ramos, as it is I imagine for all. The "simple art of murder" is not so simple in Chandler's opinion either. "It is easy to fake," but it seems to be hard to create; it "takes too much talent, too much knowledge, too much awareness" (235).

Chandler waxes romantic for such a "realist" when he describes his detective: "He must be the best man in the world and a good enough man for any world" (237). His words sound dated, but express in other words what Chicano authors also seem to feel toward their protagonists. Anaya and Corpi are called upon to write by their detectives. Hinojosa has Rafe's entire life in his head and it keeps fighting its way out. Nava, like Hinojosa, makes no claim of "hearing" his protagonist, but appears to have been obligated to explore his life. In our conversation Manuel Ramos said of Luis, "He has his issues, people say. But overall, he's the kind of guy I like too." "Too" was in response to my growing affection for this good-hearted ne'er-do-well.

Chicano authors have not used the genre to discuss serious topics, but rather they found a fit between detective fiction and themes that hold their interest. In Europe there is more interest in Chicano detective fiction than in the United States. This could be a matter of an overabundance of the mainstream genre or the fact that a few dozen authors dominate the market, or, as Anaya suggests, that the average U.S. reader is just not ready for Chicano detectives. I doubt that this lack of preparation and interest will continue. The majority of these Latino novels are worth reading and the number of authors writing in the mystery genre is burgeoning. One can only expect—considering the current variety of approaches, themes and environments—that the Latino novel will continue to be innovative and that with more authors producing this genre the readership will grow.

# 8

## Identity

### *Is a Wrap a Taco or Is a Taco a Wrap?*

Chicano literature is an example of emulation, or to strive to equal and excel. Assimilation is not simulation. To assimilate is to appropriate and transform. Hinojosa's recruitment and nurturing of *raza* educators is an example of Hispanic assimilation. So what is a wrap? It is a wheat flour tortilla tightly rolled around cold foods usually found in salads or sandwiches. The wrap is an emulation of a taco or a burrito and is the latest example of U.S. culture's assimilation of Mexican culture.

Two Chicano critics, Rafael Pérez-Torres, *Movements in Chicano Poetry: Against Myth, against Margins,* and Ramón Saldívar, *Chicano Narrative: The Dialectics of Difference,* acknowledge the pre-eminence of history in Chicano literature as the point of departure for the creative act and for its reading (Pérez-Torres 7–8, Saldívar 5–6). Their critical perspectives, however, are at odds. Whereas Saldívar relies on Fredric Jameson's Marxist concept of the political unconscious, Pérez Torres' criticism relies on postcolonial and postmodernist perspectives. Pérez-Torres links contemporary Chicano poetry with the production of culture in a postmodern environment: "postmodernism marks the end of teleological thinking in the secular sphere" (14). Teleological thinking implies the existence of a discernable pattern, an impulse towards "Project and Progress" (14). The dialectic that Saldívar traces in Chicano narrative produces a "reformulation of historical reality," an "ideology of difference" (8, 7). For Saldívar, Chicano narrative has a function; the works he analyzes "serve both a unifying communal function as well as an oppositional and differentiating end" (4). Pérez-Torres criticizes Chicano critics, not Ramón Saldívar in particular, of using Chicano "identity" and "tradition" to "essentialize" Chicano experience, which in his view is a "political act" (18).

A debate has recently been raging over literary histories and another voice has entered the forum. Samuel P. Huntington, a political scientist, describes "ideology" as "culture" (Menand 92). With his proposal of this equation, his views must be considered when writing about literature. Literature is language, and for this discussion it is the English language because the overwhelming majority of Chicano writers publish in English. The first "key element" of five[1] that Huntington uses to define U.S. culture is the English language (31–32). Culture can encompass many political persuasions, but Huntington puts all Hispanic "cultures" in the same political box:

> The persistent inflow of Hispanic immigrants threatens to divide the United States into two peoples, two cultures, and two languages. Unlike past immigrant groups, Mexicans and other Latinos have not assimilated into mainstream U.S. culture, forming instead their own political and linguistic enclaves—from Los Angeles to Miami—and rejecting the Anglo-Protestant values that built the American dream. The United States ignores this challenge at its peril [30].

Hispanics and other immigrant groups of globalization's world-wide diaspora are not the only threats to the Anglo-Protestant "creed" of the United States. Huntington claims that the following groups exacerbate the problem:

> Intellectual and political circles of the doctrines of multiculturalism and diversity; the rise of group identities based on race, ethnicity, and gender ... the growing salience for U.S. intellectual, business, and political elites of cosmopolitan transitional identities.... The United States' national identity, like that of other nation-states, is challenged by the forces of globalization as well as the needs that globalization produces among people for smaller and more meaningful "blood and belief" identities [32].

In an article published in the Modern Language Association journal in 2001, Stephen Greenblatt recognized some of these same trends in literary histories and globalization as having been influential in producing teleological narratives of marginalized, third world or postcolonial populations. However, Greenblatt's perspective significantly differs from Huntington's: he observes that these groups are producing an "ideology that we have just begun to dismantle" (Greenblatt 58). In other words Greenblatt views teleological narratives and histories, that parallel Huntington's tale of a U.S. national identity, with skepticism and fear.

The dismantled ideology that Greenblatt refers to underlies Romantic nineteenth-century literary histories, some of which were notorious for their nationalistic perspectives. His article relates an incident where he observed himself react with what could be called patriotic zeal. In a casual conversation about President Clinton's reading habits, Carlos Fuentes commented that Clinton had read *The Sound and the Fury* and, surprised by this information, South African author Nadine Gordimer suggested that the president must have read Faulkner when he was a Rhodes scholar in England. Greenblatt recalls that he forcefully declared with no evidence whatsoever that Clinton must have read Faulkner in his home state of Arkansas or when he was a student at Georgetown University (49). Oops: Greenblatt, an eminent scholar of literature, makes a statement unsupported by documentation. This bothered him.

Greenblatt then explores the nationalization of literature that reached its highest point during the Romantic period and continued, over the next two centuries, to be the norm until the 1980s. Literary histories, art histories and national histories have tended to follow the same anonymous leader: cultural sensibility. Greenblatt quotes from a scene in Jane Austen's *Mansfield Park* where the swain, Crawford, has read with great talent from *Henry VIII* and is praised for his performance of a work he claims he has never before read. Crawford says, "'But Shakespeare ... one gets acquainted with without knowing how. It is part of an Englishman's constitution'" (qtd. in Greenblatt 50). Is this what we mean when we use the common saying, "Possession is nine-tenths of the law"? Do literatures only belong to the nation, the ethnic group or religion of their creators?

For periods during the nineteenth century the French did not allow any performances of Shakespeare because his works were perceived as nationalistic (52). A curious fact, considering, as Greenblatt points out, that so many of them were drawn from foreign sources. But in eighteenth- and nineteenth-century Germany "emulation of Shakespeare shaped several of the greatest literary careers" (52). Is a wrap inherently Mexican because it is made with a flour tortilla?

The meat of Greenblatt's article concerns "origin myths." I have focused on foundational tales told by each Chicano author. Huntington focuses on the origin myth of the United States. Greenblatt had a place of origin — Vilna, Lithuania — that no longer exists; it was erased by the regimes of religious and nationalistic ideologies, first by the Fascists and then by the Soviets (55).

This is the central question of his essay:

> There must be something reassuring to the existing structure of things if emergent groups wish to recapitulate the hoariest myths of origin, but why should we endorse such reassurance? Why should we welcome the renewed imposition, now perhaps lightly seasoned with irony or cynicism, of an ideology that we have just begun to dismantle [58]?

It is obvious to me that Greenblatt and Huntington, even though they fear "origin myths" and "'blood and belief' identities" of others, do not share the same point of view. Huntington claims that the United States has one ancestor, the English protestant, and even though those of other nations have made significant contributions to the United States, they have done so because they have "assimilated" these English protestant values. This study attempts to show that the assimilation of literary forms of "origin myths" and "'blood and belief' identities" by minority populations need not be viewed with trepidation, but with intelligence.

For Greenblatt the problem with national literary histories is primarily the essentialization of identity, and he praises Pérez-Torres for writing "a different, and in my view subtler, account" than other minority literary historians (Greenblatt 62). Greenblatt's concern is that many postcolonial literary histories have appropriated late-nineteenth-century forms that "accept the hypothesis of a single, endlessly reiterated fable of identity" (58). In fact the majority of Chicano literary historians refer to the 1960s and 1970s as the "Renaissance" of Chicano literature — a "rebirth" and rupture from the past akin to the Italian Renaissance — because this period broke with the past, explored new forms and themes, but did not start with a blank slate.

Greenblatt argues that at the close of the twentieth and initiation of the twenty-first century, academic institutions are in conjunction with an assortment of marginalizing trends akin to those of the Romantic era (52). This trend is what Huntington and Greenblatt fear. Greenblatt does not support marginal or mainstream teleological histories and, with one outstanding exception, neither does Huntington.

Do we abandon the wrap and only eat sandwiches, or abandon all portable varieties of grain, meat and vegetables including the Mexican wrap, German hamburgers and Viennese hot dogs? In my opinion, the production and reading of minority teleological narratives enable the critic to more equitably judge Eurocentric ideologies that include nationalistic, religious, Marxist and capitalistic perspectives. Without access to marginal origin myths and the histories of emergent U.S. populations, the genesis myth of Judeo-Christianity and a Eurocentric interpretation of U.S. history assume the proportions of unquestioned and singular truths.

Greenblatt argues that nineteenth-century teleological narratives impose a series of steps that a culture must mount in its progress towards civilization. I have argued that Chicano detective fiction's foundational tales offer eclectic approaches to the ladder, various ways to scale it or avoid it entirely. There are numerous goals to be reached and there are *salsas* for every taste.

Chicano detective fiction appropriated a nineteenth-century European literary genre, but transformed this genre by combining it with other appropriations gathered during a nomadic history through Spain and America: pre–Columbian, Spanish, Mexican and North American travels. This is a history of assimilation and emulation.

In her study of Latin American foundational fictions, Doris Sommer notes that these have been used to promote and consolidate Latin American dictatorships of the powerful and elite. Some were written specifically as political messages that claimed to speak for the new nations, while others were romance novels that expressed a longing for intercourse between competing factions of the new republics. Latin American foundational fictions, like those of the current Baltic republics described by Linda Hutcheon, "cannot be understood as nostalgic, for there is no authentic home, no *nostos*, to conjure up.... [T]hey are about occupying a place, laying claim to authority over it, and tracing or inventing the roots that confer legitimacy on this claim" (qtd. in Greenblatt 56). This project should sound familiar to anyone who has read the "history" of Pocahontas or seen the Walt Disney movie. We "*nostos*" who write these histories do so to claim ownership of our chosen region; we, the many "nostos," need to hear all claims.

A fiction written with a specific political agenda and one written to celebrate a population's traditions are foundational fictions. Both have been used to fight against and to justify oppression.

My interest has been in establishing an analogue between the historical circumstances that provided the context for the production of Romantic national tales and detective fiction and those that have stimulated the production of Chicano detective fiction. I have sought to understand the intertextual construction, the migrations and border crossings so to speak, of Chicano mysteries in relation to those of Romantic era literatures.

Greenblatt recognizes that neither Faulkner nor Shakespeare limited their knowledge within national or cultural boundaries. He points out that literatures borrowed freely from each other prior to the Romantic era. There seems to be a problem here if we criticize contemporary marginal literatures of borrowing from a genre respected in the past and, as Huntington affirms, in the present also.

Linda Hutcheon's view of the battleground of contemporary "identity" politics is not dissimilar to Huntington's. She points out that the front is not limited by the "boundaries of the nation-state" but encompasses "a host of categories" that include ethnicity. Similar to Romantic national histories many current histories of minority literatures are written "with an eye to promoting ideological consensus" (Hutcheon 403). However distasteful the use of the teleological national narratives to promote political agendas may be, it is important to remember that they are "structured on the romantics' idealist philosophy of history, with its emphasis on the importance of origins and its assumption of continuous development" (404). She continues, "just as nineteenth-century European nationalist agendas required a teleological narrative to indicate the forward movement of progress, the minorities who aspire to 'progress' *may* also require this narrative" (406, my emphasis).

In Hutcheon's opinion, the teleological narrative is not confined to the Romantic era or even to Western thought. "In their formative moments, it would seem, nations have always made (and often remade) their histories" (Hutcheon 413). The newcomer Aztecs rewrote their history in order to justify their geographic claim to the Valley of Mexico. The teachings of Christianity incorporated the Old Testament as the initial "chapter" in the life of Christ, a teleological narrative that justified the "holy land" Crusades of the Middle Ages. The pitfalls of essentializing identity through these histories have always existed.

Hutcheon, however, reminds us that some cultures who write teleological narratives are "alert to the exclusions and entrapments as well as to the emancipatory potential" of these narratives (417). Furthermore, "The longevity and continuing appeal of the developmental model (and its ideological underpinnings) ... must be understood — in context — and not condemned outright as signs of backsliding" (417).

There are forces, ancient and modern, that are continually at work on our expressions of culture. These are "colonization, exile, emigration, wandering, contamination, and unexpected consequences, along with the fierce compulsions of greed, longing, and restlessness" (Greenblatt 62). Greenblatt concludes his article with this observation:

> [I]t is these disruptive forces, not a rooted sense of cultural legitimacy, that principally shape the history and diffusion of languages. Language is the slipperiest of human creations; like its speakers, it does not respect borders, and, like the imagination, it cannot ultimately be predicted or controlled [62].

This is the Chicano experience, just as much as it has been the experience of all humanity. But a day-old sandwich tastes just as bad as a taco made with a stale tortilla. There's the Earl of Sandwich and the *mano* and *metate*. Their products are worthy of our interest and have crossed borders with slippery habits learned from language.

Without further apologies for the teleological narrative here is another:

The founding couple in my version of the Mexican American story is not restricted to heterosexual reproduction. The Jewish, Christian and Muslim biblical tale of origin begins with a heterosexual couple, as does the current anthropological history of human origin along with many tales of ethnic and national origins. However, when one considers that the evolution of an originating equation is in itself complex, it might be more enlightening to use heterogamous reproduction as a metaphor for a starting point of origin.

Heterogamous reproduction is not the result of a singular and stable sexual act, but rather the product of a series of intercourses that differs from generation to generation. One example of how this metaphor can be employed is in an analysis of gentilics. Many that are used to describe the populations of nation states are relatively stable: the English are English; the Germans are German and the Mexicans are Mexican. But the gentilics used to describe Henry Rios' ethnicity for example, have been subject to fluctuations emanating from the historically shifting origins and demographics of the Mexican and U.S. populations. Mainstream and minority, authoritative and popular voices have proscribed these gentilics. Some are (I will not state the derogatory ones, Mexican or from the U.S.A.): Mexican or *mexicano*, Spanish, Spanish-American, Mexican American, Chicano or *mexicanoamericano*, Hispanic and Latino, any of which can preface homosexual, gay or *international*.

The usage of "Chicano" swings from generation to generation. Before the political activism of the 1960s, it was a derogatory term used by Mexican Americans to describe poor working class late-comers to the Southwest. Centuries before the term may have described the *mexica* population of the Valley of Mexico. "Chicano" is no longer derogatory and no longer describes the population of the Valley of Mexico. Many who might have called themselves "Chicano" in the 1960s and 1970s, might not do so now because of the active political commitment associated with the term. Whereas among many urban youth the term carries little political commitment, but reflects an attitude of defiant pride that might be distasteful to their grandparents.

Relative to literature, however, "Chicano" recalls indigenous, immigrant, poor, uneducated, laboring, politically astute and intellectually curious people from a place in the Southwest who migrated to and then away from the Valley of Mexico, and currently reside in the Southwest from where they continue to migrate farther north and east. These migrations have generated from a cultural matrix that undergoes change over time and is reflected in the past and present literature of this population. To imagine a singular form of reproduction as an origination point for a

Chicano foundational tale would negate the complexity of this inheritance.

The Chicano authors have had to define their particular detectives' communities in relationship to the hegemonic U.S. community in addition to delineating the community of their protagonist. Each author goes about this differently. Their definitions of community make up the matrix of an incipient, unrealized foundational tale. Each author proposes a genesis, with a refreshing caveat for those of us who may feel burdened by a *project and progress* teleological tale: the Chicano emergence myth need not be fixed, sanctioned or limited.

Some of these detective tales of origin follow nineteenth-century historiography, while others do not. These foundational narratives dialogue with each other, Romantic rebel ideology, nineteenth-century proscriptive tales of identity and the grocery lists of Formist histories of the same era. Chicano detectives are characterized by the paradox of being outsiders and insiders in the U.S. culture at large: theirs is Chicano culture, regional Mexican American culture and contemporary U.S. urban culture.

In his "Author's Note" to *Blues for the Buffalo*, Manuel Ramos communicates the acknowledgements of his Mexican American character Rad Valdez, the young detective who enlisted the aid of Luis Montez: "Rad Valdez wishes to express his gratitude for the invaluable technical assistance of several renowned sleuths including Sonny Baca, Joe Blue,[2] Rafe Buenrostro, Gloria Damasco, Henry Rios and Cecil Younger."[3] Ramos establishes a basis for my proposed dialogue between four of these detectives and his own Luis Montez. "Help" is the operative word. Chicano detective fiction is not about exclusion, and the term "popular" describes these novels.

Ramos includes in three of the titles of his *Luis Montez* novels references to American narrative musical genres; one is a "blues" novel and two sing *corridos* or "ballads." By grouping fictional detectives together with an acknowledgement from his young detective, Ramos outlines a *corrido* that I will title the "The Ballad of the Chicano Sleuth." The *corrido* is first and foremost a story of popular heroes. Ramos gathers into this group Luis Montez's fellow Chicano detective-protagonists, an Anglo Mexican, Joe Blue, and an Anglo American Alaskan sleuth, Cecil Younger. Thank you, Mr. Ramos. Your "Acknowledgements" have written the first paragraph of my conclusion.

For my ballad I've decided to construct a composite from the detective protagonists whose exploits I've followed in the body of this study. Literary histories, particularly those that have followed Romantic models, are not averse to defining the dominant characteristics of epochal heroes and heroines. What I propose is no different and should be read as these histories have been read: this is an outline that defines existing trends and is not a formula that imposes these characterizations on future protagonists.

While I select some of the characteristics that define Rudolfo Anaya's Sonny Baca, I am, however, choosing only those that all the detectives share. Baca is my template because of the five novels analyzed, *Shaman Winter* is the most obvious example of Formist and teleological narration, is undeniably romantic and is unapologetically proud of its ethnicity. Furthermore, this novel concludes with the union of a founding couple.

Among Baca's positive characteristics is his love of knowledge. He was a high school teacher before he became a detective, and in *Shaman Winter* he occupies himself and pursues his investigation of crime by reading New Mexican history. Corpi's Gloria Damasco promotes Chicano poetry and is the editor of a collection of Chicana autobiographies. Hinojosa's Rafe Buenrostro was also a high school teacher, and he and Nava's Henry Rios continue to read the English literature they studied in college. They and Luis Montez have pursued post-graduate studies in law, and he, like the others, reads, but his preference is Chicano literature and his favorite author is Oscar Zeta Acosta.

In my experience as a reader of detective fiction, and in critic Susann Samples' readings, a book-reading contemporary policeman or detective is rare (154). However, the first characteristic of the *corrido* detective is an abiding love for the written word.

The first two novels of Anaya's series introduce the reader to Baca's family who all live in or near Albuquerque, New Mexico. His widowed mother, aunt, cousins and twin brother are part of his story. The relationship between him and his family is not always smooth. His mother complains that he does not spend enough time with her, and his brother is more often than not an embarrassment to him. But Baca never questions their love for him and his connection to them. Montez has a similar relationship with his numerous siblings. Sometimes they help him during his investigations and sometimes they get in his way. His dad Jesús, however, is a constant, if sometimes cranky, fixture in his life. Rafe Buenrostro and his cousin Jehú Malacara both lost their fathers as children. They are the sons of the entire *Tejano Mexicano* community of Belken County, Texas. In *Estampas del Valle*, Hinojosa's multiple narrators trace a zigzagging family tree; all the *Tejano Mexicanos* in Belken County seem to be related. During a stop in Taos, New Mexico, in *Shaman Winter*, Baca gossips in the bar with the locals and hears that he is related to nearly every *Nuevo Mexicano* in the state. Montez also runs into lost relatives in Colorado. Gloria Damasco does not have a large family like Baca, Montez and Buenrostro, but her relationships with her daughter and her mother are close. They have a few generational differences, but both are supportive of her investigative career and occasionally help her and give advice.

Lomelí, Márquez and Herrera-Sobek point out that "the Chicano [detective] protagonist takes time to nurture personal and family relationships" (299). However, it might be more to the point, particularly when considering Rafe, Luis and Sonny, that *familia* for the *corrido* detective is inescapable. Of the five detectives only Gloria Damasco consistently nurtures her family relationships. The fact that for all five detectives these relationships are inescapable is confirmed in Michael Nava's *Rag and Bone*. Henry Rios has been missing something in his life, and in *Rag and Bone* he discovers that this element is *famila*. There are some mainstream detectives who are defined by family relationships, but as a distinguishing characteristic that identifies a detective this is a constant and consistent trait of the Chicano detective.[4]

The Chicano community figures prominently in the novels of Anaya, Corpi, Hinojosa and Ramos, but does not in the work of Nava. However, none of the detectives limit their relationships to the Chicano community and all five are helped in their investigations by Anglos and African Americans.

Baca in *Zia Summer* enlists the help of his *compadre*[5] Howard Powdrell. An expert forensic technician who works for the Albuquerque police, Powdrell also has an extensive knowledge of history, both of which he puts at Baca's service. Their relationship is warm and easy. When Anaya's third-person narrator introduces Powdrell there is no mention of his race or ethnicity. Only through the course of the novel do we learn from Powdrell himself that he is African American. He tries to convince Baca to take a break from the investigation and, with Rita, join him and his wife Maria for the Juneteenth Celebration at the State Fairgrounds. "Let's go chow down on some of Powdrell's famous barbecue ribs, fried catfish and apple pie. A man does not live on enchiladas alone," he suggests to Sonny, his *compadre* (*Zia* 233). In this passage a reader might assume that Powdrell is African American, but he still has not been described as such. It is not until the end of the novel, when Sonny, Rita, Maria and Howard have gone out to celebrate the conclusion of the case, that Powdrell makes this distinction, telling Maria, "Come on, honey, let's show these Chicanos that black folks can dance rancheras. Ajua!" (342).

Luis Montez has a similar relationship with African American Rodney Harrison. They met when Montez defended Rodney's ex-wife. Shortly afterward the rejected husband and the lawyer-detective found themselves shoulder to shoulder and drunk in the same bar. After being arrested for brawling, the two spent the night in the same jail cell where they initiated a long lasting friendship (*Buffalo* 110). Harrison owns Hot Rodney's, a casual eatery and bar with soul-food on the menu and the blues on the sound system. He helps Montez as a process server and by keeping an ear open to the gossip of Denver. In his investigation in *Blues for the Buffalo*, the detective is twice saved from close calls by Harrison's foresight. Baca's and Powdrell's relationship and Montez's and Harrison's show an equal level of depth that allows these friends to poke fun at cultural differences. Harrison quips, "You Chicanos fight over songs and what to call yourselves" (191) and Montez teases him about his restaurant's menu of "greasy roadkill" (112).

Henry Rios in Nava's first detective tale, *Golden Boy*, hires Freeman Vidor who will reappear in the series. Black detective, Freeman, and Rios never develop a personal relationship, but their working relationship immediately establishes the fact that neither allow differences in race or sexuality to prejudice judgment or interfere with the productivity of their business partnership. While discussing the first case they will work on together and what possible role homosexuality might have in the jury's verdict, heterosexual Freeman suggests that it will be hard to make the jury feel sympathetic toward a gay man.

> "You tell someone you're gay," he [Freeman] replied, "and the first thing they do after they shake your hand is get a blood test."
> "Including you?"
> "It's not on the list of my biases," he said. "You want to tell me about yours?"
> "Some of my favorite clients are black" [52].

Later, Freeman and Henry meet in a gay bar to observe and interview a witness. Conservatively dressed men make up the clientele, but Freeman enters wearing bell-bottom pants, gold chains and a pink chenille sweater that belonged to his ex-wife. Henry cannot help but laugh at him, but Freeman takes it in his stride: "Back to R&D" [Research and Development], he answers" (*Golden* 159).

In *Hidden Law*, Freeman comments on the attractions of a skimpily dressed prostitute as he and the lawyer-detective enter Henry's office on Sunset Boulevard: "You see the girls out here all day long. Don't you even get a little curious?" Henry replies flippantly that he found out everything he wanted to about girls playing "doctor" when he was six years old. Freeman replies, "Six, huh? They get better when they grow up." (127). Henry laughs. From this exchange it is obvious that theirs is an easy relationship.

Corpi's Gloria Damasco and Hinojosa's Rafe Buenrostro do not develop any friendships or long-term working relationships with African Americans. However in *Cactus Blood* and *Partners in Crime*, black characters fill minor, but key roles. During her investigation Gloria learns of a shelter run by and for Oakland's homeless. The leader and organizer of the shelter, where both African Americans and Chicanos live and work, is named Soldado or "Soldier" in English. He is described as a "dark" man (156). There are no features that distinguish him as Chicano or African American, two of the many "dark" populations of Oakland and his speech incorporates expressions from both groups (155).

In Hinojosa's novel an old African American, John Milton Crossland, who has been employed by a member of Rafe's family since 1907, discovers a dead body. Crossland is a veteran, like many of Soldado's charges, but not of Vietnam. He fought in the Cuban Campaign of the Spanish-American war of 1898 and unjustly received a dishonorable discharge (*Partners* 14). This humiliation has haunted his life. Just before his natural death he receives the news that "some professor" who had been studying his case and those of others has been able to have his dishonorable discharge rescinded and "he … died a happy man" (76). Rafe is pleased to learn this news of a man who crossed lands and lived in an area where crossing national borders is a day to day occurrence. His cousin calls to invite him to Crossland's funeral, which he attends despite the pressure of solving his current murder case (76). Significantly, Hinojosa chooses an African American to carry a surname that is representative of the experience of many minority populations.

There are very few blacks in Hinojosa's Belken County, Texas. The single other African American character in the novel is Elizabeth Tarver, who came forward to warn Jehú about the money laundering taking place at her bank. After he interviews her, Jehú realizes that, other than a few soldiers who have passed through, she and Crossland are the only African Americans he has ever known in Belken county (116). He admires her courage and proposes that his bank hire her and the other teller who came forward as soon as positions are open (153).

The relationships of Baca, Montez and Rios with the African American men who work with them, the comments of Jehú, and the story of Crossland show that respect for human dignity among the Chicano detectives easily crosses North American racist borders. Corpi's character, Soldado, extends the racial blindness of Chicano detectives by presenting a character whose color and speech are shared between communities. This is a "dark" man (*Cactus* 156) who could be of African, Mexican, Asian, indigenous North American or Sub-continent Indian, Greek or even Yemeni extraction in multi-ethnic Oakland (155).

Thus far the composite *corrido* detective has these characteristics: she reads poetry, fiction or history, and although she may be estranged from family is incapable of disassociating her identity from this inheritance. She is inclusive rather than exclusive in her relationships.

Another characteristic of detective Sonny Baca is his use of Spanish. The text of Anaya's series rarely indicates that Sonny's first language might not be English, but his speech, peppered with traditional Spanish sayings as well as contemporary Chicano jargon, indicates that he is comfortable listening to and speaking Spanish. Furthermore, one of his favorite authors is Miguel de Unamuno. Although it is not clear if he reads the Spaniard's works in translation, he is aware of his linguistic literary heritage (*Zia* 161). Corpi's narration indicates when Gloria and others are communicating Spanish. Both she and Rafe Buenrostro are fluent speakers in both languages. Montez and Rios have let their Spanish get rusty, but both can speak and understand the language to a limited degree. None of the detectives criticize Chicanos who are not fluent in Spanish and neither Montez nor Rios is ashamed of his shortcomings as a bilingual speaker, but both do at times regret their ineptitude. Rios knows that a better knowledge of Spanish would have helped in several situations, particularly in his interviews with a Central American evangelist in *Rag and Bone* (242, 245).

Language as an identifier is commonly used to distinguish a minority detective from his mainstream environment. Some examples are: Carolina Garcia-Aguilera's Cuban American detective, Tony Hillerman's Navajo detectives, Walter Mosley's African American detective, Barbara Neely's female African American detective, Alexander McCall Smith's Botswanan female detective and Arthur W. Upfield's Anglo Aboriginal detective.

The use of different registers of English and "accented" speech has been the stock and trade of the mainstream genre: classical, hard-boiled and spy-thrillers. However, in these cases language is primarily used to define hierarchies of class, social standing, ethnicity and race: in other words to create mutually exclusive stereotypical groups. In Chicano detective fiction various registers of English and the interspersing of Spanish work to unite the peoples of the urban areas the detectives visit in contrast with the use of ethnic and class jargons employed by Chandler that work to separate these segments of the population. Because they are fluent in various usages of both languages and do not employ these in a condescending or intimidating manner, the detectives are more able to understand and formalize alliances with the people they encounter during their investigations and, therefore, succeed in their profession.

The genre's most famous non-native speaker of English is Agatha

Christie's Belgian detective, Hercule Poirot. Poirot speaks the Queen's language with a heavy French accent. His English has been described as "a literal translation of school-boy French" (Chandler "The Simple" 230). This can be seen as an endearing characteristic that saves him from being too sanctimoniously all-knowing like Sherlock Holmes and protects him from blowing his cover as an investigator. He's just a curious little foreign man, not to be feared and certainly incapable of the intellectual abilities of a native Englishman. So we — the suspects and the reader — let our guard down and are caught red handed or with a red herring in our pocket. Poirot at times must rely on Captain Hastings, his English gentleman sidekick, to understand and be understood. Poirot's lack of command of English is seen as a weakness and Christie very wisely, considering her audience's fear of the foreign, does not allow him to dominate the language.

Like the majority of mainstream detectives, all the *corrido* detectives are smart, courageous and attractive and each has a good sense of humor. However, the *corrido* detective is also bilingual, is irrevocably linked to his biological family, is a life-long reader and exemplifies the practice of inclusion through his behavior. This profile describes a heroic personality in twenty-first-century United States, where monolingualism is admired, reading is seldom for recreation, nuclear families do not communicate effectively and xenophobia is again on the rise.

Américo Paredes in *With a Pistol in His Hand* uses a narrator to tell about the "good song," the *corrido*. This song was "[n]ot like these pachucos nowadays, mumbling damn-foolishness into a microphone" (34). These were songs sung by men about the heroic deeds of men. Though predominantly male, the *corrido* hero has also been female, but the story of a positive sexual partnership is rarely sung. If the love stories of Sonny Baca, Rafe Buenrostro, Gloria Damasco and Henry Rios, and the search for love by Luis Montez distinguish these detectives from the Anglo-American and British detective genres as critic Lomelí et al. suggest, their love stories also distinguish them from what has been considered one of the foundations of Chicano literature, the *corrido*. However, some *corridos*, even Paredes' example of the "Ballad of Gregorio Cortez," have, if only in the background, a reference to the hero's love of his sexual partner.

Gregorio's wife and family were jailed by the Texas authorities while he was successfully eluding the Texas Rangers. But when he heard the news of his family's plight he immediately surrendered. Times have changed. *Pachucos* are no longer singing their "damn-foolishness" and the romantic relationships of the *corrido* detective hero are more prominent than those of the hero of the "good song" that was sung at the beginning of the twentieth century.

In my analysis of these authors' works of detective fiction I have suggested that each tells of the origin and evolution of a group of Chicanos. Anaya's Sonny Baca, the most ambitious historian of the group of detectives and the one who is most attached to his free-wheeling single life style, finally agrees to settle down with his long time girl friend Rita in *Shaman Winter*. Sommer's analysis of Latin American foundational fictions posits that the foundational couple represents a fusion of political, social or racial/ethnic oppositions. It would seem that Rita, a beautiful New Mexican Chicana, who has grown up in the same town as Sonny, a Catholic with shamanistic understanding like the detective's, who cooks his favorite foods, takes care of him and is sexually compatible with him, would not represent any "opposition" to Sonny's political, social or racial/ethnic characterization.

But their union does join conflictive perspectives. Sonny is a bit of a *macho*, reluctant to diminish his privileged position. He has a hard time accepting the independence of his widowed mother in *Zia Summer*. Mom, "la jefita,"[6] has a boy friend. Sonny feels put out, even though he agrees that he has been ignoring her. Rita is the chef and owner of her own restaurant. More financially and emotionally stable than Sonny, Rita has been supporting herself and has known her spiritual self since the beginning of the series, which has not been the case for Sonny. Because she is Sonny's love, in each of the novels her life has been threatened. Their love for each other is a fact that Sonny's nemesis Raven recognized in *Zia Summer*. It takes Sonny two more novels, *Rio Grande Fall* and the length of *Shaman Winter*, to acknowledge his love and promise to marry Rita. Because of the trauma inflicted by Raven, Rita miscarries and is told that she might not conceive again. When Sonny declares his love to Rita, he accepts the fact that he may never be a father, not an easy decision for a *macho* guy (421).

Hinojosa's Rafe Buenrostro and Michael Nava's Henry Rios establish relationships that project change and also recognize parity between man and woman. In contrast to Sonny and Rita, Rafe and Sammie Jo Perkins are historical ethnic opposites in Belken County. In *Partners in Crime* they hide their relationship from families and co-workers because Sammie Jo is married and neither one is ready to accept that their union might be possible in Belken County's ethnically stratified society. Their union mitigates the historical abuses committed by Sammie Jo's family when the *Tejano Mexicano* assumes a position of authority in the Anglo Texan family. Sammie Jo defies her family's authority by marrying outside established traditions. After this experience, it would be unlikely that Sammie Jo would put up with an unequal marital relationship. She has chosen well;

Rafe is not a domineering type. Furthermore, Rafe and Sammie Jo's union affirms that both recent Anglo settlements of the mid–nineteenth century and older claims to this same area by the whole Buenrostro clan are rapidly becoming moot with the invasion of outsiders that threaten Anglo and *Mexicano* Texans alike. Only together will these populations be able to confront the new global invasion of a land that both families have shared for more than one hundred and fifty years.

Akin to Sonny, Henry Rios has played the field for many years, however, unlike Sonny, his free-wheeling years have been unsatisfying. When he meets Josh Mendel in *Golden Boy*, Henry is not sufficiently mature to accept another's love. He wants to manipulate Josh's love and be in control. Unlike Sonny's Rita, Josh will not patiently wait for Henry to mature, and he leaves. Henry is tormented by regret after he and Josh separate and this is exacerbated by Josh's painful death from AIDS. His failure to maintain his relationship and Josh's suffering motivate Henry to look into himself. In many ways he has adopted his father's domineering *macho* attitude. In *Rag and Bone*, Henry gets a second chance. Like Sonny he finds a person who is not at first glance culturally different from himself. His lover, John DeLeon, is Mexican American. However, in contrast to Henry, John is a spiritual person, an independent blue-collar professional and a bisexual father of two children.

Both Sonny's and Henry's foundational relationships erase distances between Chicanos themselves. Even though they respect women, they frequently speak and act with the mannerisms of domineering males. Henry loves a man and Sonny loves a woman who, like John, is patient with *machismo*. However, both John and Rita are able to guide their partners away from these tendencies partially because their personalities and occupations are not limited by gender-defined roles. John works in a male-dominated profession and is a great househusband who cooks and decorates. In a male dominated field, Rita takes time from her professional life as a restaurant owner and chef to care for Sonny.

The relationships that Henry and Sonny establish with John and Rita question traditional gender-defined roles within the Chicano community and highlight a changing attitude towards male dominance in the family. Sonny eventually supports his mother in her new relationship and is able to accept, even after his long and dangerous battle with Raven for the perpetuation of his own ancestry, that perhaps he and Rita will not have children, that she will not be a stay-at-home wife and that he will work for her in her restaurant. Henry has had to accept the fact that John will preserve his independence and will not move into his house or give up his family and spiritual commitments. John and Henry share love and responsibility for Henry's nephew, Angel. Henry has also had to recognize Angel's independence. No longer can the head of the Chicano household demand that its members mimic his behavior and share his convictions.

Gloria Damasco is a bit more circumspect in expressing her love for her partner Justin than are Rafe, Sonny or Henry. The consummation of Gloria and Justin's love comes as somewhat of a surprise for the reader. They have had a friendly professional relationship that has not favored either male or female prerogatives. Their union is less dynamic than the amorous unions of Sonny, Rafe and Henry. The only change in their friendly professional relationship is the sexual act.

Gloria's union with a fellow Chicano will not unite two conflicting ethnicities nor does it require that she adjust her behavior toward Justin. He is comfortable with and supportive of all that Gloria does, and she has learned facts about his life that have made his silences understandable to her. Together they present a united and stable front that contrasts with the lives of the majority of the characters in *Cactus Blood*. The other women have been subjected to trauma and tragedy that can be defined as a result of their female gender. Gloria's and Justin's relationship is the exception to the norm in this story. However, they do not purge their lives of influences outside the mainstream Chicano traditional family. This couple does not shy away from feminist perspectives or people of different sexual orientation, and as a union functions to "legitimize" marginal lives within the larger framework of the majority heterosexual Chicano community. Their stability promotes an environment that allows the marginalized to prosper and flourish. Reproduction in this foundational tale depends on the metaphorical flowering of Carlota's cactus that represents a union between Chicano activism and Chicana feminism. Justin has provided Gloria with a love that was missing in her life and now that she is whole again, Gloria can supervise the planting and care that Carlota's cactus will require.

Poor Luis Montez, twice divorced from Chicanas both times, continues to strike out with the gorgeous and intelligent *chicas* he actively pursues. Furthermore, his law practice keeps diminishing. In *Blues for the Buffalo* he is working from his home, has no secretarial help and is pushing fifty. Are his prospects for marriage or a long term relationship slim? The easy answer is, "Yes, they are."

Traditionally a woman expects that a male will support her. As he ages he will still be attractive to a woman as long as his income and assets have increased, which is not the case with Luis. He is attracted to competent and professional Chicanas. The opposites that would characterize his ideal foundational couple are drive and industry on the part of the woman and casual ease on the part of the male. Not only is the Chicano community not ready for this gender-defined role change, neither is the United States as a whole. However, Luis's perspective is not unrealistic. Even though they still lag behind men's, women's incomes have increased in the last twenty years, and more women than men are now graduating from college. This is only true for the population as a whole. Hispanic women continue to have the lowest level of education and income of any large demographic group in the United States. Reading between the lines of Luis' unsuccessful romantic escapades shows him to be a strong supporter of education and economic opportunity for Chicanas. That is the only way there will be a large enough pool of women from which he can find a partner.

In the meantime, Luis's long term relationship is with his father who, after a life characterized by drive and industry, is now living the casual ease of his retirement years. His life, however, is not without responsibilities. He is teaching his grandsons Spanish, which both their father and mother have ignored. Jesús Montez tried to teach Luis about his cultural inheritance and his goals have not changed as a grandfather. Luis's foundational male, if extended beyond Luis himself and to the characterization of the father he admires, has the responsibility to impart his culture to the next generation, and if the women Luis has chosen in the past are an example, they will share this responsibility.

The oppositions that are resolved by the unions of foundational couples in Latin American Romantic novels were generally political ones between liberal and conservative factions. Among our Chicano foundational couples that were in opposition — Sonny and Rita, Henry and John — the *macho* tendencies of the detective-protagonist were purged of traditional assumptions regarding the dominance of male prerogative in a relationship. Both detectives learned to respect the independence and productivity of their partners.

Luis Montez's unsuccessful search for a Chicana partner and Gloria Damasco's successful union with a Chicano partner underline the importance for the foundational couple to enter their union without the of burden gender-biased roles, with respect for the independence of their partners and with the knowledge and will to share Chicano history.

Foundational couples seek a stable environment where their love can flourish. In Anaya's and Corpi's fiction, if the nation state recognizes environmental concerns as the concerns of the state, the cause of stability will be furthered. For Nava and Ramos, urban America needs to be stabilized through social and political reform. Hinojosa recognizes this same concern, as do Corpi and Anaya to a lesser extent, but all three also call into account the spread of globalization and its invasive and dehumanizing tendencies. The particular perspectives of the detective stories highlight different forms of hegemonic intrusion and failures. The relationship of Luis's dreams and those between the founding couples project positive and dynamic changes within Chicano culture and in turn offer hope that from a position of relative stability their influence will not be confined to any single segment of the U.S. population.

The hero or heroine of the "Ballad of the Chicano Sleuth" will never satisfy his thirst for knowledge, recognizes his parentage, does not subject his relationships with the many peoples of the United States to prejudice, puts aside debilitating gender-defined roles, listens to language and attempts to speak to all without pretension, and strives for a stable and equal personal relationship. Hire a Chicano/a detective today. Check out their references at your local bookstore or library.

Traditionally, a study such as this one would propose a metanarrative that would fuse all the works analyzed in a cohesive teleological history. According to Dominic Strinati's overview of postmodern criticism of popular artistic expressions, the metanarrative is being questioned because in the United States and Europe of the late twentieth century "traditional sources of identity" have been fragmented (238). Strinati lists loci of identity as follows: social class, extended and nuclear family, local communities, the neighborhood, religion, trade unions, and the nation state (238). The questioning of metanarratives and the lived experience of a fragmented environment are historically familiar to Mexican Americans.

The fragmentation or loss of each of the identity sources listed by Strinati is represented in Chicano detective fiction. In Ramos' and Nava's novels Mexican Americans who have moved up the social ladder or who have been able to preserve a privileged social and economic position, such as the Vargas family in Ramos' *Blues for the Buffalo* and the Peña family in Nava's *Hidden Law*, prey on fellow Mexican Americans. In previous novels of Hinojosa's *Klail City Death Trip* series, the wealthy Leguizamón family, a business ally of the powerful Anglo Texans, showed little mercy toward the less privileged *Mexicano Tejanos*. Some at the bottom on the socioeconomic scale prey on each other in Corpi's *Cactus Blood*, Nava's *Hidden Law* and *Rag and Bone* and in the majority of Ramos' novels. The pressures of urban life in the United States exacerbate the fragmentation of upper and lower class Mexican Americans. Families are split apart by the pressures of a globalized economy in Corpi's novel and by Mexican American homophobia in Nava's novels. The Catholic religion no longer unites the majority of the characters in these novels. Traditional beliefs are undermined or affirmed in both Corpi's and Anaya's series, but have ceased to be an influential locus of identity in the community as a whole. Jesús, Luis Montez's father, is now a city dweller and his identification with the solidarity among miners is more nostalgic than actual. In his Denver neighborhood fathers and mothers are absent from home all day and Jesús looks after the children and young toughs who gather in the street. The Mexican American neighborhood is either in shambles or has been abandoned to the oldsters in the novels of Anaya, Nava and Ramos. For the young in Nava's and Ramos's novels, street gangs, rather than union jobs, serve as identity markers.

Strinati neglects to include language in his list of traditional sources of identity. Proficiency in Spanish no longer defines the Mexican American. Its loss is painful to Rios and Montez. The norm for Buenrostro, Baca and Damasco is an expressional life that bounces between Spanglish, English and Spanish, a comfortable *ménage à trois*.

Sommer's analysis of Latin American foundational fiction shows that European and North American models served as the framework for the romance novels of emergent republics. The principal difference between the European model and the Latin American product was the absence of the love triangle (*Foundational* 16). Latin American protagonists were heterosexual couples desirous of founding families. Sexual love triangles do not figure in the lives of Chicano detectives either, and these protagonists look forward to establishing families, perhaps not the traditional ones of their Latin American relations, but families nonetheless.

However, the Chicano fictions are embroiled in a literary *ménage à trois* and "American" is the third participant. Andrés Bello warned Latin America that European models should be avoided, but they weren't (Sommer *Foundational* 8). A curiously illicit relationship was established between the model and the product.

North America's love for the detective genre is the third bedfellow in Chicano detective romance. The authors have chosen as their model a genre alien to the body of Chicano literature. The challenge for each author is to make the love triangle — detective fiction, Chicano literary tradition and lived experience — compatible. They manage to accomplish this goal through a critical awareness of their surroundings. While the Chicano couple is exposed to the contradictions of the society that surrounds them, the authors identify the hazards and pitfalls that threaten a successful union and offer suggestions of what the future might bring. The authors revise the genre to accommodate their protagonists by selecting some mainstream conventions to emulate and others to discard, as did their Latin American predecessors from European romance.

Chicano detective fiction does not offer an example of a sole environment where the Mexican American, his community and the nation state will co-exist. However, each novel suggests a space where detective, community and nation state can entertain this romantic illusion.

The story of Angel, Henry Rios' nephew, the only fully developed child protagonist in the novels analyzed, is the future that has not been described. Originally Henry and his sister Elena each want to adopt Angel. Henry and Elena are very uncomfortable with Angel's background. He will not accept Elena, his biological grandmother, because he is loyal to his presumed grandmother who, from Elena's and Henry's perspective, has little to offer to Angel due to her poverty and lack of education.

Henry and Elena's educated and independent life styles are alien to Angel. He is surprised to see men cooking and cleaning because he had assumed that women were responsible for these domestic chores. Never having lived in any one home for an extended period of time, he is wary of structured environments, including schools. He is intelligent, but does not know the pleasures of reading. He is street wise and uses gang slang and intimidation tactics. He accepts his mother's evangelical Christianity without question, but is fearful of gays, having been taught that they might sexually abuse him.

The relationship that develops between Henry and Angel forces each of them to reevaluate their attitudes and actions. Through Henry, Angel discovers the pleasures of reading. Through Angel, Henry discovers that many Mexican Americans are capable of expressing love with an ease he lacks. By observing Henry's practice of law and the defense he constructs to save his mother, Angel learns to respect a form of defense that does not involve gang tactics. Henry accompanies Angel to church and finds that not all evangelical ministers are the hell and brimstone–shouting demagogues he has seen on television. He observes the minister console and encourage his Spanish speaking congregation and is better able to understand how this church has helped his niece improve her own and Angel's lives.

By witnessing the spontaneous interaction between John and Angel, Henry learns that being in complete control is not always productive. Angel finds new domestic models in the company of Henry and John: men do cook and clean and a homosexual relationship does not promote sexual abuse. Through Angel's example Henry recognizes that no matter what his or her failings have been, a parent cannot be rejected. Henry accepts that Angel will not live with him on a permanent basis and Angel becomes comfortable going between two different Chicano realities.

Henry's house is free from the danger Angel was exposed to in his previous environments. Even though his "grandmother" had temporarily given him a loving home, her house provided no defense against the intrusion of gang-related crime. The neighborhood gang, the ruin of her son's life and the purveyor of the drugs that Angel fears, murdered her in her living room. Henry provides a stable and safe environment where Angel finds intellectual stimulation and love. His mother's loving company has also become a stable environment. Her commitment to her faith complements Angel's experiences in Henry's home and completes the love necessary for his growth.

If I were to make Angel the hero of my *corrido*, this is the story I imagine writing. In Rad's company he would visit the other sleuths during his summer vacation. In his short ten years Angel has faced hardships encountered by too many children in the United States today. But despite these disadvantages he has prospered to the extent that he can comfortably cross the border that his Chicano family erected between themselves.

This is Angel's trip. Visiting Gloria and Justin in Oakland, California, and Luis in Denver, he discovers the history and the current state of Chicano activism from positive and realistic perspectives. In Oakland he meets Gloria's mom whose understanding of Mexican tradition and association with her educated daughter and granddaughter helps him resolve the conflict he perceives between the two grandmothers he has known. He is introduced into the world of creative writing. In Denver, Angel is surprised by Luis's comfortable laid back lawyerly style and realizes that not all lawyers lack spontaneity. With Luis's sons he listens to Jesús's stories and practices his Spanish.

Then Rad drives them south to New Mexico. Rita and Sonny, with Lorenza's help, teach Angel about the religious practices and beliefs that have served his ancestors for more than a millennium. Perhaps Angel finds his *nagual* in their company. In Texas, Rad and Angel stop in White Leg and visit with Sheriff Joe Blue. This is Angel's first experience in a rural area and Blue's kids take him horseback riding. Further south, Rafe takes them around town visiting the family and then across the border to Barrones. There and in Belken County Angel listens to tales of *Tejano* resistance and learns to sing *corridos*. Rafe takes him to work and he gets a firsthand look at what a Chicano does to fight drug trafficking. After meeting two Chicano policemen, the men on the beat stop looking like the guys that arrested his mom and become positive images for him.

*Tío* Luis arranges for Angel to go north. Rad puts him on a plane to Alaska where Luis's good buddy Cecil Younger takes the young city boy fishing, hiking and exploring frontier towns along the Inland Passage.

This romantic vision of Angel's future vacation highlights positive characteristics present in the people and environments described in the

Chicano detective novels. My intention is not to gloss over problems faced by the communities that Angel visits, but rather to show how these novels project a future that learns from the past but is not limited by the parameters of tradition or the sociopolitical present. Without Nava's characterization of Angel as an intelligent, resilient and highly curious child, my bucolic perspective would have been unimaginable.

In my analysis of Chicano detective fiction I began with the external form of these novels and proceeded to connect the origins of the generic tales with their ideological underpinnings. The Chicano transformations of these mystery genres were then related to the lived experience of the communities portrayed and their literary inheritance. The analysis has explored a diverse Mexican American population through their literary representations as presented in the detective genre.

It has been necessary to proceed with caution and to be aware that the knowledge of a cultural truth is elusive. Doris Sommer's cautionary advice to those of us who are competent readers warned that many "minority" literatures put up "stop signs" that the competent reader ignores. The apparent simplicity of the detective genre can beguile a competent reader into the trap of "textual conquest" and a simplistic re-writing of the author's narrative. Sommer notes that the "problems raised by presumptive, masterful understanding are both epistemological and ethical, and they ring familiar now that postmodern skepticism has lowered the volume on masterly discourses to hear some competing, even incommensurate voices" ("Textual" 143). It is my hope that my reading has suggested, but not imposed, paths for readers to investigate as they explore the novels themselves.

# Chapter Notes

## Introduction

1. The term was first applied during the Nixon administration.
2. Corpi was born in Jáltipan, Veracruz, Mexico.
3. Spanish and Native American.
4. It is better for you, too: "Chemists have isolated compounds in that herb [cilantro] that kill salmonella bacteria" (*New York Times* June 1, 2004).
5. Gloria Anzaldúa died in May of 2004.

## Chapter 1

1. For an exhaustive study of the *narcocorrido* see Elijah Wald's *Narcocorrido, A Journey Into the Music of Drugs, Guns, and Guerrillas.*
2. I use Althusser's definition of "ideology" as described by Jameson: "a representational structure which allows the individual subject to conceive or imagine his or her lived relationship to transparent realities such as the social structure or the collective logic of History" (*Political* 30).
3. Benito Juárez was full blood Zapotec Indian from the state of Oaxaca.
4. Young Mexican Americans were derogatorily called *pachucos* by their elders, had their own distinctive speech, coined words derived from Spanish and English and in the 1950s preferred rock 'n' roll to the traditional music of their elders.

## Chapter 2

1. My translation of "'Lo que se dice de alguien o de algo'" and "'anales o códices de años'" (León-Portilla *Los antiguos* 50).
2. My translation of "El establecimiento de la dualidad es el acontecimiento más transcendental en términos ontológicos para el hombre. Este desdoblamiento de la unidad separa el sujeto del objeto. El mito de la Creación distingue claramente una dualidad 'gemelar' no diferenciada que precede una dualidad diferenciada (masculino/femenino, luz/oscuridad etcétera). La segunda se obtiene a partir de la primera mediante un acto transcendental (conejo en la luna) que altera la identidad. Por lo tanto, en términos míticos el dos es ambivalente; puede expresar una dualidad gemelar muy cercana a la unidad o bien manifestar una dualidad diferenciada con carácter dinámico" (Johansson 119–120).
3. "Si quiere penetrar de veras en la conciencia náhuatl, habrá que buscar ante todo su concepto propio y específico de las instituciones culturales, que al menos en apariencia, se piensa que guardan semejanza" (León-Portilla *Los antiguos* 50).

## Chapter 3

1. The works included in the series are *Estampas del Valle* (1973), *Klail City y sus alrededores* (1976), *Generaciones y semblanza* (1977) or also titled *El condado de Belken, Korean Love Songs* (1978), *Mi querido Rafa* (1981), *Rites and Witnesses* (1982), *The Valley* (English recast of *Estampas del Valle*) (1983), *Dear Rafe* (English recast of

*Mi querido Rafa*) (1985), *Partners in Crime: A Rafe Buenrostro Mystery* (1985), *Claros Varones de Belken* (1986), *Klail City* (English recast of *El condado de Belken*) (1987), *Becky and Her Friends* (English version) (1990), *Los amigos de Becky* (Spanish version) (1991), *The Useless Servants* (1993), *Ask a Policeman: A Rafe Buenrostro Mystery* (1998) (5, 6 Zilles).

2. "[T]he use of a design, purpose, or utility as the explanation of any natural phenomenon" (*Webster's*).

3. The colonial Spanish name for the region north and south of the Rio Grande.

4. "Rafa" shifts in pronunciation to "Rafe," reflecting a shortened English vowel sound.

5. Rosaura Sánchez includes *Estampas del valle y otras obras, Generaciones y semblanzas, Korean Love Songs, Mi querido Rafa, Rites and Witnesses* and the as yet unpublished (in 1985) *Claros varones de Belken* (1986) in her "macrotext" (76, 98–99).

6. The Spanish written tradition of *estampas*, "sketches of manners," originated in the fifteenth century (Sánchez "From Heterogeneity" 78). One of Hinojosa's titles, "Generaciones y Semblanzas" is a direct reference to a "collection of sketches of famous personages of the reign of Henry III" written by Fernán Pérez de Guzmán in or around 1450 (79).

7. Sánchez describes the actions of Jehú Malacara and the episodic nature of their narration as a reference to the Spanish sixteenth-century picaresque novel, *El Lazarillo de Tormes* dated 1554 ("From Heterogeneity" 80). Jehú behaves like the "traditional pícaro-rogue," and like Lazarillo his "affiliation with the object of scorn," the Klail-Blanchard-Cooke and Leguizamón families, is a necessary step in the "exposure" of "the Valley's ruling class" (94).

8. Mariano José de Larra (1809–1837), in his article "El casarse pronto y mal," satirizes the Spanish craze for French customs.

9. See Chapter 4 for a discussion of the characteristics of detective genre.

10. The use of various "languages" specific to certain circumstances or social status.

11. Greenblatt's concern is that many postcolonial literary histories have appropriated the late nineteenth-century forms that "accept the hypothesis of a single, endlessly reiterated fable of identity" (58).

## Chapter 4

1. "The point is that the commonplace theory of detective fiction as an inherently conservative genre fails to recognize that it is based on assumptions about the demographic composition of a readership and the ideological perspective of that readership and that if understood in a different cultural and demographic context, the detective fiction formula could as easily serve a politically radical and social transformative function" (Libretti 67).

2. Significantly, Chevalier Auguste Dupin relies on the generosity of his independent American friend and chronicler to pay the rent. Poe's tales were much better received in France than in the United States, perhaps because his detective-hero is not an American mythological hero. Charles Baudelaire's translations of Poe introduced his work to Europe (see Carlson).

3. The detective story "reached a remarkable degree of specialization.... It is therefore a good example of the overdevelopment of one element of narrative [hermeneutic organization] at the expense of others: it is possible to tell a story in such a way that the principal object of the reader is to discover, by an interpretation of clues, the answer to a problem posed at the outset. All other considerations may be subordinated to this interpretative, or, as I shall call it, hermeneutic activity" (Kermode 179).

4. "Gadamer's claim is that art has been systematically excluded from the sphere of truth by the hegemonic discourse of the natural sciences. ... Particularly important is the notion of play or game (*Spiel*), which has the potential to overcome the subject/object dichotomy. In a game we give ourselves over to a set of rules beyond any individual subjectivity. We do not confront the game as an object but rather participate in it as an event. And in this participation the subject is itself transformed. Our relationship to art is analogous: we do not confront the art work as a subject cognating an object; instead, we participate in the game that constitutes genuine art and are ourselves transformed. Indeed, for Gadamer play is

the truth and essence of authentic art" (Holub 380).

5. In 1973, the 1965 contract signed by grape growers of Kern County, California, with AWOC (a Filipino labor union that had enlisted the help of UFW's César Chavez) expired. Instead of signing a contract with a representative union, the growers brought in the AFL-CIO in an attempt to form a new farm labor union and to immobilize a workers' strike. The AFL-CIO's primary interest was in the livelihood of its truckers. The involvement of the AFL-CIO initiated "an acrimonious jurisdictional dispute" that was not resolved until 1975. Violence was not uncommon on the picket lines during this conflict (Gonzalez 198–200).

6. "She has no head. In its place two spurts of blood gush up, transfiguring into enormous twin rattlesnakes facing each other, which symbolize the earth-bound character of human life. She has no hands. In their place are two more serpents in the form of eagle-like claws, which are repeated at her feet: claws which symbolize the digging of graves into the earth as well as the sky-bound eagle, masculine force. Hanging from her neck is a necklace of open hands alternating with human hearts. The hands symbolize the act of giving life; the hearts, the pain of Mother Earth giving birth to all her children, as well as the pain that humans suffer throughout life in their hard struggle for existence. The hearts also represent the taking of life through sacrifice to the gods in exchange for their preservation of the world. In the center of the collar hangs a human skull with living eyes in its sockets. Another identical skull is attached to her belt. These symbolize life and death together as parts of one process. ... In her figure, all the symbols important to the religion and philosophy of the Aztecs are integrated" (*Borderlands* 47).

## Chapter 5

1. See chapter 1, note 4.

2. See Introduction, note 3.

3. Many Chicanas see their Indian mother as a woman of intelligence whose coupling with the Spaniard, rape or consensual, describes a strong figure.

4. Oscar Zeta Acosta disappeared in 1974

while sailing on a friend's boat off the coast of Mazatlán, Mexico (Acosta, Marco "Afterword" 201).

## Chapter 6

1. The word "*bracero*" comes from the Bracero Program of regulated immigrant labor from Mexico that was in effect from 1942 to 1964. It is a Spanish word for someone who works with his arm or *brazo*.

2. I discuss Samuel P Huntington's "Anglo-Protestant" culture in my conclusion.

3. "Mexican relatives criticized my parents for letting me 'lose it'—my culture, they said. (So it was possible to lose, after all? If culture is so fated, how could I have lost it?) Many years later, complete strangers—Hispanic readers and academics, even non–Hispanic readers and academics—picked up the taunting refrain. As if culture were a suitcase left too long unclaimed. I had lost my culture. The penalty for my sin was a life of inauthenticity. Then they commenced hurling coconuts—all those unchivalric taunts that are the stock of racial and sexual and patriotic bullies" (*Brown* 130).

4. "[T]hrough him [the detective] we are able to see, to know, the society as a whole, but he does not really stand for any genuine close-up experience of it" (Jameson "On Raymond" 127–128).

5. The title is taken from W.B. Yeats' "The Circus Animals" quoted in the epigraph: "...Now that my ladder's gone, / I must lie down where all the ladders start, / In the foul rag-and-bone shop of the heart."

6. For the last 17 years "ACT UP [has been an] adverse, non-partisan group of individuals united in anger and committed to direct action to end the AIDS crisis. We advise and inform. We demonstrate" (ACT UP New York).

## Chapter 7

1. All figures are from the U.S. Census quoted in the *2004 New York Times Almanac*.

2. "Chola" is adjective that refers to young Chicanas. In the case of Rita, it refers to her speech, love of dancing and her style of dress. And it shows, even though she does

not speak fluent Spanish, that she is not dis-
tant from her cultural roots.

  3. Interview questions:

    1. Would you describe yourself as an ac-
tive promoter of social, educational
or political opportunities? If so, could
you describe your efforts?

    2. When writing detective fiction do you
have a vision of a core audience? If so
could you describe this audience?

    3. Are you a reader of detective fiction?
If so, who are your favorite authors
and which tales of detective fiction
are your favorites?

    4. To a greater or lesser degree, in all of
your detective novels you portray
Chicanos or Mexican Americans and
their communities. To what extent
are the communities you portray
reflective of your observations of
contemporary reality?

    5. Many authors of genre fiction who
are also authors of "serious" literature have used pen names when publishing genre fiction. If you considered this option why did you decide
not to use a pen name: Or was this an
option you did not consider, and if
so why?

    6. For Mr. Anaya, Ms. Corpi and Mr.
Hinojosa: would you describe the experience of writing detective fiction
as different from that of your "serious" writing? If so, in what way? If
not, why?

    7. For Mr. Nava and Mr. Ramos: writ-
ing, for a lawyer, in comparison with
other nonliterary professions, is an
obligation. Is there any connection
between your legal writing skills and
experiences and your skills and experiences as a writer of fiction?

    8. Do you have another detective novel
soon to be published, are you currently working on another detective
novel or do you plan to write another
detective novel?

    9. If you were to give a seminar in
writing detective fiction what guidelines would you outline for your students?

    10. Do you feel that detective fiction is in
any way more accessible to the gen-
eral reading public than a nongenre
work of fiction? If so, in what way? If
not, why?

  4. I have used italics to present the words
of the authors in these interviews, instead
of quotation marks, for easier reading.

  5. "Raza" refers to Mexican Americans
and has grown to include other Latinos in
the United States.

  6. Nava's responses, as recorded by Gambone, are italicized rather than enclosed by
quotation marks for easier reading. Page
references direct the reader to Gambone's
text.

  7. "The natives believe that the famous
Doña Marina, Cortés's Indian mistress, his
interpreter, adviser, and strategist in the
conquest of Mexico, was born in Jáltipan
and is buried there, under a large artificial
mound on the outskirts of town, from
where she will return one day to free the Indians of the curse she brought upon them"
(Covarrubias 40).

## Chapter 8

  1. "[…] the English language; Christianity; religious commitment; English concepts of the rule of law, including the responsibility of rulers and the rights of
individuals; and dissenting Protestant values of individualism, the work ethic, and
the belief that humans have the ability and
the duty to try to create a heaven on earth"
(Huntington 31–32).

  2. The sheriff in Max Martínez's *White
Leg* and *Layover*.

  3. The private investigator in John Stra-
ley's Alaskan mystery novels.

  4. Included in this group are Apodaca's
John Garcia, Limón's George Sueño, Mar-
tínez's Joe Blue, Ortiz Taylor's Yolanda
Ramírez, Means Ybarra's Pete Escobedo,
Troncoso's Helmut Sanchez and Gaspar de
Alba's Ivon Villa.

  5. *Compadre*, literally "co-father," de-
notes one member in a relationship with
characteristics of a familial bond.

  6. *La jefita*, "little chief," is an expression
commonly used to refer to the woman of
the house in a tongue-in-cheek manner.
She is not *el jefe*, "the chief," who is male,
or *la jefa*, who is a domineering female.

# Bibliography

Abbott, Megan E. *The Street Was Mine: White Masculinity in Hardboiled Fiction and Film Noir*. New York: Palgrave Macmillan, 2002.

Abella, Alex. *Final Acts*. New York: Simon and Schuster, 2000.

Acosta, Marco Federico Manuel. "Afterword." *The Autobiography of a Brown Buffalo*. New York: Penguin, 1989, pp. 201–204.

Acosta, Oscar Zeta. *The Autobiography of a Brown Buffalo*. New York: Penguin, 1989.

*Act Up New York*. www.actupny.org. 12 August 2004.

Acuña, Rodolfo. *Occupied America: A History of Chicanos*. New York: Harlow, 2000.

Alas, Leopoldo. *La Regenta*. Mexico: Editorial Porrúa, 1990.

Alewyn, Richard. "The Origin of the Detective Novel" in *The Poetics of Murder: Detective Fiction and Literary Theory*. Eds. Glenn W. Most and William W. Stowe. New York: Harcourt, Brace, Jonanovich, 1983, pp. 62–78.

Almaguer, Tomás. "Chicano Men: A Cartography of Homosexual Identity and Behavior" in *The Lesbian and Gay Studies Reader*. Eds. Henry Abelove, Michèle Aina Barale, and David M. Halperin. New York: Routledge, 1993, pp. 255–273.

Alonso, Ana Maria, and Maria Tersa Koreck. "Silences: 'Hispanics' AIDS, and Sexual Practices" in *The Lesbian and Gay Studies Reader*. Eds. Henry Abelove, Michèle Aina Barale, and David M. Halperin. New York: Routledge, 1993, pp. 110–126.

Alurista, et al. "Plan Espiritual de Aztlán" in *Aztlán: An Anthology of Mexican American Literature*. Eds. Luis Valdez and Stan Steiner. New York: Knopf, 1973, pp. 14–48, in Pérez-Torres, Rafael. *Movements in Chicano Poetry, Against Myths, Against Margins*. New York: Cambridge University Press, 1995.

Alvar, Manuel. *Romancero viejo y tradicional*. México, D.F.: Editorial Porrúa, 1987.

"American Library Association's Challenged and Banned Books." www.ala. org/NavigationMenu/Our_Association/offices/Intellectual_Freedom3/ Banned_Books_Week. 17 April 2002.

Anaya, Rudolfo. *Albuquerque*. Albuquerque: University of New Mexico Press, 1992.

_____. *Bless Me, Ultima*. Berkeley, CA: TQS Publications, 1991.

_____. *Rio Grande Fall*. New York: Warner Books, 1996.

_____. *Shaman Winter*. New York: Warner Books, 1999.

_____. *Zia Summer*. New York: Warner Books, 1995.

Anzaldúa, Gloria. *Borderlands/La Frontera, the New Mestiza*. San Francisco: aunt lute books, 1987.

_____, and Cherríe Moraga, eds. *This Bridge Called My Back, Writings by Radical Women of Color*. New York: Kitchen Table: Women of Color Press, 1983.

Apodaca, Rudy S. *The Waxen Image*. Mesilla, NM: Titan, 1977.

_____. *Pursuit*. Bloomington, IN: Rudy Apodaca, 2003.

Bailey, Matthew. "Oral Composition in the Medieval Spanish Epic." *PMLA* 118.2 (2003), pp. 254–269.

Barvosa-Carter, Edwina. "Breaking the Silence: Developments in the Publication and Politics of Chicana Creative Writing, 1973–1998" in *Chicano Renaissance: Contemporary Cultural Trends*. Eds. David R. Maciel, Isidro D. Ortiz, and María Herrera-Sobek. Tucson: University of Arizona Press, 2000.

Boling, Becky. "The Reproduction of Ideology in Ana Lydia Vega's 'Pasión de historia' and 'Caso Omiso.'" *Letras Femeninas*, XVII:1–2 (1991), pp. 89–97.

Brown, Marshall. *Preromanticism*. Stanford: Stanford University Press, 1991.

Calderón, Héctor. "Rudolfo Anaya's *Bless Me, Ultima*: A Chicano Romance of the Southwest" in *Rudolfo Anaya: Focus on Criticism*. Ed. César González-T. La Jolla, CA: Lalo Press, 1990.

Carlson, Eric W. "Introduction" in *Critical Essays on Edgar Allan Poe*. Ed. Eric W. Carlson. Boston: G.K. Hall, 1987, pp. 1–34.

"Carolina Garcia-Aguilera." *Voices from the Gaps*. http://voices.cla.umn.edu/newsite/authors/GARCIAAGUILERAcarol. 21 March 2004.

Castillo, Ana. *So Far from God*. New York: Plume, 1994.

Catalán, Diego. *Arte poética del romancero oral, Parte primera, Los textos abiertos de creación colectiva*. Madrid: Siglo Veintiuno editores, 1997.

Chandler, Raymond. *Farewell, My Lovely*. New York: Vintage, 1988.

_____. "The Simple Art of Murder" in *The Art of the Mystery Story: A Collection of Essays*. Ed. Howard Haycraft. New York: Simon and Schuster, 1946, pp. 222–237.

Cisneros, Sandra. *The House on Mango Street*. New York: Vintage, 1991.

_____. *Caramelo*. New York: Alfred A. Knopf, 2002.

Colón, Leslie Santiago. "Ana Lydia Vega" www.angeltire.com/ny/conexion/ana_lydia_vega.htm. 21 March 2004.

Corpi, Lucha. *Black Widow's Wardrobe*. Houston: Arte Público Press, 1999.

_____. *Cactus Blood*. Houston: Arte Público Press, 1995.

_____. *Crimson Moon*, A Brown Angel Mystery. Houston: Arte Público Press, 2004.

_____. *Delia's Song*. Houston: Arte Público Press, 1989.

_____. *Eulogy for a Brown Angel*. Houston: Arte Público Press, 1992.

Covarrubias, Miguel. *Mexico South: The Isthmus of Tehuantepec*. New York: Alfred A. Knopf, 1946.

D'Emilio, John. "Capitalism and Gay Identity" in *The Lesbian and Gay Studies Reader*. Eds. Henry Abelove, Michèle Aina Barale, and David M. Halperin. New York: Routledge, 1993, pp. 467–476.

Díaz Roig, Mercedes. *Romancero tradicional de América*. México, D.F.: El Colegio de México, 1990.

Duff, David. "From Revolution to Romanticism: The Historical Context to 1800" in *A Companion to Romanticism*. Ed. Duncan Wu. Malden, MA: Blackwell, 1998, p. 23.

Eagleton, Terry. "Introduction: What Is Literature?" in *Literary Theory: An Introduction*. Oxford, England: Basil Blackwell, 1983.

Earle, W. Hubert. *Cacti of the Southwest.* Tempe, AZ: Rancho Arroyo Book Distributor, 1986.

Eco, Umberto. *The Name of the Rose.* Trns. William Weaver. New York: Harcourt Brace, 1994.

_____. "Narrative Structures in Fleming" in *The Poetics of Murder: Detective Fiction and Literary Theory.* Eds. Glenn W. Most and William W. Stowe. New York: Harcourt, Brace, Jonanovich, 1983, pp. 93–117.

Estill, Adriana. "The Pleasures of Closure: Chicano/a Detectives and Questions of Identity," Chicano Detective Fiction Conference, University of New Mexico, Albuquerque, 2000.

Fabre, Genviéve. "Introduction" in *European Perspectives on Hispanic Literature of the United States.* Ed. Genviéve Fabre. Houston: Arte Publico Press, 1988.

Fernández, José. "Hispanic Literature: The Colonial Period" in *Recovering the U.S. Hispanic Literary Heritage.* Eds. Ramón Gutiérrez and Genaro Padilla. Houston: Arte Público Press, 1993, pp. 253–264.

Flys-Junquera, Carmen. "Murder with an Ecological Message: Rudolfo Anaya and Lucha Corpi's Detective Fiction" in *Revista Canaria de Estudios Ingleses* 42 (2002), pp. 341–57.

Frye, Northrop. *The Secular Scripture: A Study of the Structure of Romance.* Cambridge, MA: Harvard University Press, 1976.

Fuentes, Carlos. *La muerte de Artemio Cruz.* México D.F.: Fondo de Cultura Económica, 1993.

Gambone, Philip. "Michael Nava" in *Something Inside: Conversations with Gay Fiction Writers.* Madison: University of Wisconsin Press, 1999.

Garcia-Aguilera, Carolina. *Bloody Secrets: A Lupe Solano Mystery.* New York: G.P. Putnam, 1998.

Gaspar de Alva, Alicia. *"Desert Blood/The Juárez Murders,* Synopsis." Houston: Arte Público Press, 2004.

Gladhart, Amalia. Review of *Cactus Blood,* by Lucha Corpi. *Letras Femeninas* 22:1–2 (1996), p. 254.

Gómez-Quiñones, Juan. *Chicano Politics, Reality and Promise, 1940–1990.* Albuquerque: University of New Mexico Press, 1990.

Gonzales, Manuel G. *Mexicanos: A History of Mexicans in the United States.* Bloomington: Indiana University Press, 1999.

Gosselin, Adrienne Johnson. "Multicultural Detective Fiction: Murder with a Message" in *Multicultural Detective Fiction: Murder from the "Other" Side.* Ed. Adrienne Johnson Gosselin. New York: Garland, 1999, pp. 3–14.

Greenblatt, Stephen. "Racial Memory and Literary History." *PMLA* 116:1 (2001), pp. 48–63.

Griswold del Castillo, Richard. *North to Aztlán: A History of Mexican Americans in the United States.* New York: Twayne, 1996.

Grossvogel, David I. "Agatha Christie: Containment of the Unknown" in *The Poetics of Murder: Detective Fiction and Literary Theory.* Eds. Glenn W. Most and William W. Stowe. New York: Harcourt, Brace, Jonanovich, 1983, pp. 252–265.

Handel, Peter. "Latino Noir" in *Armchair Detective* 27 (1994), pp. 220–221.

Hart, John Mason. *Revolutionary Mexico: The Coming and Process of the Mexican Revolution.* Berkeley: University of California Press, 1997.

Haycraft, Howard. "Murder for Pleasure" in *The Art of the Mystery Story: A*

*Collection of Critical Essays*. Ed. Howard Haycraft. New York: Simon and Schuster, 1946, pp. 158–177.

Herbert, Rosemary, Catherine Aird, and John M. Reilly, eds. *The Oxford Companion to Crime and Mystery Writing*. New York: Oxford University Press, 1999.

Hill, Jane H. "Hasta La Vista, Baby: Anglo Spanish in the American Southwest" in *Critique of Anthropology* 13:2 (1993), pp. 145–176.

_____. "Language, Race, and White Public Space" in *American Anthropologist* 100:3 (1999), pp. 680–689.

Hinojosa, Rolando. *Ask a Policeman: A Rafe Buenrostro Mystery*. Houston: Arte Público Press, 1998.

_____. *Estampas del valle y otras obras*. Berkeley, CA: Quinto Sol Publicaciones, 1973.

_____. *Generaciones y semblanzas*. Berkeley, CA: Justa Publications, 1979.

_____. *Korean Love Songs*. Berkeley, CA: Justa Publications, 1978.

_____. *Mi querido Rafa*. Houston: Arte Público Press, 1981.

_____. *Partners in Crime: A Rafe Buenrostro Mystery*. Houston: Arte Público Press, 1985.

_____. *Rites and Witnesses*. Houston: Arte Público Press, 1982.

_____. *The Valley*. Ypsilanti: Bilingual Press, 1983.

Holquist, Michael. "Whodunit and Other Questions: Metaphysical Detective Stories in Postwar Fiction" in *The Poetics of Murder: Detective Fiction and Literary Theory*. Eds. Glenn W. Most and William W. Stowe. New York: Harcourt, Brace, Jonanovich, 1983, pp. 149–174.

Holub, Robert C. "Hermeneutics." *The Johns Hopkins Guide to Literary Theory and Criticism*. Eds. Michael Groden and Martin Kreiswirth. Baltimore: Johns Hopkins University Press, 1994, pp. 375–382.

Huntington, Samuel P. "The Hispanic Challenge" in *Foreign Policy*. March/April 2004, pp. 30–45.

Hutcheon, Linda. "Interventionist Literary Histories: Nostalgic, Pragmatic, or Utopian?" in *Modern Language Quarterly* 59:4 (1998), pp. 401–413.

Irons, Glenwood, ed. "Introduction" in *Feminism in Women's Detective Fiction*. Toronto: University of Toronto Press, 1995, pp. ix–xxiv.

"Interview with Martín Limón." *Troutworks, Inc.* www.mysteryguide.com. 1998. 12 July 2004.

Jameson, Fredric. *The Political Unconscious*. New York: Cornell University Press, 1982.

_____. "On Raymond Chandler" in *The Poetics of Murder: Detective Fiction and Literary Theory*. Eds. Glenn W. Most and William W. Stowe. New York: Harcourt, Brace, Jonanovich, 1983, pp. 122–148.

Johansson K., Patrick. "Análisis estructural del mito de la creación del sol y de la luna en la variante del *Códice Florentino*" in *Estudios de Cultura Nahuatl*. 24 (1994), pp. 93–123.

Kaemmel, Ernst. "Literature Under the Table: The Detective Novel and Its Social Mission" in *The Poetics of Murder: Detective Fiction and Literary Theory*. Eds. Glenn W. Most and William W. Stowe. New York: Harcourt, Brace, Jonanovich, 1983, pp. 55–61.

Kermode, Frank. "Novel and Narrative" in *The Poetics of Murder: Detective Fiction and Literary Theory*. Eds. Glenn W. Most and William W. Stowe. New York: Harcourt, Brace, Jonanovich, 1983, pp. 175–196.

Kindade, Richard P., and Dana A. Nelson. *Historia y antología de la poesía española 1150–1650.* Tucson: Department of Spanish and Portuguese, University of Arizona, 1998.

Krauze, Enrique. *Mexico, Biography of Power: A History of Modern Mexico, 1810–1996.* Trans. Hank Heifetz. New York: HarperCollins, 1998.

Krutch, Joseph Wood. "Only a Detective Story" in *The Art of the Mystery Story: A Collection of Critical Essays.* Ed. Howard Haycraft. New York: Simon and Schuster, 1946, pp. 178–185.

Langham, Jeffrey. "Subject to Interrogation" in *Multicultural Detective Fiction: Murder from the "Other" Side.* Ed. Adrienne Johnson Gosselin. New York: Garland, 1999, pp. 143–164.

Lantigua, John. *Player's Vendetta: A Little Havana Mystery.* New York: Signet, 1999.

Larra, Mariano José. "Costumbres. El casarse pronto y mal" in *Artículos de Costumbres.* Madrid: Espasa Calpe, 1996, pp. 107–120.

Leal, Luis. "El corrido de Joaquín Murrieta: origen y difusión." *Mexican Studies/ Estudios Mexicanos.* 11 (1995), pp. 1–23.

León-Portilla, Miguel. *Literatura del México antiguo.* Caracas, Venezuela: Biblioteca Ayacucho, 1985.

_____. *Los antiguos mexicanos.* México, D.F.: Fondo de Cultura Económica, 1993.

Libretti, Tim. "Lucha Corpi and the Politics of Detective Fiction" in *Multicultural Detective Fiction: Murder from the "Other" Side.* Ed. Adrienne Johnson Gosselin. New York: Garland, 1999, pp. 61–81.

Limón, José. *Dancing with the Devil.* Madison: University of Wisconsin Press, 1994.

_____. "Dancing with the Devil: Society, Gender, and the Political Unconscious in Mexican-American South Texas" in *Criticism in the Borderlands: Studies in Chicano Literature, Culture, and Ideology.* Eds. Hector Calderón and José David Saldívar. Durham, NC: Duke University Press, 1991, pp. 221–235.

_____. *Mexican Ballads, Chicano Poems: History and Influence in Mexican American Social Poetry.* Berkeley: University of California Press, 1992.

Limón, Martín. *Buddha's Money.* Bantam Dell, 1998.

_____. *Jade Lady Burning.* Soho Press, 1992.

_____. *Slicky Boys.* Bantam Dell, 1997.

Lomelí, Francisco A., Teresa Márquez and María Herrera-Sobek. "Trends and Themes in Chicana/o Writings in Postmodern Times" in *Chicano Renaissance: Contemporary Cultural Trends.* Eds. David R. Maciel, Isidro D. Ortiz, and María Herrera-Sobek. Tucson: University of Arizona Press, 2000, pp. 298–302.

López, Enrique G. "The Intersection of Ethnicity and Sexuality in the Narrative Fiction of Three Chicano Authors: Oscar Zeta Acosta, Arturo Islas, and Michael Nava." Dissertation, Ohio State University, 1998.

Maciel, David R. "Introduction" in *Chicano Renaissance: Contemporary Cultural Trends.* Eds. David R. Maciel, Isidro D. Ortiz, and María Herrera-Sobek. Tucson: University of Arizona Press, 2000, pp. xi–xxxiii.

"Manuel Ramos." http://hometown.aol.com/mrriter/newtest10.htm. 25 May 2004.

Martí, Samuel. "Simbolismo de los colores, deidades, números y rumbos." *Estudios de cultura náhuatl*-vol II UNAM (1960), pp. 93–120.

Martínez, Max. *Layover.* Houston: Arte Público Press, 1997.

_____. *White Leg.* Houston: Arte Público Press, 1996.

"Max Martínez, one of the best 100 best writers in Texas history" in *Hispanic vista.com, Inc.* www.miskutonic.org/rara-avisa/. 13 May 2004.

McGuire, Randall H. "The Mesoamerican Connection in the Southwest" in *Kiva* 46:1–2 (1980), pp. 3–38.

Menand, Louis. "Patriot Games" in *The New Yorker.* 17 May 2004, pp. 92–98.

Mendéz, Miguel. *Peregrinos de Aztlán.* Tempe, AZ: Bilingual Press/Editorial Bilingüe, 1991.

Mendoza, Vicente T. *El romance español y el corrido mexicano estudio comparativo.* México, D.F.: Imprenta Universitaria, 1939.

Menéndez-Pidal, Ramón. *Flor nueva de romances viejos.* Buenos Aires: Espasa, 1938.

Mignolo, Walter D. "Posoccidentalismo: el argumento desde América Latina." *Teorías sin disciplina. Latinoamericanismo, poscolonidad y globalización en debate.* Eds. Santiago Castro-Gómez and Eduardo Mendieta. México, D.F.: Porrúa; San Francisco: University of San Francisco, 1998, pp. 31–58.

Miller, Mary Ellen. *The Art of Mesoamerica, from Olmec to Aztec.* London: Thames and Hudson, 1996.

Napier, Robert S. "An Interview with Martín Limón" in *Over My Dead Body!* 1:1 (1993).

Nava, Michael. *The Burning Plain.* New York: G.P. Putnam's Sons, 1997.

_____. *The Death of Friends.* New York: Bantam Books, 1996.

_____. *Goldenboy.* New York/Los Angeles: Alyson Publications, 1996.

_____. *The Hidden Law.* New York: Ballantine Books, 1996.

_____. *How Town.* New York: Ballantine Books, 1992.

_____. *The Little Death.* New York/Los Angeles: Alyson Publications, 1986.

_____. *Rag and Bone.* New York: G.P. Putnam's Sons. 2001.

"Nava (Michael) Papers" *Online Archive of California* www.oac.cdlib.org/findaid/ark:/13030tf5159p0p0/bioghist/48. 19 June 2004.

*The New York Times 2004 Almanac.* Ed. John Wright. New York: Penguin Reference, 2003.

Novoa, Bruce. "New Chicano Literature: Manuel Ramos" in *Voices of Mexico* 65 (2003), pp. 115–117.

Noyes, Alfred. "The Highwayman" in *The Standard Book of British and American Verse.* Ed. Nella Braddy. Garden City, NY: Garden City, 1932, pp. 711–714.

Ortiz Taylor, Sheila. *Coachella.* Albuquerque: University of New Mexico Press, 1998.

*The Oxford Study Bible.* Eds. M. Jack Suggs, Katharine Doob Sakenfeld, and James R. Miller. New York: Oxford University Press, 1992.

Padilla, Genaro M. *My History, Not Yours.* Madison: University of Wisconsin Press, 1993.

Paredes, Américo. *A Texas-Mexican Cancionero.* Urbana: University of Illinois Press, 1976.

_____. "The United States, Mexico and *Machismo*" in *Journal of the Folklore Institute* 8:1 (1971), pp. 17–37.

_____. *With His Pistol in His Hand.* Austin: University of Texas, 1958.

Paredes, Raymund. "Mexican-American Literature: An Overview" in *Recovering the U.S. Hispanic Literary Heritage.* Eds. Ramón Gutiérrez and Genaro Padilla. Houston: Arte Público, 1993.

Paz, Octavio. *El laberinto de la soledad.* México: Fondo de Cultura Económica, 1989.

Pérez-Torres, Rafael. *Movements in Chicano Poetry, Against Myths, Against Margins*. New York: Cambridge University Press, 1995.

Perkins, David. *Is Literary History Possible?* Baltimore: Johns Hopkins University Press, 1992.

Pitt, Leonard. *The Decline of the Californios, a Social History of the Spanish-Speaking Californians, 1846–1890*. Berkeley: University of California Press, 1970.

Poe, Edgar Allan. "The Murders in the Rue Morgue" in *Edgar Allan Poe: Tales of Mystery and Imagination*. New York: The Heritage Press, 1941, pp. 336–366.

_____. "The Mystery of Marie Rogêt" in *Edgar Allan Poe: Tales of Mystery and Imagination*. New York: The Heritage Press, 1941, pp. 198–241.

Porter, Dennis. *The Pursuit of Crime; Art and Ideology in Detective Fiction*. New Haven, CT: Yale University Press, 1981.

Ramos, Manuel. *The Ballad of Gato Guerrero*. New York: St. Martin's Press, 1994.

_____. *The Ballad of Rocky Ruiz*. New York: St. Martin's Press, 1993.

_____. *Blues for the Buffalo*. New York: St. Martin's Press, 1997.

_____. "Chicano detectives." Rara-Avis Archives. www.miskutonic.org/rara-avisa/. 8 Oct 2002.

_____. *The Last Client of Luis Montez*. New York: St. Martin's Press, 1996.

_____. "Max Martinez." Rara-Avis Archives. www.miskutonic.org/rara-avisa/. 12 May 2004.

_____. *Moony's Road to Hell*. Albuquerque: University of New Mexico Press, 2002.

_____. "The Postman and the Mex: From Hard-boiled to Huevos Rancheros in Detective Fiction." http://hometown.aol.com/mrriter/Webpage7.htm. 8 Oct 2002.

Rebolledo, Tey Diana, and Eliana S. Rivero. *Infinite Divisions: An Anthology of Chicana Literature*. Tucson: University of Arizona Press, 1993.

Reyman, Jonathan Eric. "Pochteca Burials at Anasazi Sites?" in *Across the Chichimec Sea*. Carbondale: Southern Illinois University Press, 1978, pp. 242–259.

Rivera, Tomás. "Richard Rodríguez's *Hunger of Memory* as Humanistic Antithesis." *MELUS* 11: (1984), pp. 28–33.

_____. *…y no se lo tragó la tierra*. Houston: Arte Público Press, 1992.

Robertson, Donald. *Mexican Manuscript Painting of the Early Colonial Period, the Metropolitan Schools*. Norman: University of Oklahoma Press, 1994.

Rodriguez, Richard. *Brown: The Last Discovery of America*. New York: Viking, 2002.

_____. *Days of Obligation: An Argument with My Mexican Father*. New York: Penguin Books, 1992.

_____. *Hunger of Memory: The Education of Richard Rodriguez*. New York: Bantam Books, 1983.

Romano-V., Octavio Ignacio. "The Historical and Intellectual Presence of Mexican Americans" in *El Grito* 2(2) (1968), pp. 32–46.

Rosaldo, Renato. *Culture and Truth: The Remaking of Social Analysis*. Boston: Beacon Press, 1989.

Ruiz de Burton, María Amparo. *The Squatter and the Don*. Houston: Arte Público Press, 1993.

Saavedra, Ángel de. *Obras Completas de D. Ángel de Saavedra, Duque de Rivas, de la Real Academia Española. Tomo 2, El Moro espósito*. Madrid: Biblioteca Nueva, 1854.

Sáez, Pilar Bellver. Review of *Zia Summer* by Rudolfo Anaya. *World Literature Today* 70:2 (1996), p. 403.

Saldívar, José David. *Border Matters: Remapping American Cultural Studies*. Berkeley: University of California Press, 1997.

_____, ed. "Our Southwest: An Interview with Rolando Hinojosa" in *The Rolando Hinojosa Reader*. Houston: Arte Público Press, 1993, pp. 180–190.

_____, ed. "Rolando Hinojosa's *Klail City Death Trip*: A Critical Introduction" in *The Rolando Hinojosa Reader*. Houston: Arte Público Press, 1993, pp. 44–63.

Saldívar, Ramón. *Chicano Narrative: The Dialectics of Difference*. Madison: University of Wisconsin Press, 1990.

_____, ed. "*Korean Love Songs*: A Border Ballad and Its Heroes" in *The Rolando Hinojosa Reader*. Houston: Arte Público Press, 1993, pp. 143–157.

Saldívar-Hull, Sonia. "Feminism on the Border: From Gender Politics to Geopolitics" in *Criticism in the Borderlands: Studies in Chicano Literature, Culture, and Ideology*. Eds. Hector Calderón and José David Saldívar. Durham, NC: Duke University Press, 1991, pp. 203–220.

Samples, Susann. Review of *Partners in Crime: A Rafe Buenrostro Mystery*, by Rolando Hinojosa. *Hispanic Journal* 9:2 (1988), pp. 153–154.

Sánchez, Rosaura. "From Heterogeneity to Contradiction: Hinojosa's Novel" in *The Rolando Hinojosa Reader*. Ed. José David Saldívar. Houston: Arte Público Press, 1993, pp. 76–100.

Santiago, Soledad. *Room 9, a Novel of Suspense*. New York: A Perfect Crime Book Doubleday, 1992.

Santiago-Colón, Leslie. "Ana Lydia Vega." www.angelfire.com. 21 March 2004.

Siepmann, Katherine Baker, ed. *Benét's Reader's Encyclopedia*, 3rd ed. New York: Harper and Row, 1987.

Simpson, Amelia. *Detective Fiction from Latin America*. Cranbury, NJ: Associated University Presses, 1990.

Singh, Amritjit, and Peter Schmidt. "Identities, Margins and Borders I" in *Postcolonial Theory and the United States*. Eds. Amritjit Singh and Peter Schmidt. Jackson: University Press of Mississippi, 2000, pp. 3–69.

Smith, Alexander McCall. *The No. 1 Ladies' Detective Agency*. New York: Anchor Books, 2002.

Sommer, Doris. *Foundational Fictions: The National Romances of Latin America*. Berkeley: University of California Press, 1991.

_____. "Resistant Texts and Incompetent Readers." *Poetics Today* 15:4 (1994), pp. 523–551.

_____. "Textual Conquests: On Readerly Competence and 'Minority' Literature" in *Modern Language Quarterly* 54:1 (1993), pp. 141–154.

Soto, Gary. "Rodriguez Meditates on His Mixed Roots." *San Francisco Chronicle* 1 Nov. 1992, pp. 1, 10.

Soyka, David. "A Conversation with Eric Garcia." www.sfsite.com/06a/eg105.htm. 2 July 2004.

Taboada, Antonio Prieto. "El caso de las pistas culturales en *Partners in Crime*" in *The Americas Review* 19:3–4 (1991), pp. 117–132.

Tatum, Charles. *Chicano Popular Culture: Que Hable el Pueblo*. Tucson: University of Arizona Press, 2002.

_____. Review of *Partners in Crime: A Rafe Buenrostro Mystery*, by Rolando Hinojosa. *World Literature Today* 60:3 (1986), p. 470.

"Thrilling Detectives." www.thrillingdetective.com. 8 Oct. 2002.

Townsend, Richard F. *The Aztecs*. New York: Thames and Hudson, 1993.

Troncoso, Sergio. *The Nature of Truth*. Evanston, IL: Northwestern University Press, 2003.

Valdez, Luis. *Luis Valdez — Early Works: Actos, Bernabé and Pensamiento Seprentino*. Houston: Arte Público Press, 1994.

Vigil, Ernesto B. *The Crusade for Justice: Chicano Militancy and the Government's War on Dissent*. Madison: University of Wisconsin Press, 1999.

Villanueva-Collado, Alfredo. "Growing Up Hispanic: Discourse and Ideology in *Hunger of Memory* and Family Installments" in *The Americas Review*. 16:3–4 (1988), pp. 75–90.

Villatoro, Marcos McPeek. *Home Killings: A Romilia Charcón Mystery*. Houston: Arte Público, 2001.

*Webster's Third New International Dictionary of the English Language Unabridged*. 1965.

Weiss, Michael J. "The Salsa Sectors" in *Atlantic Monthly* 279: May (1997), p. 85.

White, Hayden. "Introduction." *The Historical Imagination in Nineteenth-Century Europe*. Baltimore: Johns Hopkins University Press, 1973.

Wilder, Laura Ingalls. *Little House on the Prairie*. New York: Harper Collins, 1981.

Ybarra, Ricardo Means. *Brotherhood of Dolphins*. Houston: Arte Público Press, 1997.

Zamoyski, Adam. *Holy Madness: Romantics, Patriots and Revolutionaries, 1776–1871*. London: Weidenfeld & Nicolson, 1999.

Zilles, Klaus. *Rolando Hinojosa: A Reader's Guide*. Albuquerque: University of New Mexico Press, 2001.

# Index

221

120, 133; social concerns in *LM* series 200, 201–202; transformation of hard-boiled genre 121, 131, 133, 134; women in *LM* series 113, 116, 118, 199–200

*Raven* 34, 35, 36, 37, 41, 42, 43, 48, 50, 51, 54

La Raza Unida Party (LRUP) 119–120

reading, as leisure activity 1, 7, 124

Rechy, John 18, 123

*Reconquista* 20, 21, 22, 23

resistant texts 3, 205

*Rio Grande Fall* 31

*Rita* 34, 35, 50, 53, 54, 192, 197, 200, 204

Rodriguez, Richard 14, 15, 123, 126–128, 136, 147

romance literature 7, 26, 32–33, 45, 63–64, 80, 82–83

*romancero* 20–22, 24

Romanticism: hero/heroine 7, 12, 25, 64; historical era 9, 46–47, 64, 65; historical narrative 2, 7, 15, 44–46, 63, 184, 187–88; identity and 25; Spanish 21–22

Sahagún, Fray Bernardino de 40, 49

Saldívar, José David 15, 56–58, 74

Saldívar, Ramón 15, 18, 32, 123–125, 183

*Sammie Jo* 67, 76, 197, 198

Sánchez, Rosaura 57, 58

Santiago, Soledad 157–158

*Shaman Winter* 8, 31, 35, 41, 42, 49, 191

Sommer, Doris 3, 7, 15, 25–26, 53–54, 59, 106, 187, 202, 205

*Sonny Baca* 3, 9, 31, 33, 34, 35, 36–37, 39, 43, 47, 49–51, 190, 191, 192, 194, 195, 196, 197, 198, 200, 204

Spanish epic poetry 20–21

Spillane, Mickey 112

*The Squatter and the Don* 8, 19, 26–28, 30

Strinati, Dominic 201, 202

Taboada, Antonio Prieto 56, 67, 71, 74

Tatum, Charles 56

Tezcatlipoca 43, 47, 48

Tlacaélel 48, 52, 98

Toltec (or the city of Tula) 9, 42, 43, 51–53

Tonantzín 99

Treaty of Guadalupe-Hidalgo 28, 30

Troncoso, Sergio 155–156

United Farm Workers (UFW) 85, 86

urbanization 10, 16, 64, 66, 75, 131

U.S.–Mexico border 66, 100–101, 102

Valdez, Luis 18

Vasconcelos, José 127

Vega, Ana Lydia 158–159

Villatoro, Marcos McPeek 162–163

Virgin of Guadalupe 99, 103

Ybarra, Ricardo Means 153–154

Zamoyski, Adam 7, 45, 46, 47

*Zia Summer* 31, 35, 42

Zia sun 42, 47